# John Bianchi
# An American Legend
# 50 Years of Gunleather

## by Dennis Adler

Publisher's Suggested Retail Price: $39.95

### About The Cover:

John Bianchi is the central figure in this popular image of "The Cowboys," which depicts the year 1881 with a small group of Texas cowboys camped in front of a chuck wagon and pondering the long dusty Chisholm Trail from Fort Worth to Abilene. The original full color image was shot in 1981, and was the last of five iconic posters in the Bianchi series. "The Cowboys" was one of the most intricate of the images and featured an authentic chuck wagon that would end up being the centerpiece for one of the largest displays in the Bianchi Frontier Museum.

# Publisher's Note

ISBN 10: 1-886768-88-9
ISBN 13: 978-1-886768-88-8

Blue Book Publications, Inc.
8009 34th Avenue South, Suite 175
Minneapolis, MN 55425 U.S.A.

GPS Coordinates: N 44° 51 28.44, W 93° 13.1709

Orders Only: 800-877-4867, ext. 3 (domestic only)
Phone No.: 952-854-5229
Fax No.: 952-853-1486
General Email: support@bluebookinc.com
Web site: www.bluebookinc.com

Since Blue Book Publications, Inc.'s phone system is equipped with voicemail, you may also wish to know extension numbers and email addresses which have been provided below:

Ext. 10 – Beth Schreiber, Operations Manager .................................... beths@bluebookinc.com
Ext. 11 – Katie Sandin, Operations ....................................................... katies@bluebookinc.com
Ext. 12 – John Andraschko, IT Director .......................................... johnand@bluebookinc.com
Ext. 13 – S.P. Fjestad, Publisher .......................................................... stevef@bluebookinc.com
Ext. 15 – Clint H. Schmidt, Art Director..............................................clints@bluebookinc.com
Ext. 16 – John Allen, Associate Editor....................................................johna@bluebookinc.com
Ext. 17 – Zachary R. Fjestad, Guitar/Amp Author............................ zachf@bluebookinc.com
Ext. 18 – Tom Stock, CFO....................................................................toms@bluebookinc.com
Ext. 19 - Cassandra Faulkner, Executive Editor .......................... cassandraf@bluebookinc.com
Ext. 22 – Kelsey Fjestad, Operations .....................................................kelseyf@bluebookinc.com

Office hours are 8:30 am – 5 pm, CST
Monday-Friday

Distributed in part to the book trade by Ingram Book Company and Baker & Taylor.

Distributed throughout Europe by Deutsches Waffen Journal
Rudolf-Diesel-Strasse 46
Blaufelden, D-74572 Germany
Website: www.dwj.de

## CREDITS:

**Photography & Text** – Dennis Adler

**Designer & Art Director** – Clint H. Schmidt

**Editorial** – James Arness, Dennis Adler, and S.P. Fjestad

**Communications** – Matt Whitaker, General Manager, Frontier Gunleather

**Proofreading** – Charles Priore, Jr., Kelsey Fjestad, David Kosowski, and Cassandra Faulkner

**James Arness Publicist** – Ginny Fazer

**Additional Photography** – Taylor Sherrill and Clark Fogg

**Printing** – Kwong Fat Offset Printing Co., Ltd, Hong Kong

## ACKNOWLEDGEMENTS:

Dave Snowden, Chief of Police, Beverly Hills, CA

Nicolette Bianchi – my devoted wife for her support and gracious hospitality during the preparation of this book.

James Arness

Ethan Wayne

Published in the United States of America, printed in Hong Kong.

# John Bianchi — An American Legend
# 50 Years of Gunleather

A Biography by Dennis Adler

# Introduction

## by James Arness

James Arness, legendary Western TV star from *Gunsmoke*, portrayed Matt Dillon for 37 years.

There are few names better known in the gunleather industry than John Bianchi. His remarkable innovations in holster designs and his lifelong fascination with Western history are as legendary as the millions of holsters that bear his name worldwide. For more than half a century his product design breakthroughs have had a powerful influence on three generations of police officers, the military, and sportsmen the world over, not to mention his celebrated recreations of Western gun rigs made famous in films and on television, including my own holster and belt from *Gunsmoke*.

Back in 1955 when I started playing Matt Dillon on TV, John Bianchi had not made his first production holster. By the time I filmed the last of five *Gunsmoke* movies for CBS in 1992, I had been portraying Matt Dillon for 37 years, during which John Bianchi had become world renowned for his innovative holster designs and top quality gunleather.

I first became acquainted with John during the quarter century run of the Hollywood cowboys Golden Boot Awards foundation, for which John had served on the Board of Directors for a number of years. We met in 1989 when we were both serving on the U.S. Marshal's Bicentennial Commission in Washington, D.C. I saw him as a fellow kindred spirit, since John, like myself, had been drawn to the military at a young age and it was there that we had both learned the camaraderie and disciplines that would remain with us throughout our lives. His "star" on the Palm Springs Walk of Stars attests to his national and international recognition. His friendships with legendary film stars like George Montgomery, Monte Hale, Roy Rogers, Dale Evans, Gene Autry, Dale Robertson, Kelo Henderson (the star of *26 Men*, one of the earliest TV Westerns), and particularly Duke Wayne and the Wayne family have lasted a lifetime. It was the Duke who convinced me to sign with CBS and star in *Gunsmoke*; little did I know then that it would become the longest running dramatic series in TV history. It was with an appreciation for the history of motion pictures, television, and the American West that many years later John Bianchi would embark on a monumental venture, building an extraordinary museum of historic memorabilia from the Old West, films, and TV. One of the finest museums of its kind in the world, it later provided the foundation for what would evolve into the current Autry National Center in Los Angeles. It all sparked from John's imagination and devotion to the heritage of our American West.

It seems appropriate that on the 50th anniversary of John Bianchi's remarkable career and his contributions to the industry and his country that this fascinating biography finally comes to light. It reveals the trials and tribulations he encountered during his long career as a police officer, and as a soldier in the National Guard and U.S. Army who rose through the ranks to become a Major General in command of the California State Military reserve.

John Bianchi has been a major supplier to the Hollywood film industry. His gunleather products have been seen in Western TV series and films, police dramas, and action adventure films. More recently, his innovative design for the U.S. Military's standard sidearm holster can be seen on the nightly news being worn on the hips of our brave soldiers and in documentaries covering the United States Military in every theater of combat around the world for the last 25 years.

Late in John's career, he returned to his original love of the Old West and began making a special line of handcrafted Western holsters and gun belts. John Bianchi's Frontier Gunleather is dedicated to producing Old West style belts and holsters with a focus on authenticity, both for the original rigs worn in the 19th century and for those made famous on television and in the movies. As a result, he has inspired another long list of cult followers and loyal fans around the world.

Some years ago John presented me with a faithful reproduction of my original Arvo Ojala gun belt that I wore for more than 20 years as Marshal Matt Dillon in *Gunsmoke*. Arvo, who had been friends with John since the late 1950s, designed a benchmark TV Western style holster for me that not only became Matt Dillon's trademark rig, but later inspired one of John's most popular holsters. I have enjoyed working with John over these many years and especially appreciate his eye for quality, authenticity, and attention to detail in the reproduction of my James Arness "*Gunsmoke*" Tribute gun rig.

John has been a friend and inspiration to many others throughout his long career, and I am not alone in my admiration. This carefully composed biography of John's life by noted author and firearms historian Dennis Adler is a must-read for all who believe in the American Dream and success story. I know I do, and I know readers will join me in wishing John well as he continues to pursue his passion for Western history and great gunleather.

*James Arness*
*"Matt"*

James Arness

James Arness has been associated with John Bianchi since the Golden Boot Awards foundation honored the *Gunsmoke* star in the early 1980s. They both served on the U.S. Marshal's Bicentennial Commission in Washington, D.C., and most recently have collaborated on a *Gunsmoke* Matt Dillon commemorative gun belt being offered by Bianchi's Frontier Gunleather. This CBS promotional photo pictured the entire Gunsmoke cast: James Arness, Amanda Blake, Ken Curtis, Milburn Stone, and a very young Burt Reynolds. (Photo courtesy James Arness)

# *Preface*
## by S.P. Fjestad

*"I wish to preach, not the doctrine of ignoble ease, but the doctrine of the strenuous life. …Far better it is to dare mighty things, to win glorious triumphs, even though checkered by failure, than to rank with those poor spirits who neither enjoy much nor suffer much, because they live in that grey twilight that knows not victory nor defeat."*

— Theodore Roosevelt, Speech at the Hamilton Club, April 10,1899

The greatest American I have ever met was Joe Foss. The second greatest is John Bianchi. It is apparent after even one dinner with John that four key personality traits stand out like giant marble pillars that have supported both his business and family since he was a child – they are leadership, integrity, discipline, and performance.

This project got started with a cell phone call from Wayne Sheets, the NRA's long time Director of Endowments. As usual, he got right to the point. "Steve, I'm in Palm Springs, and I have John Bianchi next to me. He wants his biography published, and I think you're the right guy for this job."

The project sounded exciting, and I felt there was only one person that had the photojournalist skills necessary to write and photograph this important biography on one of America's industrial icons. I quickly called Dennis Adler, and he was on board almost immediately. After several extended trips to interview John at his house in Rancho Mirage, Dennis had almost everything he needed. Our talented art director, Clint Schmidt, designed and laid out the landscape format in a month, and Charles Priore, Jr. did a clinical job of proofing and editing. The rest, as they say, is history.

John Bianchi is the living, breathing, modern day example of Horatio Alger – a man who has literally pulled himself up by the leather boot straps, except that in John's case he also made them!

John Bianchi (I), Nikki Bianchi (seated), and S.P. Fjestad at a recent NRA Convention.

He typifies what seems lost in contemporary America. Bianchi is a man, who with the humblest of beginnings but a will to experiment, built a business that began in a simple garage and then blossomed into a multi-million dollar company. He has exhibited and continues to do so, those qualities of a true American: grit, resolve, tenaciousness, determination, entrepreneurship, and the honest risk taking that is all but gone from our current psyche.

Thinking out of the box cannot be used to describe him, as he threw out the concept of a "box" decades ago and invented a completely new way of looking at challenges. Between circa 1964-1992, John developed more new handgun holster designs, innovations, and fabrication technology than everything done previously in the 20th century.

Some of John's industry firsts include:

- Being responsible for the creation of the first ambidextrous safety for the Colt Model 1911 pistol.
- Being a CEO that actively starred in his company's advertising and promotional materials. And this was long before Lee Iacocca started appearing in Chrysler television commercials and advertisements.
- Inventor/designer of countless carry and concealment holsters, plus researching and designing the ambidextrous UM84 (Universal Military 1984) holster for the military's Beretta M9 sidearm. It remains the standard issue sidearm holster for the U.S. Armed Services.
- Opening the first large scale museum featuring major artifacts of Western Americana in unique, diorama settings.
- Coining the word "Histograph," referring to images taken to look like historical photos from the Old West, and the terminology "gunleather."

After reading this biography, one of my disappointments is never having had the opportunity to see the original Bianchi Frontier Museum located in Temecula, California. Like everything John has accomplished in his life, when the doors opened in 1982, everything was perfect. Make sure you read Chapter Seven thoroughly and pay special attention to the images – the Western aura this museum created remains unmatched in American history.

John Bianchi is much more than a businessman. He has served his country with honor and distinction. He has been the leader in preserving the great Old Western heritage that so many just take for granted today. He has attained the academy's highest degree – the Ph.D. Generous to a fault, what he has given away in his lifetime with no strings attached surpasses even simple philanthropy. He has come to the aid of many in need and his close-knit family will attest to this and to so much more.

All of us owe him a great debt of gratitude, for he has staunchly defended our Second Amendment rights by the many charitable acts he has performed throughout his life. I am very proud to have published his biography and to be able to call him a friend.

In short, John Bianchi *personifies* the word legendary.

*S.P. Fjestad, Publisher*

# Foreword
## by Dennis Adler

After writing more than 35 books on subjects as varied as 1930s Duesenbergs, the saga of the Porsche family, the first book ever published on the history of Winchester shotguns, and another dozen assorted books on collectible firearms, taking on a biography seemed a daunting task because everyone I have ever written about had passed away long before I was born. Now I was facing a living legend, a man I had known through his work for almost 20 years before I met him for the first time in 1998. Then as now, John Bianchi was an easy person to like. He embodied all of the characteristics I had grown to respect in so many of the heroic individuals I have written about for more than 30 years.

When I began working on this book, John and his lovely wife Nikki invited me into their home like I was an old friend, even though John and I had little more than a passing relationship at gun shows and NRA events where we often met. Yet here I was more than a decade later standing in his home office in Rancho Mirage, California, and glancing across the vast floor to ceiling book shelf behind the desk that once occupied the executive suite at Bianchi International. There among his favorite books, aligned on sides so the spines would be easier to read, was the book I had autographed to him in 1998. But that, as you will come to realize from this book, is typical John, a man who honors and respects relationships however humble or great. On an adjacent wall are letters and photos from John Wayne, and in his living room a Lucite framed shadowbox holds one of the Duke's favorite vests and hats, a gift from the Wayne family. Elsewhere are mementos from other famous Western stars, military leaders, and U.S. Presidents. They are not there to impress visitors, but rather to remind John of the people who welcomed him into their lives in one way or another.

When you consider that John Bianchi's name has graced more than 40 million gun belts, holsters, and accessories, including the majority of holsters in use today by every branch of the U.S. Military and foreign governments the world over, it is not surprising that the Bianchi brand is as familiar to firearms enthusiasts today as Colt, Smith & Wesson, and Winchester. There is barely a contemporary pistol or revolver holster in use that has not been improved upon or invented by John Bianchi over the last half century. That in itself is something of a benchmark, but there is much more to this man than his gift for working in leather. He is a symbol of the American Dream and the belief that anything is possible.

As we sat and talked over days, weeks, and then months, we discovered a lot in common, which helped me to better understand the story of John's life. He is one of those rare individuals you come across who always sees the bigger picture, has a plan, and finds a way to execute that plan against all adversity. As readers will discover, John Bianchi's life has not been without adversity. His story is compelling, much like John himself when you sit and talk with him. His boundless enthusiasm for his lifelong careers have made him, like the famous

Author Dennis Adler, in a photo shoot for *Guns of the Old West* magazine, is shown wearing a Bianchi Frontier Gunleather "Fort Apache" Collection gun belt, holster, and knife sheath. The 3rd Generation Peacemaker pictured was engraved by John J. Adams, Sr.

people he became associated with, a legend in his own lifetime. Yet he is the antithesis of that famous line from *The Man Who Shot Liberty Valance*: "When the legend becomes fact, print the legend." John Bianchi is that legend, and it is my honor to tell his story.

*Dennis Adler*

Dennis Adler

## CHAPTER

*Growing Up in the Golden Age of Movie Westerns*

### The Influence of a Gun Belt

We all have a destiny. Some of us never realize it until later in life, but a fortunate few get a glimpse when they are young. At the age of twelve, John Bianchi got that glimpse when he made his first holster. What, one might ask, would encourage a young boy raised in New York City to fashion a western holster from scrap leather? The answer, as John Bianchi recalls, was a cap gun and a rodeo. He closes his eyes for a moment to recall an event that would ultimately set the course of his life.

"My first recollection," recalls Bianchi, "was attending a rodeo at Madison Square Garden, which I believe was one of the last years my dad served on the New York City Police Department. For the first time I saw real cowboys and Indians. I was thrilled," says Bianchi with childlike enthusiasm. "I had seen them in the movies, but this was for real, right there in front of me! And for a kid who was eight or nine years old, I was just overwhelmed and impressed. As we walked out of the arena there were a number of vendors selling novelties and I spotted a cowboy belt on one of the tables. My dad bought it for me and I still hold a vivid image of the design of that belt and the buckle, and how it was constructed," he says more than sixty years later.

"A couple of years after the rodeo we relocated to Southern California, and I was still wearing that cowboy belt. It was a cherished possession that influenced my interest in leather. After we moved to Monrovia, California, I came across a factory near the elementary school I was attending. They made heavy-duty work gloves, and after school I would take a shortcut through an alley that went past the Morrison Glove Factory. Out back there were mounds of leather scraps waiting to be hauled off. Some of the trimmings were pretty good size pieces, so I would pick up the larger pieces and take them home. I don't know what I used to cut that leather but I managed to cut tough industrial grade leather and make bags, dog collars, belts, anything I could imagine that I could put together, I'd just cut it out, no instructions, no guidance. I just had this passion for fabricating things out of leather. I was hand stitching everything, I mean, I had no idea what a saddle stitcher even looked like, and I made my first, what I thought was a cowboy holster, based on what I had seen in the movies."

That first holster, as John recalls, was made to fit his western cap pistol. He based the holster's styling on the belt his dad had bought for him at the Madison Square Garden rodeo. "I remember cutting slits in the belt to duplicate what we know today as a 'Buscadero' style rig. The slits were cut so I could put the loop of the holster I was making through the belt, just like the cowboy movie holsters I had seen." Of course, as John would learn years later, the movie holsters were a 20th century contrivance. But at the time, his first holster was as real as any from the days of the Old West and his cap pistol the very essence of a Colt Peacemaker.

After John Bianchi, Sr. retired from the New York City Police Department, the family headed south to Florida. "We had relatives there, one of whom had become very ill and had to go into the hospital. My aunt called my dad, knowing that he was a very enterprising, do-it-all-guy, and he dropped everything, loaded the family on a train, and we went from New York down to Southern Florida to help. I remember gazing

Old family photo from around 1908 showing John's paternal grandmother in front of his great grandfather's shoemaking shop in Brooklyn. "As family legend goes, my great grandfather died on the day I was born," says John. "He was a highly trained European custom shoe maker. The family always thought there was a genetic link to my leather crafting aptitude."

John at age three in 1940 with his first cap gun and cowboy outfit, what John dubbed his "first gunfight." "My dad was with the New York City Police Department during World War II."

One of John's favorite photos, wearing his dad's duty holster and revolver. "I was maybe eight or nine and my dad had taught me safe gun handling by then. He let me wear his uniform hat too. I don't know if I ever made the connection with that period of my life and later wanting to become a police officer, but it's interesting to look at it now and wonder," says Bianchi.

out the window of the train and looking at all the shacks that were right smack along the railroad line, little shanty towns of poor, migrant workers. I'd never seen anything like that and it left an impression on me. Here it was, America, and these people were starving to make a living. When we got to Florida my dad stepped right in and began helping run my aunt and uncle's restaurant."

As a young boy, John refers to himself as having been "…a roamer, a free spirited kid. I would leave in the morning and be gone all day. I'd take off for one adventure or another, and I was only about nine years old, but my folks knew I was a responsible kid and didn't worry; of course, times were different back then. I can remember going down to the docks and watching troop ships coming back from Europe into one of the big ports in Florida, and I'd see the men lining up on the sides of the ships. They were so thrilled to be back; the war was over and they were so excited that they were waving American flags and throwing their hats and other uniform items into the air and off the ship. Some of them would hit the water and wash ashore and I'd wade out and get them. I thought that was a great find! My mother didn't. She'd look at me and say, 'What are you going to do with this junk?' 'I don't know mom, the soldiers are coming home!'"

The Bianchi family stayed in Florida for about a year before returning to New York. In 1948 John's father got a call from his uncle in California telling him to come out west. 'It's the golden state of opportunity,' he told my dad. 'There are orange trees on every corner.' Well, my dad, being ambitious, decided to drive out. Being the oldest of the three kids, I went with him. My dad's goal was to find work or a business opportunity first, and then have my mother and sisters come out by train."

"I can remember as we traveled from New York to California. We drove along a lot of Route 66, through farming communities in the Midwest, through other big cities that I'd never been exposed to, and then through the southern states, Texas, New Mexico, and Arizona, where I got a real taste of the last vestiges of the Old West. Driving through the Southwest was a real eye-opening experience for me. It took a day and a half just to drive from east to west Texas and then into New Mexico. There were still American Indians who lived on the reservations, who came into El Paso and Albuquerque and places like that, and you could see them, they would come into town with their wares, their blankets, and their silver. I can remember the chief, or the braves would walk ahead of the squaws who would carry whatever it was they were selling, or if they were coming back from the trading post, they walked two paces behind. And there were still real cowboys who rode horses into town and you'd see them along the highway all the time. There were old timers I saw in El Paso and Albuquerque, as I recall, who had guns stuck in their waistbands or strapped on their hips! They were still wearing old hats, Stetsons and different versions of cowboy hats. These were people who were born in the late 19th century when the Old West was still very much alive, so they still bore that look and perception of the way the world was. I thought I had died and gone to heaven; these were real Cowboys and Indians. All I had seen up to that point in my life were in the movies or the rodeo, and now right here in front of me was the real thing," says Bianchi with the same look of fascination he must have had as a child. He smiles broadly and

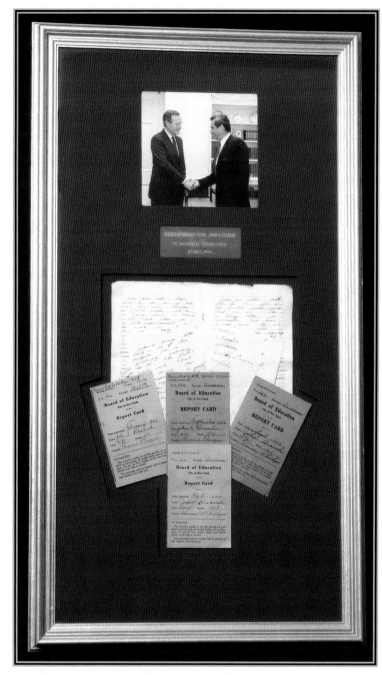

This framed picture with a photo of John and President George H.W. Bush in the Oval Office in 1990 shares space with three letters from John's grade school teachers telling his parents that he could not keep up with class work and held very little promise for a successful future. "We moved so frequently that I barely went to the same school two years in a row. I hated those years in school and I was never a very good student until later in life when I learned the value of a good education. I wonder what those teachers would think if they knew I have a Ph.D today!" John left high school five months early to go on active duty in order to qualify for Korean War veterans' benefits under the G.I. Bill. He used all of his G.I. Bill education benefits to earn his B.A. in Police Science and Administration.

shakes his head knowingly. "It was an experience that made a lifelong impression on me. No one will ever see that again."

The Bianchi family was in California for about a year before John's mother began to get homesick for New York. "It was a traumatic experience," he recalls. "My father always accommodated my mother; she was kind of the decision maker. So my dad sold the house we had bought and we moved back to New York." John rolls his eyes and laughs, "My mother wasn't back there two weeks when she said, 'Holy cow, did I make a mistake! I want to go back to California.' It was obvious that the contrast in lifestyle between the East and West Coast had made an impression on my parents that they hadn't realized until we moved back to New York. The difference in lifestyle back in those days, that was true through the 1960s," says John, "was that for every thousand miles you went east from California you stepped back ten years. After seeing California in the late 1940s, going back to New York was like living in the late 1920s in terms of how people thought, acted, and dressed. It was a different way of living life; it was a huge difference back then. My dad and I got back in the car and drove across country again, and he started over, looking for work and a place for us to live. He decided to settle in Monrovia."

When they returned to California the second time, John's father had to begin looking for work all over again and the family moved into a small, 500 square foot apartment. There wasn't enough sleeping space, so John, being the boy, had the optional "bath tub" suite for about a year. "We didn't have a hammer and nails to fasten the boards together that I had made into a platform over the tub for my blankets and pillows. Every so often the boards would separate and I'd fall through into the tub!" For a family of five, it was very cramped quarters while John Senior got back on his feet and started his grocery business in 1949.

Growing up in Southern California in the late 1940s and early 1950s was probably one of the best places for an impressionable young boy with a passion for the Old West. This is where the Western movies John had watched in New York theaters were being made, and what remained of the real Old West wasn't too far away. Even Monrovia had a western heritage and an annual Western Days celebration in the 1950s.

John had his belt, handmade holster, and cap pistol; all he needed now was a pair of real cowboy boots and a Daisy Red Ryder BB gun.[1] "I didn't get my first pair of cowboy boots until I was maybe twelve, and I didn't get the BB gun until about a year later," recalls Bianchi, but both remain memorable events in his life.

"I can't tell you how thrilled I was to get my first pair of real cowboy boots, the kind they wore in the movies, and then one day I was walking back home about nine p.m. after seeing a Roy Rogers movie. As I passed the local hardware store, there was a Red Ryder BB gun in the window, the first production since the end of the war! During the 1940s Daisy had discontinued BB guns and switched to war time production. I'll never forget seeing the Daisy in the window. I ran all the way home to tell my dad that BB guns were available again! That Christmas I got my Red Ryder and I was a

John's dad on the New York City police force in the early 1940s. "He was also an Air Raid Block Warden during World War II. His job was to make sure all the lights in the neighborhood were turned off every night and that all the cars had the top half of their headlights blacked out. New York was always anticipating the possibility of an air raid."

real cowboy! I had my boots, my original cowboy belt from Madison Square Garden, the holster I had made, and my cap pistol six-shooter." Long before Jean Shepherd penned his classic *In God We Trust, All Others Pay Cash*, which led to the screenplay for 1983's film classic *A Christmas Story*, John Bianchi got to be a real life Ralphie Parker and find his own Red Ryder lever action air rifle under the Christmas tree.

Bianchi's parents contributed to his cowboy infatuation by getting him a fine-looking western hat and shirt. "I remember my mom bought me this maroon and gray high-quality cowboy shirt," says John, pausing to reflect on the memory. He settles back in his chair to eulogize the virtues of 1950s clothing. "This is when the cowboy shirts were made of gabardine," he says, raising both hands as if measuring the sense of quality. "Today most of them are imported and you can't find good quality western wear unless it is custom made. This was an original gabardine shirt, the same material the stars of the B Westerns clothing was made from. I had that shirt all through my pre-teen years. There's a picture of me when I was about eleven or twelve wearing that outfit with my belt and holster, my Levi's with the cuffs rolled up like John Wayne, and my Red Ryder BB gun. It was taken during Western Days in Monrovia. My dad even dressed up in his own western outfit for it."

Back in the early 1950s John Bianchi was immersed in the Old West like most boys his age who went to Saturday matinees or had access to that new contraption called a television. "As a kid I went to see all the black and white B Westerns with stars like Johnny Mack Brown, Monty Hale, Bob Steele, and later, Roy Rogers," says Bianchi, reciting his childhood silver screen heroes. "Around 1950 they came on TV with reruns from the movies that were made in the 1940s. I can't recall seeing William Boyd [Hopalong Cassidy] in a movie theater but I remember watching him on the very, very primitive small black and white television we had. I can still picture the way the cowboys dressed and the holsters they wore, with their horses and the silver on the saddles. All of it made a lasting impression on me." He pauses for a moment and continues in a more somber voice. "There was a message back then with the Lone Ranger, Hoppy, Roy Rogers, and all the others that evil never triumphs. They were all morality plays, and

This was taken in May 1949 during Monrovia Western Days, a big Western celebration. That's the western belt John's father bought for him at the Madison Square Garden rodeo, the holster John hand made for his cap pistol years later, and the Red Ryder BB gun he got the previous Christmas. "I had the same size waistline for years," laughs John, looking back at the old photo. Notice how John rolled up the cuffs on his jeans the way John Wayne did in the movies.

John's father got into the Western spirit too during Monrovia Western Days. "He was wearing the same holster he used as a New York City police officer. I remember the design of that holster so well," says John. "It was far from being a western holster, but he did have a Colt Single Action he borrowed for the festival. When he left the police force he had to turn in his issued Colt Official Police .38 revolver."

in the end the white hat won and they righted all the wrongs that occurred during the storyline. I think that is sadly lacking today in the images kids follow. We had black and white images literally and figuratively; the good guys wore white hats and the bad guys wore black hats, except, of course, for Hopalong Cassidy," says Bianchi, laughing at his own contradiction.

William Boyd made the black hat famous (from his first big screen film in 1935 to the small screen from around 1948 to 1954) and opened the door for a lot of black hat TV heroes like Hugh O'Brian's portrayal of Wyatt Earp, Richard Boone as Paladin in *Have Gun Will Travel*, and James Garner in *Maverick*, but the lesson was still the same. Regardless of the color of the hero's hat, good always triumphed over evil, at least in the movies of John Bianchi's youth. "It was a great period to grow up in."

Growing up with a policeman for a father gave John a lifelong role model. "He was on the New York City Police Department all through the war years. He was the hardest working man I ever knew, he worked ten, twelve hour days and was always looking for better opportunities" says Bianchi, "and that inspired me. As a kid, even before we moved to California, I was always looking for a job to make money. I remember shoveling snow in the winter time, raking leaves in the fall, and selling subscriptions door to door for *Look* and *Life* magazine when I was eight years old. Role models for us kids in those days were the kids who were a couple of years older and had real jobs, and I would piggyback with the big kids if an older friend had a job shoveling snow or raking leaves, I'd tag along and help. I delivered newspapers; I did anything and everything to make a buck. For kids in those days, that was a sense of self worth. 'Well what do you do?' 'Well I got a job!' Today kids don't have jobs. My grandkids, who are all very successful college grads, never had a job when they were young. They never learned what it was like to work for pennies and nickels and dimes. That work ethic stayed with me all my life and I learned it from my father. He taught me that hard work and good luck are inseparable, the harder you work the luckier you become. Once we finally settled in Southern California, my dad went into the grocery business and later the food service industry because he believed that people had to eat three times a day."

Even in California the Bianchi family moved around. "I had a hard time in grade school because we moved to wherever my dad could get the best job, so it was hard to keep up with the schoolwork. After we settled in Monrovia and I entered high school, I thought we had moved for the last time and I wouldn't have to change schools again. Then one day my dad came home and said, "We're moving to Upland, California, about thirty miles away. And I said to my parents, I'm not moving again. I'm not changing schools. My folks gave me a great deal of latitude in those days. They knew I was hard working and reasonably dependable, so when we moved to Upland I stayed in my same school in Monrovia and hitched a ride back and forth every day for three years! It was in the very early 1950s and people were a lot more trustworthy back then. A lot of times I'd get picked up by the same people going back and forth to work. I don't think you could do that today."

This early family photo shows John with his mother, father, and his two sisters, Mary Lou and Jane. It was taken by their house in Monrovia, California, around 1951.

"When I'd get home from school, usually around six, I'd go right to work in my dad's little grocery store doing whatever was needed. I didn't have a driver's license at the time but I'd make grocery deliveries in the evenings in an old World War II Army ambulance that the store owned," recalls John with a laugh. "That was life for me and I just went about it every day. Those were interesting and challenging years."

For a kid who was a roamer, Southern California in the late 1940s and early 1950s was a never-ending adventure. Reflecting on 1950, the year John enrolled in the NRA, he recalled a weekend adventure with his .22 caliber Winchester take down slide action rifle. "If I wasn't doing something for my dad, I'd make myself a sandwich, strap on my GI canteen and go hiking in the mountains around Upland." Sometimes John's adventures were daunting, if not remarkable. "One morning a friend of mine who was a little older decided we should have an adventure. I knew about an old ghost town north of Barstow, California, called Calico. It was an Old West mining town so we decided to go and see it. I packed my Winchester .22 rifle in a blanket and we got together some canned fruit and things to eat and packed it in a laundry bag. 'How we going to get there?' he asked. I said, 'Let's hop a freight going through to Ontario, California, and jump off at Barstow.' So we caught a train heading that way and stayed on until we got to Barstow around midnight. It was August and super hot. We just had some blankets to sleep on and we made camp on a little rise overlooking Barstow. Unknowingly, in the dark we had laid our blankets down on top of an ant hill and we soon realized we had a big problem! We got up to brush off the ants and heard sirens and saw red lights flashing in the town below. Unable to sleep, we packed up our stuff and decided to investigate. When we got to where the police cars had gathered we stood there like a couple of amazed kids until one of the policemen asked us what we were doing out on the street in the middle of the night. I said, 'We're hiking to Calico to explore the old ghost town.' The policeman asked if our parents knew where we were; I said they did but he decided to call and make sure! When we got to the police station he phoned my dad and woke him up in the middle of the night to ask him if he knew where his kid was. My dad said, 'He's out hiking, it's all right.' So we asked if we could sleep on a bench in the lobby of the police station for the rest of the night and they let us stay. The funny thing is, the policeman never looked in the laundry bag where I had my Winchester .22 rifle!"

The next morning John and his friend got out on the highway and hitchhiked to the road that led off the highway to the old ghost town. "We could see it from a distance on the hillside about five miles away, and we started walking. We misjudged the distance and the high temperature in the desert. After a couple of miles we dropped from exhaustion and managed to flag down a passing flatbed pickup truck with some miners going up to explore the hills. They dropped us off at the ghost town with a warning to watch out for rattlesnakes and scorpions. We courageously responded, 'Don't worry, we've got our .22' and headed off toward Calico. We sadly discovered that the 'historical' old town was in absolute shambles and the buildings we had hoped to camp out in were uninhabitable! We had envisioned staying in some old hotel room or saloon, but there wasn't anything left. The afternoon temperatures were in the range of 110 to 115 degrees and it was becoming unbearable. We found shelter for the night in an abandoned mine

John with his mother Louise, photographed at Fort Ord, California, when he was on active duty with the U.S. Army in February 1955. "It was freezing that day and then the wind came up. Fort Ord was right on the coastline and the wind was coming in off the ocean. We both had our coats wrapped tightly around us. I had just graduated from an advanced infantry course," recalls John.

shaft, which was dark and cool, and the next morning we decided to get the hell out of there and head back to the railroad tracks to hop a freight home. We managed to hitch a ride back with another truckload of miners who dropped us off right at the highway. Then we hitchhiked back to Upland with a traveling salesman who had been gambling all night in Las Vegas. He had a new Pontiac with an automatic transmission. He asked if either of us knew how to drive or had a license. My friend said yes, so the guy let him drive and he climbed into the back seat and passed out. Neither of us knew how to use an automatic transmission or had a license! Being older, my friend tried to figure out the automatic transmission and when we got the car going we realized we had no idea how to get back to Upland. Somehow we managed to get near home on Highway 66, and we woke the guy up. He left and we walked the rest of the way back, so ending our seventy-two hour adventure."

John always participated in whatever his dad was doing. "I worked in his grocery stores, and in his industrial food service business. Up until the time I joined the police department, except for my military service, I always worked for my dad. He always said, 'follow your dreams but wear work gloves.'"

John's mother, as he describes her, was a "typical old world Italian. She spoke English and Italian and was ever so dedicated to whatever business my dad was involved in. She was there morning, noon, and night working side by side with him. She instilled in my two sisters and me a sense of reliability and the understanding that we all had to contribute to the family's well-being. She taught us manners and respect. She was a very loving, hard working woman. What's interesting is that when I went into business for myself she had an empty nest, because my two sisters, Jean and Marylou, were grown and had lives of their own. So my mother decided to come and work at my gunleather shop in Monrovia. She took it upon herself to take care of all our incoming mail and she operated the Bianchi mailroom for the next thirty-five years! She opened thousands and thousands of letters. She started at five in the morning, would go to Mass every single day, then on to work, usually before I got there. Because she opened up the mail, she saw the complaint letters too, and she would read them and get furious, 'How could this happen!' she'd say. My mother carried a big red pen and she would circle the problem, a defect, a missed delivery, or someone didn't return a phone call, she'd circle these things and be waiting outside my office tapping her foot when I got in. 'It's eight thirty, nice of you to drop by! The office opens at eight, not eight thirty, you have to set an example for the workers and besides that, did you see this?' and she'd push the letters in front of me. I'd say that they should be given to customer service and she'd come right back with 'You've got to know what's going on!' So everybody knew when I came in a little late, they'd warn me, 'Your mom's waiting up front and she's getting a little impatient….she's tapping her foot and leaning against your office door, and she's going to give you hell when you get there.' So I knew what was coming," says John, as he bursts into laughter. "It was like a comedy routine, but she was very supportive of me. She stayed with the company three or four years after I left!"

John Bianchi, Sr. would also play a big role in the operation of his son's up-and-coming holster making business and in the creation of Bianchi International, serving as Chairman of the Board after the company moved to Temecula. "He attended all of the trade shows, was really great with people, and the life of the party. He was 'Mr. B' and everyone loved him." But decades before those memorable days, John Bianchi, Jr. got yet a second glimpse of his future when he enlisted in the National Guard at the age of fifteen! ✂

John holds the "legendary" Winchester Model 62 pump action .22 rifle that accompanied him on several of his hiking adventures as a kid in the 1950s. "Because it was a take down model I could wrap it in a blanket and tie it to the handlebars of my bicycle. I used to ride five miles to the San Gabriel Valley shooting range to practice. This was the same .22 we took on our adventure to Calico Ghost Town." John says that the old 1940s Winchester is still in almost perfect condition.

[1] Named for the comic strip cowboy character Red Ryder (who also appeared in numerous films between 1940 and 1950, and on television in 1956), the BB gun is still in production despite the fact that the comic strip was cancelled in 1963. Thanks to Jean Shepherd and *A Christmas Story*, the Red Ryder is arguably the most famous BB gun in American history.

CHAPTER

# *Soldier, Policeman, Holster Innovator*

## Turning Life's Experiences into a Career

John had set his sights on joining the U.S. Army at a very early age. "It was the tail end of the Korean War and I was still in high school. I was kind of restless," John says with a laugh. "I had come to realize there was no future in being a cowboy." Still chuckling with the idea that had filled his head for years, he laments, "They just weren't hiring cowboys and I didn't have a horse." He even thought about going into acting but at the heart of it all was a sense that the military might be his calling. "I was fascinated with military history and I decided I was going to join the Army. Trouble was, I was only fifteen. I went to the recruiting station and the recruiting sergeant says, 'How old are you kid?' and I said, [as John goes to a falsetto voice] 'I'm seventeen sir.' And he says, 'You don't look seventeen. Go get your birth certificate.' So I went home. I couldn't find my birth certificate so I went back to the recruiter and he says, 'You know kid, why don't you go down to the National Guard, they don't look as closely as we do at your age.' I think he was just trying to politely get rid of me, but I went to the National Guard, picked up the enlistment forms, and brought them home. 'Dad, you've got to co-sign for me,' I begged, and he looked at me, 'But you're not seventeen, you're only fifteen.' I said 'All you have to do is sign here. I'll fill in the rest.' Anyway, after a while I talked my dad into signing me up. I filled in my birth date as 1935 instead of 1937 and I joined. It was probably the most rewarding part of my youth. I virtually lived in the National Guard Armory and gravitated to the military culture, discipline, and education. It was like an early form of R.O.T.C. I served in the National Guard for two years and when I actually turned seventeen, I went on active duty in the regular Army for the next three years." John had also convinced a friend, John "Jack" Mills, to enlist in the National Guard with him. "We were both fifteen at the time! Years later I would convince Jack to join the Monrovia Police Department. He stayed for thirty years and retired a Lieutenant. Today he is a Municipal Court Judge in Bullhead City, Arizona."

Back in 1955 when John went on active duty, the Cold War was heating up and he got assigned to the Alaskan Command, America's first line of defense. "Alaska was not yet a state. I was assigned to air base defense, ski troops, and the 2nd Infantry Division. I'll tell you, for a California boy accustomed to warm weather, the brutal Alaskan winters were a memorable experience. At the time the Army was still equipped with old World War II uniforms and had dilapidated World War II equipment, so we were ten years behind in the development of arctic clothing and shelters. Ironically, we were stationed at an Air Force base assigned to air base defense, which consisted of ski patrols along the 'DEW Line.' The 'DEW Line' was the Distant Early Warning system that prevailed at that time in our national defense strategy. We monitored Soviet movements to forestall any invasion that might come across the Bering Sea. The arctic patrols were brutal because our clothing wasn't suited for the sub-zero temperatures. When we camped we had to leave our weapons outside in the cold because if we took them into the tent, where it was warmer, and then went outside they would sweat and freeze up. While the rest of us slept one man would stand guard outside by a small fire, and each of us had to take turns in two-hour shifts. The whole thing began to remind me of an old Jack London short story I had read as a kid called *To Build A Fire*, about surviving in sub-zero temperatures. I think that kind of came back to haunt me because the character in the story died!"

John in uniform after he joined the Army National Guard in 1953. He was still in high school. "We were still wearing World War II uniforms at that time. That's my dad's 1948 Cadillac in the background."

On duty during summer camp with the National Guard in 1953, John got a taste of real military life. "That's a Korean War Jeep I'm standing with."

In the summer of 1953, John was only 15. He was already in the National Guard having changed the year of his birth from 1937 to 1935. "I practically lived at the National Guard Armory back then," says John. "I was in Heavy Mortar Co., 223rd Infantry Regiment of the 40th Infantry Division. The Company had just returned from a tour of duty in Korea when I joined. As a result of my reserve duty date I qualified as a Korean War veteran, although I never had the opportunity to serve there."

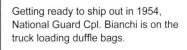

By 1955 John was on active duty. Here he is at Ft. Lewis, Washington, practicing with a .30 caliber water-cooled Browning machine gun.

His adventuring spirit rose once more while stationed at Ladd Air Force base in Alaska. He volunteered for paramedic rescue, which entailed learning how to parachute out of a plane. "I joined the Midnight Sun Skydivers; it was a sort of combined parachute club and rescue organization, and I made five jumps. The first one was in the middle of winter and it was 40 below. We used a Cessna 170 with two jumpers in back and two more sitting in the open doorway with the door removed. No seatbelts, we just sat there in our gear waiting for the jump master to tap you on the shoulder, and out you went. It was so cold that when we got over the drop zone I didn't feel the tap, never felt it, and they told me later that the jump master just pushed me out the door. I opened my chute and came down in a cow pasture just outside of Fairbanks and sprained my ankle! I had to wait six months to make my second jump. The second jump we made at midnight in June and the sun was still up in the sky. I jumped with another kid who was from Long Beach, California. We drifted way off course and he got caught in a tree some thirty feet off the ground. Somehow I managed to get him loose and help him down the tree. It was pretty funny now that I look back on it. I made three more jumps and that was it."

On the arctic patrols, which lasted up to ten days, John and his fellow GIs carried packs that weighed fifty to sixty pounds and often had to pull an *ahkio*, a small, Finnish-style snow sled often used in Alaska. "We didn't have sled dogs, so three or four GIs were hooked up with harnesses to pull the sleds. We had to carry all of our food and bedding on *ahkios*. When we were out on patrol we kept packs of raisins in our inside

Getting ready to ship out in 1954, National Guard Cpl. Bianchi is on the truck loading duffle bags.

On active duty in late 1956, John was assigned to the Alaskan Command, 9th Infantry Regiment, 2nd Infantry Division Ski Patrol Fairbanks. "This photo was taken the following spring in 'mild' weather," recalls John. "In the winter we often patrolled in temperatures of 40 and 50 below zero."

Louise and John Bianchi, Sr. celebrated their 25th wedding anniversary in Monrovia in 1959. John was already a member of the Monrovia Police Department, having left active military service in 1957.

John on the Monrovia Police Department in 1964. "I was assigned to traffic duty at the time."

John on an accident investigation in 1965 wearing the infamous "lost gun" border patrol style rig developed in the 1930s by Bill Jordan. As John recalls, "I kept experimenting with it to come up with a faster approach for drawing, and I had too much forward cant so that the gun lost its center of gravity and one night on a routine vehicle stop as I was searching the car I leaned over and the gun fell out of the holster and slipped to the back of the seat cushion. It was only after we'd let them go that I noticed my gun was missing! We had to race after these guys, stop them again, get them out of the car for another search so I could find the gun," says John with a laugh. "The driver was sitting on it and never knew."

The Monrovia Police Department is where John Bianchi started his law enforcement career in the late 1950s. John is in the top row, fifth in from the right, almost directly under the "5". (Photo courtesy Rick Baratta)

pockets to eat as energy snacks. We had to keep them in an inside pocket or they'd freeze hard as bullets. We needed them for the sugar and iron content. To this day I hate raisins!" says Bianchi with a laugh. "But it was a rewarding experience. I learned a lot and have an appreciation for the maturing process. The values I learned during those years stayed with me. I'd been in Alaska for eighteen months and at that point I didn't think I wanted to be a full-time soldier. I thought, 'Well, I've got to make a living,' so I decided to follow in my dad's footsteps and go into law enforcement, but also stay in the Army as a reservist."

When John came off active duty late in 1957, he got married and a year later joined the Monrovia Police Department. "I can remember the seven years I was on the Monrovia Police Department. I was going to school on the GI Bill, I had a custom holster operation out of my garage, and I was still working part time driving for my dad. I had a very busy life."

John eventually earned a bachelor's degree in Police Science and Administration, and later, during some of the busiest years of his life, went back for a master's and a doctorate in Business Management.

While he was a member of the Monrovia Police Department, John was pursuing what he then referred to as his "hobby craft" making holsters on his kitchen table. As a uniformed officer he wore a traditional border patrol style rig developed by Bill Jordan in the 1930s. "I kept experimenting with it to come up with a faster approach for drawing, such as a more radical tilt to the holster, but I had too much forward cant, and the gun lost its center of gravity, only I didn't know it at the time. One night we were on patrol and we stopped a suspicious car with four passengers. We pulled the driver and passengers out of the vehicle so I could search it, and as I leaned over the driver's seat, which was all tattered with the stuffing poking through, the gun fell out of the holster and slipped to the back of the cushion. We didn't find anything in the car and let the suspects go." A few moments later as John took a deep breath and put his hands on his hips, he realized, "…there was no gun in the holster! I knew what must have happened so we had to race after these guys, stop them again, and get them out of the car for another search. They weren't too happy about that. I found my revolver at the back of the seat cushion. The driver had been sitting on it and never knew! So a great lesson was learned that day about holster cant," says John with a laugh. "I never told anybody and I retired that holster when I left. Later I mounted it in a shadow box display and donated it to the Monrovia Police Department exhibit hall."

Back when he began making holsters, John's first customers were his fellow officers. "I'd make a holster at night, take it to work the next day and sell it. Next day I'd do the same thing. I was making traditional style belt holsters for some of the detectives and that's when I realized there was a need for high-performance concealment carry holsters, which for the most part didn't exist. Most of the police holsters back then were bulky, and even the holsters the detectives used were cumbersome. There weren't any sophisticated designs that did the job and I became acutely aware of it. The manufacturers that existed at that time were simply not responding to consumer needs. They'd say, 'We've been

A newspaper clipping from the Monrovia News Post showing John with the two car garage where he started Bianchi Leather in Monrovia. "I was still on the police force and making holsters part time. I must have made over a thousand holsters in that garage over the three years we lived in that house, which I bought on the G.I. Bill for $12,000.

Tool board that John has today which holds all of his original tools used to make holsters by hand. "The shears are actually sail making shears, but I didn't know that back in the 1950s when I picked them up in a junk store!" Also shown are the original maker's mark stamps John used to mark the first holsters manufactured in Monrovia. Many of the same style tools are still used today.

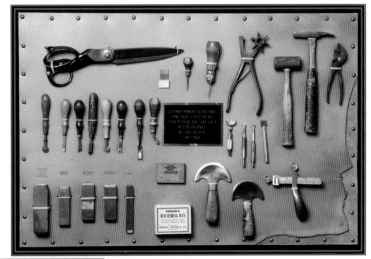

John sits in his home office today with the left-handed No. 2 basket weave holster that he made for himself around 1959. Over the years it had been sold and he'd forgotten about it. "One day about twelve years ago I'm looking through a pawn shop in Indio (a town near Palm Springs) and I almost choked. I saw this left-handed No. 2 holster and thought, 'That can't be mine.' I picked it up, turned it over, and it was marked with my old brand stamping from Monrovia. It was the very same holster I'd made on my first Landis No. 1 saddle stitching machine in 1959. I gave him $5 for it."

doing it this way for the past thirty years, my grandfather made it this way and it was good for him, it's good for me.' So I had discovered a niche and I saw an opportunity. I was hungry for any little bit of leather work I could get, so I listened carefully to the needs and the desires of the users and took it one step further. I was constantly refining the techniques and asking myself, 'How do you make these belt holsters more concealable, more comfortable and secure, and still have them practical for rapid access?' Nobody had addressed it before with any degree of sophistication."

In the 1950s most plain clothes law enforcement officers were carrying little five-shot S&W Chiefs Special and Colt .38 caliber Detective Special revolvers. These were also the typical off-duty guns for uniformed officers. "Very few people carried auto pistols off-duty in those days," says Bianchi. "Another popular gun was an S&W two-inch M&P revolver. It was a medium frame gun, with a big bulky grip, totally impractical for the purpose. So I began making holsters for these guns, and the more I got into it the greater the need. The market just expanded. Starting with one little one-inch by one-column ad in *Gun World* magazine, which cost $39, we launched our first one-sheet sales brochure which, had three models; a model No. 1, model No. 2, and model No. 3 holster.

"The No. 1 was for a Colt single action, a high-performance western holster with an exposed triggerguard. The No. 2 was the Speed Scabbard for the Colt Model 1911A1 automatic, a high-performance, very concealable, very minimalist compact holster. The No. 3 was for double action revolvers and had a hammer shroud and sight protector. The market was changing very quickly and the No. 3 evolved into a thumb break snap, which revolutionized the design of holsters. In those days nobody offered a thumb snap over the hammer protector. The new No. 3 was smooth on the outside. There was no snap or safety strap attached to the outside of the holster. Instead I reversed the concept; it was a thumb snap from the inside, so you could easily break it open when drawing the gun."

Bianchi put out a B&W single page brochure to accompany the first $39 ad in 1959. "Jack Lewis and Ray Rich had just launched *Gun World* magazine and the response to the ad was pretty good. A lot of people were asking for the brochure, actually a lot more than I had expected. People were writing in and asking for the free brochure. Well, they cost a couple of cents to print; a stamp was seven cents, an envelope was a couple of pennies, and I realized I couldn't afford it. When the time came to do another ad, I decided to charge a dime for the brochure. People said, 'You can't do that! Everybody else's little brochure is free. Why would they send you a dime?' I said, 'I don't know but I can't afford to send them out for free anymore.' So I charged a dime. Boom! All we could sell. Those orders came in every day. Those dimes paid the printing, envelope, and postage."

John's fellow officers were not only his earliest customers but also a big help to his expanding holster business. "One of my partners, Rick Baratta, hand built my first real work bench. He went on to become a firearms instructor, establishing training standards for law enforcement that are used nationally and internationally. He now teaches firearms tactics in South Africa. Bill Tubbs came up through the ranks to become the department's Chief of Police before he retired. Another friend, Carl Ball, became Chief of the Santa Fe Railroad Police Department after leaving Monrovia, and Jane Millet, the beloved 'mother hen' of the department, retired after fifty years service. Another partner, Jack Moorhead and I worked the streets together. We saw the best and worst of people, and hardly a day goes by that I don't think back about the adventures we shared and survived. We really were a tightly knit group. There was an unspoken bond of trust and loyalty that existed. We worked, played, laughed, and cried together. We truly were a 'Band of Brothers' and many of us still keep in touch even after fifty years. Never forget your roots."

When John first started making holsters, he did everything by hand and it wasn't without its risks, as he found out in 1959. John was juggling two careers as a police officer and holster maker, and his wife Donna was ready to deliver their first child. "She said, 'I know you're working nights, but remember, should you get the call that I'm ready to go in and deliver you have to come home.' 'You can count on me,' I said, 'I promise I'll be there.' Well, she calls the dispatcher, and it's March of '59, and they never call me on the radio! She phones the station again; they never put the request out. At the last minute she has to call her father to take her to the hospital to deliver our first child." John stops and smiles. "Now the plot thickens," he says nodding his head. "I go to the hospital and she says, 'You promised you'd be there to take me to the hospital.' I said, 'Honey, the message…I never got the radio call, they never let me know.' She says, 'All right, we're coming home on Thursday. Promise me you'll be here to pick us up.' I looked her straight in the eyes and promised, 'You can count on me, you've got my word. Nothing will prevent me from being there.' They were to release her at three o'clock in the afternoon. At twelve noon, on Thursday I'm working on a little work bench and I'm cutting leather with an inappropriate knife. I slip and I drive the knife into my thigh, right to the bone. I figured I'd hit an artery because blood was going everywhere. I rushed into the kitchen, barely made it into a chair and I'm sitting there looking around for something to use as a tourniquet. I look across the kitchen and I see a towel. I'm thinking, 'I've got to stop this flow of blood or I'm going to bleed to death.' I stagger over to the sink, get the towel, and stagger back to the chair and the towel isn't big enough to make a tourniquet! I can just barely get one twist into it. I call the police dispatcher, and tell him, 'I'm hurt bad. Please don't send an ambulance, just send a car.' They send a car, pick me up, and rush me to the hospital, the same hospital where I'm supposed to pick up Donna and the baby! Just as I'm going into the emergency room, she's being released, and they have to send a doctor down to tell Donna that I've been incapacitated and that I'm in the emergency room being stitched up! So she has to call her dad to take her home. Second time," John puts his fingers to his lips and shakes his head. "Donna never let me live that down. I still have the scar on my leg to this day."

By the early 1960s John's product line expanded and it was time to start charging 25 cents for the brochure. "And again the detractors said, 'Ah, this kid has gone off his rocker. Nobody is going to spend a quarter for that brochure when they can get brochures free from everyone else.' I didn't know what I didn't know," laughs John. "I charged a quarter. Orders still kept coming in. The catalog grew in size and in a couple

Family photo taken in the early 1980s of John with his parents and two sisters. John's parents were living in Fallbrook, California, and working for Bianchi International. John, Sr. was Chairman of the Board and Louise Bianchi was still in charge of processing all incoming correspondence, a job she had for over twenty-five years!

Photo of John's parents at his mountain cabin "Stonewood Lodge" in Lake Arrowhead, California. "My mother and father were born on the same day, June 24, 1911, and married on their birthdays in 1934. It was very efficient, two birthdays and a wedding anniversary always on the same day," laughs John.

A collection of badges including John's very first from the Monrovia Police Department, which was presented to him twenty years later when they found badge No. 3 while cleaning out the department vault. Other badges consist of his U.S. Marshal's badge while serving on the Bicentennial Commission, his Riverside County Sheriff's Department Reserve badge, and badges from law enforcement agencies and police departments for which John had served as a consultant over the last forty years.

of years it was time to go to 50 cents. That posed a new challenge because most people would put two quarters in an envelope and we became concerned about the security of two loose quarters sliding around inside. So, came the big question, can we go from a quarter to one dollar? Aaugh…" John hollers, throwing his hands upward, "…nobody ever heard of it! A dollar for a catalog? But we did it. I went to a dollar and printed my first two-color brochure for gunleather in the mid 1960s."

Bianchi was still working full-time as a police officer and making holsters on his off hours, only now he had expanded into a two car garage and even got a little publicity from the local newspaper. "I was making holsters morning, noon and night. If I wasn't on duty I was making holsters."

The product line was now large enough that John had a company name, Combat Action Holsters "Protector Brand" by John Bianchi. His third brochure appeared in 1963 with a full line of handcrafted holsters for single action revolvers, double action revolvers, and semi-autos. It included one of the most famous holsters in the world, the Model No. 2 Speed Scabbard for the Colt 1911. "It's been in production for over fifty years," Bianchi says proudly. "I got the idea in 1958 from a slim eyeglasses case that I happened to see on somebody's belt. I don't know that I'd ever really paid that much attention to them before, but for some reason the belt case caught my eye that day. I even had one at home, so that evening I took my Colt 1911 and tried to fit it into the eyeglasses case. I was amazed. It slipped in and it was a perfect fit!"

What John liked the most about the shape of the eyeglasses case was its slim profile and the way it hugged a wearer's belt. He designed a prototype belt holster about the same size and shape, only he left the triggerguard exposed like he had on his No. 1 western rig. "This had never been done before by any of the little custom operations making holsters for the Model 1911, mainly because in the 1950s the big .45 semi-autos were not popular concealed carry guns. Up to that time no one had devised a way to carry a 1911, which weighs 2.44 pounds loaded, in an open style holster," explains Bianchi. "The Speed Scabbard was able to solidly retain a Model 1911, with the grips and triggerguard exposed, and without using a safety strap. The trick was to balance out the gun's center of gravity in the holster. When the Speed Scabbard came out it became the first commercially successful, high-production concealed carry holster for the Model 1911 ever made. Later on when we went into higher production, we added a version with a safety strap, and from there the next evolution was to go with a thumb snap." The original 1958 design has been duplicated by holster makers the world over for half a century.

Prior to the Speed Scabbard, production holster designs for the 1911 hadn't changed much since the gun was introduced. Most were large belt holsters based on early military designs, western holsters, or heavy weight shoulder holsters developed in the 1920s and 1930s.

Back in the 1950s, being a police officer wasn't exactly the most lucrative field. "As a patrolman for the Monrovia Police Department, I was taking home, (after deductions)

$67 a week, and we had to buy our own uniforms and equipment! There was no paid overtime, but if they allowed it, which was rare, we got accumulated time off for all the hours we worked overtime," says Bianchi with a chuckle. "In fact, going through my files I found the original receipt I signed for equipment when I went on the department. They gave you an option of taking a gun from the gunroom, which nobody would do because most were worn out junk guns, so everybody went out and bought their own. But they did give you a nightstick, handcuffs, and a raincoat, but you had to buy your own belt and holster, even if you took one of the hand-me-down revolvers from the gunroom, unless you wanted an old rig left behind by one of the retired officers. But they were so worn out, if you had any sense of pride you'd buy a new Sam Browne rig, which back then with all of the accessories sold for $36."

By the 1960s John was making enough money from the sale of handmade holsters that he began thinking about leaving the police department and going full time as a holster maker. "It was 1964 or 1965 when I finally thought I could make a go of it. I had a friend, Neil Perkins, who knew I was thinking about leaving the department, and he said, 'Why don't we go into business together?' We took a shot at it but it didn't last very long. We had different philosophical approaches to what we were doing and we parted company after a couple of years. Neil and I had started out together as Safari, Ltd. which became Safariland after Neil and I went our separate ways. We had our own styles and ideas and became highly competitive, but there was more than enough business for us both," says Bianchi.

When he finally left the Monrovia Police Department to strike out on his own, John had saved $1,700 in retirement funds after seven years on the force. "I took the money, paid taxes on it, made two house payments in advance, sold our 1962 Pontiac Catalina that I was making payments on and bought a little compact Pontiac model for $600 cash. Donna and I paid off all our bills and I started the business with zero in the bank! To say that I was nervous and paranoid would be an understatement! Every morning the first thing I would do was rush to the post office and check my box for mail orders. Nobody had credit cards back then, so I usually got checks or money orders. Then I'd have to see if there were enough orders to cover expenses for that day. Some days we made it, some days we didn't, but I did everything possible to make sales, even going around and selling holsters to local dealers, and eventually it became more and more successful. We also got a lot of favorable publicity because we were doing what had never been done before. We were coming out with designs and styles that were really nicely crafted. Back then, a holster sold for maybe $10. Somehow we managed to sell enough and the business grew and continued to grow all throughout the 1960s." But not without some setbacks, some of which John laughs about today but were very serious at the time.

"When I was operating out of our garage, I had done a week's production and had left it out to dry in the air. The garage door was open; it was sunny and beautiful out. My neighbor behind me had pigeons, and one day he left them out and they came to roost in my garage while I was at work at the police department. I get home that night and they had crapped all over my leather. Pigeon crap all over my stuff," exclaims John, throwing his hands up in the air in mock frustration. "They stained all of it. I was working so hard, forty to sixty hours a week, carrying a full load in college and also still working as a relief driver for my dad's company. I'll never forget, I stood there and said, 'This is it. I've had it.' I could hardly make ends meet and this just seemed like too much. But the next day I was reenergized and thought I'd give it one more try."

By the mid-1960s, John Bianchi Combat Action Holsters had expanded from a carport to a one car garage, then to a two car garage, and finally into a small storefront in Monrovia. "I remember it was funny sometimes because when I'd order materials the sales rep would deliver them to Bianchi Leather, and it was just a garage behind the house!" The first store front, actually an old real estate office, was John's second retail outlet. He never had a chance to move into the first one.

"When I first started looking for a small storefront, I drove around looking at vacancies and found what I thought would be a perfect location. It was owned by a foreign lady who spoke very little English. We talked about the rent and finally I said, 'OK, I'll take it' and gave her my business card. She looked at it and said 'Bianchi?' as if it was a question. I said 'yes' and she replied, 'Is that Italian?' I said it was, and she shook her head. 'I can't rent this to you. My husband hates Italians!' I told her, 'My parents were born here and my grandparents came here from Italy.' She said, 'I'm sorry, I cannot rent to you.' And that was the end of my first storefront! I found another old real estate office across the street and that became the first home of Bianchi Leather on Foothill Boulevard in Monrovia."

John had progressed from hand stitching to using an old hand operated Landis No. 1 saddle stitcher (which he still has), to his first electric Campbell/Randall saddle stitcher (or heavy needle work sewing machine), which he was leasing. "I think I paid about $16 a month to lease it, and along with my hand tools proceeded to make as many holsters as I could by myself." There were still some almost comical setbacks. Once when John was working with Neil Perkins, they had completed an entire day's work and decided to break and go to lunch. In the alleyway behind the storefront they had a 4x8 sheet of plywood set atop two 50-gallon drums, and had laid all of the holsters out in the sun to dry. "When we got back from lunch we went out into the alley and all the stuff was gone! Turned out the trash men had come and thought it was there to be thrown away so they scooped it all up and that was the end of it! I mean we were working hand-to-mouth back then to make ends meet and again I thought, 'The odds are against me, I can't live like this,' but I took a deep breath, got myself up, dusted myself off and started all over again." John laughs and says, "We just started making them again."

The one thing John had going at the time was that there was no real competition for his holsters. "There was nothing else like what we were making. Everything we produced we sold." In time John had sold enough and had a large enough clientele to take the next step and become a major manufacturer. ✍

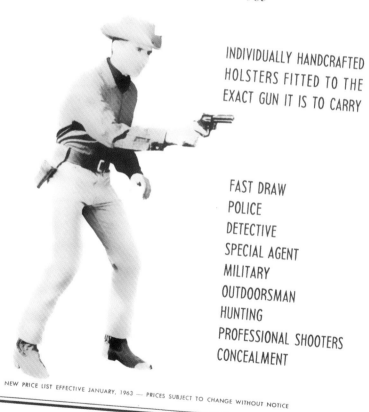

# COMBAT ACTION HOLSTERS
## Made By
### *John Bianchi*

*Protector Brand*

INDIVIDUALLY HANDCRAFTED HOLSTERS FITTED TO THE EXACT GUN IT IS TO CARRY

FAST DRAW
POLICE
DETECTIVE
SPECIAL AGENT
MILITARY
OUTDOORSMAN
HUNTING
PROFESSIONAL SHOOTERS
CONCEALMENT

NEW PRICE LIST EFFECTIVE JANUARY, 1963 — PRICES SUBJECT TO CHANGE WITHOUT NOTICE

### WHY DO PROTECTOR BRAND HOLSTERS COST MORE?

This question is often asked. The answer is simple. Protector Brand Holsters, by John Bianchi are made from only the very finest select grade of eastern tanned cowhide in a weight commensurate with the size of the gun it is to carry. We use the best dyes, oils, waxes and hardware in the finish of the holster. Each holster is individually hand crafted and fitted to the exact gun it is to carry.

Mass production is a term unknown here in our custom shop. We believe in **Quality** rather than **Quantity**. Pride of workmanship is evident in every piece of leather that leaves our shop and every holster is unconditionally guaranteed against defective materials or workmanship.

For the most part, our holsters are confined to the weapons in the "Combat Weapon" class, usually the larger calibers used by law enforcement officers and other professional shooters. The holsters in this class are designed with speed and safety in mind. We continually field test and design new holsters in an effort to always bring our customers the very latest features in handgun leather.

Whether you are a law enforcement officer who lives by his gun, or a sportsman who thinks enough about the shooting sport to get the finest holster in the field, Combat Action Holsters by Protector Brand will fill your every need. . . . .

### ASK THE MAN WHO HAS ONE

JEFF COOPER, National authority on combat shooting, knows the importance of quality holsters.

Protector Brand Combat Action Holsters by John Bianchi catalog from January 1963. "By 1963 I had a full line of products and this was the first multiple page catalog. It sold for 25 cents." John's innovative holster line in 1963 included the Belly Band deep concealment rig, the Agent upside-down shoulder holster inspired by the original Berns-Martin, the Jeff Cooper combat holster for the .45 caliber Model 1911 as well as western and Civil War style holsters and the benchmark No. 2 Speed Scabbard for the Model 1911. "The Speed Scabbard laid the foundation for all commercial 1911 holsters by all makers from that time forward."

## FAST NOT FANCY

### Model No. 3 COMBAT REVOLVER HOLSTER

The combat revolver holster was designed especially for police officers. The holster features a unique sight and hammer protector, the full value of this feature is appreciated by policemen who have to carry a revolver at all times. The sight and hammer guard prevents snagging your clothing and arms, and yet does not hamper your fast draw. The holster needs no safety strap as the gun is hand molded in the holster. The rig rides close to the hip for full concealment. This is the type of holster recommended by most police officers. This model is especially favored on the range by professional combat shooters.

| Plain | Basket Stamp |
|-------|--------------|
| $6.95 | $7.95 |

### Model No. 4 COMBAT REVOLVER HOLSTER

Only difference in this holster is the exposed hammer and sight, for those shooters that want a plain revolver holster. Otherwise it is the same as Model No. 3.

| Plain | Basket Stamp |
|-------|--------------|
| $6.50 | $7.50 |

Safety strap optional at .75 cents.

Both holsters are available for all Colt and Smith & Wesson double action revolvers, 4 inch barrels only.

## THE "COOPER COMBAT" HOLSTER FOR THE .45 AUTOMATIC PISTOL

### Model 45

Designed by Jeff Cooper, national authority on handguns and combat shooting. The Cooper Combat holster was perfected after 25 years of study and testing by Jeff Cooper. The holster was designed with three purposes in mind. 1. Competition Combat Shooting. 2. Uniform wear. 3. Field use. Without a doubt this is the fastest holster in the competition class ever designed. Quick draw "hits" by Jeff Cooper in ½ second have been made and photographed. The holster has numerous features not found in other holsters. A covered trigger guard enables the shooter to draw the gun without danger of a premature shot. The holster is fully lined and has a metal

insert between the lining and the outside so the holster can be formed around the hip. The special "fly-off" safety strap both secures the pistol and blocks the hammer action, yet flys off at the touch. The new theory of the forward rake design of the holster minimizes the rotation of the barrel into firing position, thus saving valuable time and keeps the muzzle pointed away from your leg at all times. The holster has two leather "rails" sewn into it to keep the front sight from dragging on the holster.

Made only by John Bianchi, quality craftsmanship guaranteed.

Available for revolvers on special order.

Matching gunbelt available, see belt no. 1.

| Plain | Basket Stamp |
|-------|--------------|
| $18.50 | $20.00 |

---

## THE "LAWMAN"
### Model 1

The Lawman Single Action Revolver holster is the ultimate in speed and comfort. It has gained the respect of both lawmen and sportsmen in recent years. Holster features, molded custom fit and rawhide hammer safety loop. The holster rides high and close to the body like a fast rig should. The holster is canted slightly forward for the FBI quick draw.

Made For Most Popular Single Actions.

| | Plain | Basket |
|---|-------|--------|
| 5½ inch barrels or less | $ 7.50 | $ 8.50 |
| 6 to 7½ inch barrels | $ 8.95 | $ 9.95 |
| Buntline Special | $12.50 | $14.50 |

Full leather lining (optional on special order) | $ 3.95

Safety strap 75 cents extra.

See section on gun belts for a matching belt for this holster.

## BIANCHI POLICE SPEED HOLSTER
### Model 999

The border patrol style police uniform holster has been found to be the most popular and practical police holster in use today. This is a natural for police combat shooting. Most authorities recognize it as the fastest police holster ever designed. This particular model is hand made from the best materials available. The holster has a metal insert in the shank so it can be bent to suit the shooters preference. This model features the forward cant for speed shooting. The holster rides fairly high so it will not cause discomfort while riding in patrol cars or on horseback. Comes with standard 2¼ inch belt loop.

| | Plain | Basket |
|---|-------|--------|
| 4 inch barrels | $13.00 | $14.00 |
| 5 inch barrels | $14.00 | $15.00 |
| 6 inch barrels | $15.00 | $16.00 |

Add $1.50 for same type with swivel.
Hand sewn plug in bottom | $1.50
Full leather lining | $3.50

Note: This model is fully custom made to your specifications. We keep none on stock.

Colt and Smith & Wesson revolvers only.

### Model No. 5 DETECTIVE SPECIAL

Here is one of the most popular plainclothes holsters on the market. A good sturdy compact fast draw holster for the plainclothes officer.

Holster features FBI type draw, and a simple hammer protector to prevent hammer from snagging your coat and clothing. The gun is wet fitted to the holster for a glove like fit. Although no safety strap is needed, you may order one installed for only .55 cents. The Model No. 5 holster is available for all Colt and Smith & Wesson 2 and 3 inch barrel double action revolvers.

| Plain | Basket Stamp |
|-------|--------------|
| $5.95 | $6.95 |

### Model No. 6 WAISTBAND HOLSTER

An old time favorite for those that want maximum concealment and security. The holster is made from soft leather and is worn inside trouser waistband and fastens to your belt with a durable brass snap, fits belts up to 1½ inches. Works best with the small frame 2" Bbl revolvers, although some men prefer to carry the big .45 Auto and other large revolvers in it. May be worn in front or in rear near hip pocket.

Plain finish natural color only

$4.95 2" bbl.        $5.50 4" bbl.

## .45 SPEED SCABBARD
### Model No. 2

Here is the favorite speed holster of professional gunmen. Designed especially for the Colt .45 Auto, it features extra heavy duty construction, FBI forward tilt for fast draw and double stitching at points of strain. No bulk or excess leather, the holster holds the gun without a safety strap. Available for all .45 and .38 cal. automatics. Specify what model you have when ordering.

Also available for the new Smith & Wesson Model No. 39 9mm Automatic.

Safety strap .75 cents extra.

| Plain | Basket Stamp |
|-------|--------------|
| $6.95 | $7.95 |

## THE "RANGER" HOLSTER
### Model No. 7

The Ranger .45 Auto holster is the most unique combat holster made for the .45 Automatic. It was especially designed for law enforcement and military use. The feature of this holster enables the wearer to carry his gun with the hammer down and the chamber empty. When the need arises, you can draw the gun, when it is partially drawn, the muzzle is pushed down into the special pocket around the trigger guard, thus forcing the slide back and jacking a round into the chamber. This is all done with the drawing hand as shown in pictures. With a little practice this is remarkably fast.

Safety strap .75 cents extra.

| Plain | Basket Stamp |
|-------|--------------|
| $7.50 | $8.50 |

Note: Should be worn on a 1½ inch gun belt or larger.

## Civil War Army Holster Model 1861

Out of the colorful pages of American history comes this hand made, authentic reproduction of the actual Union Army Holster. Remade to the actual specifications of the original holster. This model features the brass stud and hand sewn plug in bottom of holster. The model 1861 will fit all the old Colt percussion revolvers and all the modern replicas. This will also accommodate the 7½ inch Colt Single Action Army. Available in either black or brown, right or left hand cross draw.

Smooth plain finish        $14.50

## The Gunfighters Special Model 1880

Here is the famous old holster of the south west, originally made for the Colt Single Action only, it is now available for all Colt and Smith & Wesson Revolvers. This model features a full lining with strap and a nickel buckle around holster and a rawhide tie down. Holster will fit any western or standard gun belt. Truly the finest most rugged holster of the type made today.

| Barrel lengths up to 6 inches | $17.50 |
| Barrel lengths 7½ to 12 inches | $20.50 |

Note: This holster is made from select 8 oz. leather with a full lining of 7 oz. leather. The heaviest holster made. Oil treated and hand rubbed to insure long wear.

Plain finish, tan or black.

## SPECIAL AGENT HIDE OUT RIG!
### Model No. 9

The special agent shoulder holster is the most practical way to carry a short barrel revolver. The rig is small and comfortable, it lays the gun close under your armpit. As for speed, I defy any man to surpass the speed of this holster. We have tried them all and have found that the special agent fills all the needs of an undercover agent. This model is particularly popular for detectives, undercover agents, government officers and military personnel. The holster features a special piece of heavy duty elastic across the front. The gun is held in by the tension of the elastic under the most vigorous conditions, when you draw the gun it comes out smoothly and quietly. The harness is made from top grain soft elk hide and is adjustable to your size. Here is a holster that you can pack in your suitcase, glove compartment or pocket, when you want a hide out rig it's there when you need it. No bulky springs or clamps to bend or rust, the special agent is a real natural for the professional gunman.

Tan plain finish only

| | |
|---|---|
| 2" bbl. | $12.95 |
| 3" bbl. | $13.95 |

For All Colt and Smith & Wesson Guns (small frame)

Give height and weight when ordering

Excellent for the police officer who carries a second gun

## GUNBELTS CUSTOM MADE

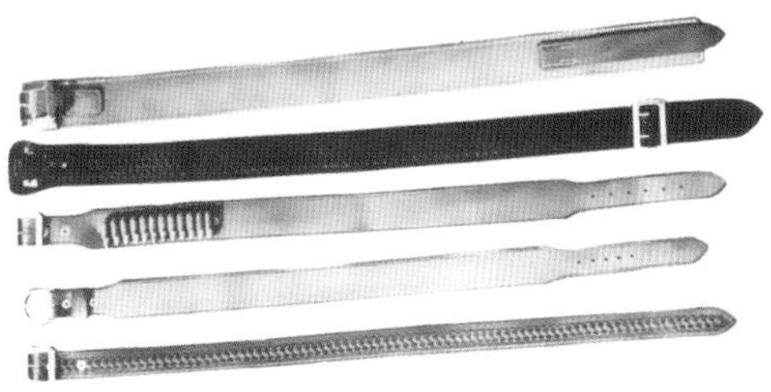

| Model No. | | Plain | Basket |
|---|---|---|---|
| 1. | 2½ inch wide gunbelt with 1½ buckle straps. Fully lined and saddle stitched. Large western nickel silver buckle. | $17.50 | $21.50 |
| 2. | Sam Brown Police duty belt, full lining and saddle stitching. Comes with your choice of chrome or brass buckle. | $12.50 | $15.50 |
| 3. | 2¼ inch gunbelt, tapered down to 1½ inch buckle end, comes with your choice of 12 bullet loops. Additional loops up to 24, are 15 cents for each extra loop. | $10.00 | $13.00 |
| 4. | Vaquero belt, from old California. A rugged 2 inch heavy duty trousers belt. Comes with authentic solid brass buckle. Perfect for outdoor wear. | $ 7.50 | $ 9.75 |
| 5. | Regular pants belt, 1½ inch wide heavy strap leather. | $ 5.50 | $ 6.75 |

### Cartridge Slide 12 Loop

Plain $6.00

Basket $6.75

Calibers .38-.44-.45

### Quick 6

Snap open-6 pak for fast loading

Plain $3.50

Basket $4.00

Calibers .38-.44-.45

### 6 Loop Snap-On

Plain $3.25

Basket $3.75

Calibers .38-.44-.45

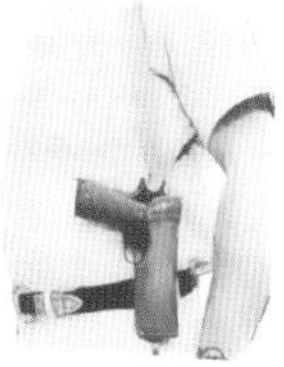

## MODEL 3-IN-1 MILITARY — POLICE SHOULDER RIG

The model 3-in-1 is a practical holster for the automatic pistol, it enables the shooter to have one holster that can be worn as a shoulder holster, cross draw belt holster or straight belt holster. Only one buckle holds the harness for fast change from belt to shoulder rig. The harness is made from heavy duty elk hide, yet it is soft and pliable for long and comfortable wear. The holster fastens to your pants belt on one side and the harness fastens on the other side. The harness forms a figure 8 in the middle of your back for adjustment and proper support. The holster has a stiff metal rod sewn along the top portion of the holster so the rig keeps its shape under all conditions. This is an excellent field or combat holster because of its versatility. This model is not recommended for use as a concealment rig.

Available for:

All Colt automatic pistols in calibers .38 and .45

All automatic pistols of similar frame size Model No. 39 Smith & Wesson 9M/M

Plain finish, black or brown with grey harness $14.50

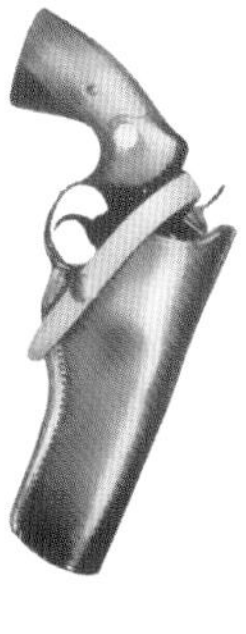

## MODEL NO. 10 OUTDOORSMAN HOLSTER

The outdoorsman holster is a heavy duty holster made especially for rugged outdoor use. It is made from 10 ounce cowhide and comes equipped with a safety strap. The holster has a double welt sewn down the seam for extra support. This model comes with a standard belt loop of 2¼ inches, unless specified otherwise. Made especially for the heavy frame magnum and other large caliber revolvers.

| | Plain | Basket Stamp |
|---|---|---|
| 4-5" bbls. | $ 7.50 | $ 8.50 |
| 6-7½" bbls. | $ 8.50 | $ 8.95 |
| 8⅜" bbls. | $10.00 | $12.00 |

Specify gun make, caliber and barrel length.

## THE "BELLY BAND" Model 8

**Original by John Bianchi**

For years undercover agents and police officers have searched for a holster that was capable of concealing a gun under the most critical conditions. Now, after considerable research and field testing, Protector Brand Holsters has developed the ultimate in a concealment rig. The Belly Band is made from a special piece of heavy elastic band with a soft glove leather pouch type holster, that holds the gun close to the body for maximum concealment. The band actually contracts and expands with your breathing for comfort and reliability. The band is worn around the midsection slightly above the stomach. This rig was designed for the small frame 2 inch barrel revolvers and small automatics.

When ordering, give the measurement around your middle.

Washable, white elastic and natural color glove leather $12.00

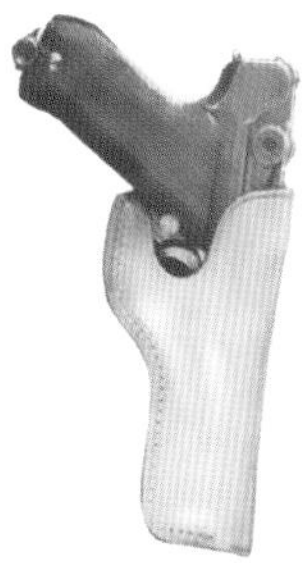

### Luger Holster Model "88"

By popular demand we have added the luger holster to our line of combat holsters. The same fine quality and workmanship goes into this model as all other Protector Brand holsters. Features cut-out portion near trigger guard and slight forward tilt for fast draw.

| | Plain | Basket |
|---|---|---|
| For 4 inch barrel Lugers | $7.50 | $8.50 |

Safety strap optional at .75 cents

Add $1 for each inch over 4 inch bbl.

For special orders or appointments with John Bianchi, telephone ELliott 9-1848. If you call long distance, be sure to call person-to-person.

## ORDER INSTRUCTIONS

### Read Carefully

Be sure to include; PRINT ALL INFORMATION CLEARLY

1. Make and model of gun. Include barrel length and caliber.
2. Holster style and model number.
3. Color and finish of holster. (tan or black) (Plain or Basket Stamp)
4. Belt slot width desired. 1½, 2¼, or 3 inch.
5. Safety strap, if desired.
6. When ordering belts, give waist size (be exact) and width of belt.
7. PRINT YOUR NAME AND RETURN ADDRESS CLEARLY ON ORDER.

Our fast delivery service will amaze you. In many cases we ship retail orders 5 days after received.

If you would like your order shipped AIR MAIL, be sure to indicate this on your order, and include additional money to cover the cost of air mail postage. Check your postal rates for the approximate cost.

You may send your personal check, bank draft or money order.

California residents add 4% sales tax. No orders under $5.00.

Sorry

WE DO NOT SHIP C.O.D.

Please do not request holsters for foreign made or outdated pistols, as we can only make holsters for guns that we have here in our shop. We maintain a comprehensive arsenal of American made weapons, but we can not hope to stock every gun made. Therefore we ask that you do not order holsters for guns not mentioned in the catalog.

**PROTECTOR BRAND HOLSTERS**
**Box 217**
**509 Hacienda Dr., Monrovia, Calif., U.S.A.**

**JOHN E. BIANCHI**
**MAKER**

Veteran police detective Jack Donihoo of Dallas, Texas demonstrates fast draw with .45 automatic.

Photography by Carl Ball

A montage of guns, catalogs, and events from John Bianchi's life. At top, his Winchester Model 62 takedown .22 pump rifle (serial no. 263722); below that, a Bianchi catalog from 1965 and an original order blank. To the left of the rifle stock is John's Special Investigator's badge and I.D. card; below, the signature gun belt, holster, and Colt Single Action (serial no. 272452) worn by John in many of his ads and personal appearances; a rare early Safari Ltd. catalog from 1965-66; a custom holster John made for his own S&W Bodyguard revolver (serial no. 201540); at lower left an original 1963 Protector Brand Bianchi sales catalog; two photos of John on the Monrovia police department in 1963; a photo from his first Army assignment in Alaska from 1956; the original left hand Speed Scabbard that he made for his 1911 .45 Government Model (serial no. 334045) in 1959, lost and found again in a pawn shop thirty years later. At far lower right, a photo of the first Bianchi manufacturing plant in 1967 along with John's portrait; and far right, a 1968 Bianchi catalog and photo of John with his original Monrovia Police Department duty holster in a shadow box. He presented it to the Monrovia Police Department in 2000.

Shown with several early Bianchi catalogs, this early handcrafted western holster was made when John Bianchi was producing them in his garage. The holster is marked "Combat Action Bianchi Protector Brand". (Photo by Bob Arganbright courtesy *Combat Handguns* magazine)

# 3
## CHAPTER

# *The Evolution of Bianchi International*
## From a Kitchen Table to a Worldwide Industry Leader

By the mid-1960s Bianchi had ten different designs in production, including the X15 shoulder holster, another innovative design that, like the No. 2 Speed Scabbard, became a Bianchi Leather trademark. "All the existing shoulder holsters for the 1911 were pretty uncomfortable back then. I collected old holsters and I wondered, 'Why anyone would put a one-inch strap on a gun that weighs two pounds and put it over their shoulder?' So I said, why not put a wider leather strap over the shoulder and distribute the weight more evenly? I don't know why, but no one had ever done it! Now you can't find a shoulder holster anywhere that doesn't have the wide, innovative curved shoulder strap and elastic straps for comfort and ease."

Bianchi's design for the original X15 shoulder holster shifted the weight distribution of the 1911 by 40 percent. "Instead of a narrow one-inch strap supporting the entire weight of the gun we used a three-inch strap, thereby dispersing the weight over a greater area and making it more comfortable to carry."

The X15 used a leather-covered spring steel framework holster so the gun could be pulled easily from the shoulder rig. At the time it was introduced Bianchi could not order enough pieces to have the spring steel framework manufactured, so he had to order spring wire on a six-foot coil and fabricate each spring by hand with a cold chisel on an anvil. "I'd cut it off, put it in a vice, and with a hammer over a piece of pipe, tap and form the spring into shape. I developed a technique for fitting the spring into the holster. Necessity was always the mother of invention. I had no other way, I had to fabricate each holster spring by hand. It was a good design and the holsters sold. The X15 shoulder holster became a world standard and remains so after fifty years."

Bianchi has designed and invented most of the contemporary holsters in use today. He holds seventeen holster patents and a total of 200 patents, copyrights, and trademarks. "Those patents controlled a large portion of the modern police security holsters made. We innovated. We took police duty holsters…" John pauses to make his point…"there were no police security holsters," he explains, "we took police holsters out of the dark ages and into the 20th century. Holsters didn't even have thumb break straps until we introduced them. As a result, we pretty much dominated the market."

The first large Bianchi facility was in a rezoned commercial section of Monrovia. "In order to get the financing to construct a building, you had to buy the lot. It was $6,000 and I managed to come up with enough to purchase the property. In 1966 we built a 4,000 square foot building. We needed the space and I had to do something, but let me tell you, I was scared. We got 100 percent financing on the building and I'll never forget the first day I walked into the totally empty structure. I looked around and thought, 'Holy hell, how are you going to pay for this? Now you bit off more than you can chew.' But we filled the space and production increased, employees increased, and within two years we had outgrown the facility! I had twenty employees and we were working full schedules to meet demand."

By the late 1960s Bianchi had stopped selling mail order and was selling to wholesalers and retailers. "We were now extending credit and buying supplies in quantity. Everything was tied up in receivables and inventory and there was a constant quest for working capital

The Bianchi Holster Company opened its doors in Monrovia, California in 1967. This was the first new building that John had built and comprised 4,000 square feet. "It seemed very large when we moved in, but we outgrew it in two years!"

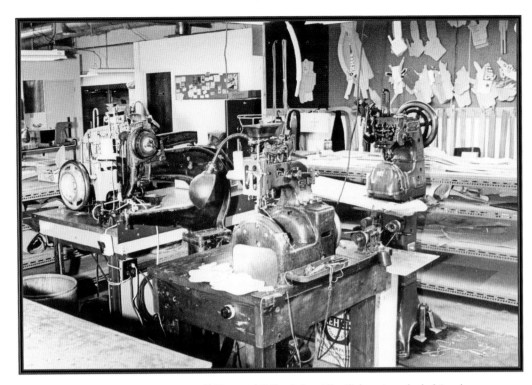

In Monrovia John was using some "100 year old" Randall saddle stitchers to make holsters by hand. Note the hand cut holster patterns hanging on the back wall. "At that time we were employing thirty-five people," recalls Bianchi, "and we were working full-time, plus over time, to keep up with orders."

John, at far left, discusses gun belts with Bianchi production manager Richard Gerfen (far right) and John Lutes II, Midwestern sales representative. By 1968, the Bianchi Holster Company was turning out 100 units a day, and averaging a total of 25,000 gun belts and holsters annually.

because we needed a bigger building again." John looks down and smiles to himself. "This was scary," he says with a nod. "The contractor that built the first building said he had another lot on Foothill Boulevard. He said, 'I'll make you a deal. I'll take the equity you have in your 4,000 square foot building and sell you the new lot and then you can get 100 percent financing on a new manufacturing facility.' The new property was large enough to accommodate a 10,000 square foot building. Somehow we pulled it off. I really didn't know anything about real estate, financing, or anything like that, but it was surprising how many people were offering help and advice. No money, just advice," John quips. "We built a great building, two stories up front with offices upstairs and production facilities in back. In the next two years we went from thirty-five employees to sixty-five and we'd outgrown the 10,000 square foot building. By now we were selling thousands and thousands of holsters."

By the late 1960s and early 1970s things were rapidly changing in Monrovia and the San Gabriel Valley. "Things were becoming depressed. Schools districts were depressed. It wasn't a place where we thought we wanted to raise our children. Hope, born in 1959, Shirlene, born in 1960, and John, Jr., born in 1963, were all of school age, and Donna was determined to put them in good schools," recalls John. "Our fourth child, Elizabeth, was born in 1973. We looked at it rather pragmatically; here was an opportunity to bust out of this urban environment where there was one building right next to another and no room to expand and look for a better place to work and live.

The Bianchi shipping department in Monrovia was always a busy place in the 1960s. Sales rep John Lutes II, at far right, looks over outgoing orders with sales and shipping staff. Note the new catalog on the table at far left. "This was our first full color cover catalog, a first for the holster industry," says Bianchi.

"I started a relocation site search. I cast a wide net. I went as far north as central California, Nevada, Arizona, and parts of Southern California in the San Diego area. Every weekend my general manager, Richard Gerfen, and I would get in the car and we would just drive and look for a community that was wholesome to raise a family and had some reasonably priced industrial land. We kept coming full circle and one day someone said, 'Hey, you ought to go down and look at Rancho California down by Temecula in Southern Riverside County.' I'd never heard of it, so we drove down to Temecula on Sunday. It was a hot August afternoon. It was nothing but a barren prairie and the beginning of a subdivision industrial park. Old Town Temecula was like the back lot at Warner Bros. Dusty streets, no activity. We stopped for gas and got a Coke; Richard looked at me and we couldn't get out of town fast enough. We got back in the car, drove to San Diego, couldn't find anything there, and as we were driving back, something was haunting us about the overall Temecula Valley. We went back to the industrial park area, looked around again, and decided there was potential."

Kaiser Aetna, (Kaiser Steel, Aetna Life Insurance) was the developer of what was once the Vail Cattle Ranch, covering nearly 100,000 acres. "It was divided up into an industrial park on one side of the highway (later to become the Interstate 15 corridor) and on the other side was to be the residential commercial area. My wife Donna and I looked it over and decided we could move to nearby Fallbrook, where the schools were

The table is covered with X15 shoulder holster blanks awaiting assembly. "The X15 was the most successful mass produced shoulder holster of its time and went on to influence shoulder holster designs for the rest of the 20th century. The X15 is still made to this day," says Bianchi.

really good, and I found a prime piece of commercial real estate in Temecula, seven acres, right off of the highway. I still didn't know anything about dealing in land and went to the sales office to ask how much the property would cost. They said $23,000 for the seven acres. Today, one acre costs $200,000!" John takes a deep breath and then almost whispers, "Twenty-three grand was a lot of money. I looked at our accounts receivable, I looked at all our stuff, and I just didn't know how we could do this. I went back to the developers and said, 'You know I don't have the cash, but let me make a proposal to you.

John's father was also working at Bianchi after retiring from his own business. Here he is looking over gun castings used to wet fit holsters. "My father went on to become Chairman of the Board by the time we had moved operations to Temecula," says John. "He stayed active in the company until he was eighty years old."

We have a 10,000 square foot building we built two years ago. The land is paid for and we have equity in the building. We'll trade you the equity we have in our building for the land in Temecula, and once we have the land clear we can get 100 percent financing on the construction.' The salesman says, 'You're crazy. We have 100,000 acres here, why would we want your building up in Monrovia? We're developing this land down here.' I said, 'I've got sixty-five employees and they all need a place to live. I'm going to guess that maybe half of them will relocate with us and you want to sell homes, rentals, apartments, and condos.' He said, 'Yeah, but I don't think the corporate office will go for it.' I said, 'Try it.' So we went back a week later and he said the Oakland office of Kaiser had said no. They're not interested in the trade. A month goes by and we went back again. I dropped into the office and I said, 'I know the corporate office said no, but this time write it up on a formal offer. You take the equity in our building, we will lease it back from you while we build the new building, and then we'll vacate it. In the meanwhile you'll have a year lead time to sell or release our current building.' He looks up and says, 'Well, I don't know, I'll run it up to the office. I'll try.' A week goes by and I call back down there. The gal that answers the phone says, 'Oh, he doesn't work here anymore.' And I said, 'What about the offer we sent up to the Oakland office? She says, 'I don't know, there's a new manager up there.' I asked if she had his name and number. She gives it to me and I call. The guy says that he's new on the job and doesn't know what's going on. So I said, 'Look, we have a deal in the offing. The manager in Temecula accepted it

and was waiting for you to sign off on it and now he's not there anymore.' John covers his mouth as if holding back a laugh, but it's more like astonishment recalling what happened next. "This guy signs off on the offer. 'Sounds like a good deal to me.' He signs off on it! And here I am again, no cash. I'm dealing with blue sky but I went ahead, hired a contractor, and got 100 percent financing on a 30,000 square foot building."

When the new facility was completed, John moved one section at a time from Monrovia to Temecula. "The first time I walked into that cavernous complex I thought that I had over built, but as the machinery was moved in and work stations set up and we added people and equipment to meet demand, everything fell into place. But at the start we were cash poor and I didn't take a salary for months so we could make payroll. The first department we moved in was finished goods. We manufactured in Monrovia and every week we would ship everything we did that week to Temecula for warehousing and shipping. The next month we moved another department, incrementally bringing the company down until everything was there. I didn't know that wasn't the way to do it. Technically, what we did couldn't be done in a normal business model, but I did it like a military operation. I assigned each of the department heads in the Monrovia factory a job. Your job is to see that the equipment in area one is tagged and moved into place in Temecula. We had tape and chalk marks on the floor so everyone knew where each

John (at right) discussing new product designs with his father at the first Monrovia factory in 1967. "He was very involved in every aspect of the business and was active in sales and public relations. He was a real people person and everyone loved 'Mr. B', as he was called. He was really laid back in the way he dealt with people. We would go to trade shows and everyone would say, 'Why can't you be more like your dad?' recalls John with a laugh. "I was always hard driving and goal oriented. Everything was on the line back then."

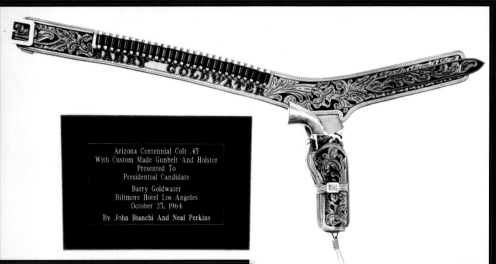

Arizona Centennial Colt .45
With Custom Made Gunbelt And Holster
Presented To
Presidential Candidate
Barry Goldwater
Biltmore Hotel Los Angeles
October 23, 1964
By John Bianchi And Neal Perkins

Back in 1964 when John was still working for the Monrovia Police Department and making holsters from his garage, he handcrafted a gun belt for then Presidential candidate Barry Goldwater. "My partner at the time, Neil Perkins and I met him at the Biltmore hotel in Los Angeles on October 23, 1964. It was my 28th birthday. We presented him with the holster; on the back was inscribed 'Protect our right to keep and bear arms.'" Also shown is a letter from Senator Goldwater sent to John prior to their meeting and the presentation of the holster. "By the time we met with him in October it was clear that he would not win the upcoming November election." After the presentation, a newspaper article appeared in the *L.A. Times* about Bianchi's meeting with the Senator. "I was called on the carpet by the Monrovia Chief of Police for participating in partisan political activities, which was prohibited by department policy at that time!"

## United States Senate
WASHINGTON, D.C.

Dictated en route to Phoenix, September 2, 1964
Transcribed in Washington, September 8, 1964

Mr. John E. Bianchi
President
Safari, Ltd.
945 West Foothill Boulevard
Monrovia, California

Dear Mr. Bianchi:

As a collector of guns, both old and modern, you can't know the thrill that was mine on receiving a letter from such an esteemed producer of holsters as you. I have been collecting guns most of my life and I think I have about fifty in the group now, ranging from French sixty calibre black powder and ball to the most high powered rifles. When we first built our new home outside of Phoenix I had an extensive range system set up, but the encroachment of civilization has gradually forced me back to the position where I only fire into a Detroit bullet cap now.

I would certainly enjoy receiving the presentation that you suggest. However, I am at a loss to know just where this might be accomplished. I will be in Los Angeles on September eighth, but I know this is too short a notice, so possibly this could be worked out at some later appearance in California, which I assure you will be numerous.

With best wishes,

Barry Goldwater
Barry Goldwater

After outgrowing two facilities in Monrovia, in 1970 ground was being broken for the new Bianchi manufacturing plant in Temecula, California. Pictured are, John (at far left), a representative from Kaiser-Aetna, John Bianchi, Sr., and the local realtor.

A picture of the Temecula plant around 1975, when the company was still called Bianchi Leather Products. "The first building, before we started adding on, was 30,000 square feet. As we outgrew it, we added another 15,000 square feet in 1972 and continued to add a 5,000 square foot second story mezzanine over the next five years. We had our own internal construction crew," says Bianchi, "and over 350 employees."

piece of equipment went. Slowly but surely, every department head did their job. There was no confusion, no disasters. We just followed the plan and moved, and through it all we never missed a payroll or a delivery," John says proudly. "Then we realized where we were, in Temecula, still a small town and miles from anywhere. We were, for the most part, the biggest part of the community. That's when we discovered that the simple things we were used to in Monrovia weren't that simple any longer."

John discovered that there weren't any local plumbers or electricians, any tool and die makers, or machinists. There wasn't even a post office. "You had to get everything from Riverside." John shakes his head knowingly. "Big problem. The solution was to systematically bring in-house all of those skill levels. So maybe the electrician did two jobs, maybe he also worked in the machinist department and he was also the company electrician, so everyone learned to multi-task, and we became totally self-contained. We operated as a substation for the post office and processed our own mail. It was metered and everything, out the door," John says with a wave of his hand. "Plumbing, construction, it was all in-house. If we needed an office, a ten by twelve room, we had the crew on site to build it. It would take three or four days, tops."

This time, when Bianchi Leather Products outgrew its facilities, which happened two years after moving into the new 30,000 square foot building, John had the land and the people to handle the expansion. "When we went down to Temecula we had just a

fraction of the labor force we had in Monrovia. A lot of the workers couldn't make the move; a few drove down every day for months, while others relocated right away. By the time we expanded for the second time in Temecula we had 350 employees."

Bianchi Leather Products (later Bianchi International) wasn't like most businesses from the very start. John had his own style of management and his own standards for customer service. "We revolutionized the manufacturing in our industry. We did things that had never been done before. We had to meet demand. Historically, the people who were making gun belts and holsters in those days weren't concerned with quick service and prompt delivery, and they didn't have new catalogs almost every year. Some hadn't published a new catalog in five years. That's the way the industry was serviced. I wanted to change all that. For example, rarely did a catalog show a holster with a gun in it. They'd show a picture of the holster with no gun in it. We wanted buyers to see what the gun looked like in the holster, how it fit. So we were earning business by doing the job better."

John was making constant improvements at every level. "After salaries, every dollar of profit was reinvested in new equipment, new designs, more efficient layout of manufacturing, and better service to the customers." By the end of the 1970s, Bianchi had established a manufacturing production philosophy that was goal oriented.

An aerial view in 1982 shows the then 50,000 square foot manufacturing facility, and to the far left the Frontier Museum building, which was completed and opened in spring 1982.

"We had target objectives. Each department head would sit down with marketing and make a projection, 'I'm committing to sell x number of each model in the next year and that means we have to produce so many a day in each version.' This was done by every department head for every model holster being produced. In that way the department heads participated in establishing production goals in conjunction with the marketing people. It was all coordinated. It was unusual in the 1970s for employees to have a voice in management, but we mandated it and it worked. We even included the maintenance department in meetings in order to have the necessary supplies on hand when we were

hiring new employees. As a result, everyone took great pride in keeping everything clean and all the machinery operating at peak efficiency. It showed in the end product."

What John had learned from the experiences of building his company became the basis for his doctoral dissertation. It was based primarily on marketing and corporate structure and included a variety of business protocols along with what John described as the "bell curve." "I took a very complex socioeconomic condition and developed it into a bell curve to monitor the performance after the successful selection of a manufacturer's

# SALES AGREEMENT

WALTER W. COLLINS (the "Seller") and BIANCHI LEATHER PRODUCTS, INC. (the "Purchaser") hereby enter into a sales agreement in respect to the following property and on the following terms and conditions:

1. Seller hereby certifies that he is the sole and exclusive owner of the BERNS-MARTIN HOLSTER COMPANY (the "Company") and all its related assets; and that no limiting legal agreement exists to prevent the sale or distribution of said assets to a second or subsequent party(s).

2. Seller hereby sells to Purchaser and Purchaser hereby purchases from Seller, BERNS-MARTIN HOLSTER COMPANY including without limiting the generality of the foregoing:

   a. All patents, trademarks, copyrights, and rights to patents, trademarks, and copyrights as the Company may hold;

   b. All designs and patterns for holsters;

   c. All leather working equipment, both machinery and hand tools, owned by the Company;

   d. Certain photographs of the founders of the Company and other pertinent historical data relating to the Company; and

   e. All right, title, and interest to and in the name "BERNS-MARTIN HOLSTER CO."; and

3. Purchaser hereby deposits with the Seller the sum of One Thousand Dollars ($1,000) and other good and valuable consideration. The balance of the purchase price is to be paid at the consummation of this agreement.

4. Seller agrees to stand responsible for all debts of the Company, of which Seller has notice and which are outstanding on the date hereof. Seller shall indemnify and hold harmless Purchaser from liability resulting from any and all such debts as may exist on the date hereof. Purchaser shall not make any payment in regard to any such liability outstanding on the date hereof which may be asserted against the Company without giving notice to Seller of such liability.

5. Purchaser shall not be indemnified by Seller for any liability in respect of the Company arising subsequent to the date hereof.

6. Seller shall not be required to file any report or to make any payment of any tax, franchise tax, or license fees in respect of the Company.

WITNESS our hands and seal on this ___ day of **April 4, 1974**
(month) (year)

_Walter W. Collins_
Walter W. Collins, President
Berns-Martin Holster Company
P.O. Box 13835
Atlanta, Georgia 30324

_John E. Bianchi_
John E. Bianchi, President
Bianchi Leather Products, Inc.
100 Calle Cortez
Temecula, California 92390

_Colleen Mabry_
Notary Public

_W. Peter Vanderhaal_
Notary Public    3/27/74

On April 4, 1974, John achieved one of his dreams, acquiring the legendary Berns-Martin Holster Company of Atlanta, Georgia. "The signing ceremony included the legendary Elmer Keith, author of many firearms industry books and articles. I wanted to purchase Berns-Martin because of its historical significance," recalls Bianchi. "I had always admired their designs and early innovations."

Pictured with John are Elmer Keith and Richard Gerfen.

[...] RELEASE
[ATL]ANTA, GEORGIA
MONDAY, MARCH 25, 1974

An historic union of two of the biggest names in gun holsters occurred in Atlanta, Georgia at the NATIONAL RIFLE ASSOCIATION convention at the Marriott Motor Hotel on Sunday, March 24th when John Bianchi, President of Bianchi Leather Products, the worlds largest manufacturer of holsters announced the acquisition of the famous Berns-Martin Leather Company of Atlanta, Georgia, founded in 1925.

Signing this historic agreement was Mr. Walter W. 'Blackie' Collins, President of Berns-Martin, and editor-publisher of the American Blade magazine. Mr. Collins is a recognized knife designer and will be leaving Berns-Martin to devote full time to publishing American Blade. Mr. Bianchi announced the relocation of the Berns-Martin Company to Temecula, California where it will be merged with Bianchi Leather Company. No business interuption is expected.

On hand to witness the signing was Elmer Keith, recipient of the 'Outstanding Handgunner Award' last year and popular shooting sports writer for over 50 years. Elmer Keith was responsible for many of the holster designs that made Berns-Martin famous for over half a century.

Back in the Monrovia facility John had mastered production techniques that allowed workers to use efficiency in assembly to turn out a surprising number of high-quality holsters and belts daily. When they made the move to Temecula, each department head was responsible for establishing the same set up in the new, larger facility. "The first department we moved in was finished goods. We manufactured in Monrovia and every week we would ship everything we did that week to Temecula for warehousing and shipping. The next month we moved another department, incrementally bringing the company down until everything was there. I didn't know that wasn't the way to do it. Technically, what we did couldn't be done in a normal business model but I did it like a military operation."

Workers at the Temecula plant assembling part of the UM84 holsters for the Beretta Model 92. Bianchi International turned out more than 39,000 for both military contracts and civilian sales.

One of the company's longtime employees, Ken Maynard, is shown at the Temecula plant with stacks of ballistic nylon specially manufactured to produce the military M12 (UM84) holsters. "The ballistic nylon was laminated over closed cell foam, which provided a protective padded pouch for the military's new Beretta 9mm service pistol," explains Bianchi. "We had the first government contract to manufacture them.

representative. How do you manage them, how do you get them up the bell curve, how do you keep them at the peak of the bell curve, and then, what happens when they go down the slippery other side?"

John used his proven motivational skills to run his entire company for many years. "It was more than just business management. It was total integration of the workforce and managers. When I used to work for my dad as a food service delivery truck driver, I'd call on factories and businesses in this big industrial complex. I noted that the secretaries had their noses stuck in the air and they took their coffee over here. The engineers did their thing over here, the factory workers somewhere else. The management people never associated with the working level people. There was no homogenization. And I thought, 'You know, this is dumb. If I were a manager I'd break down those barriers.' I put that in the back of my head. When I was on the police force we had some good leaders in the department, good role models, but still the policies and the culture of the organization could be improved. And I thought again, 'If I ever get in a position where I make those decisions, I'd do this differently and that differently.' Sooner or later it happened and I was able to recall those experiences. What I did at Bianchi International was born out

of necessity, not just a whim. I had to maximize the performance of our people. I had to make sure the morale was elevated so they would follow me through all my eccentricities. They had to believe in what I was doing, otherwise they'd say, 'Oh that crazy guy, what's he going to do now...' but by involving everyone in everything so they all knew and understood what everybody was doing, it worked. If one department head had a problem, he could go to the next department head and say, 'Hey Bill, I've got to work overtime, I need a couple of extra guys,' and he'd get them. Everyone helped each other.

"We had four or five annual company events that everybody looked forward to and was involved in. There was no separation from upper and middle management right down to the janitorial staff. We had a big chili cook off every year where everyone contributed ingredients. They signed up for it about a week in advance, and we'd have the cooks ready to put it all together. I'd stand there with a half gallon of water in a tequila bottle and I'd pour a little in the pot every time a group came through with their ingredients, and I'd keep pouring it in there." John breaks into a laugh. "By noon people would say, 'Boy I had a second helping of that chili and that tequila really got to me!' We also had a Cinco de Mayo costume event, a tractor race where teams worked to make

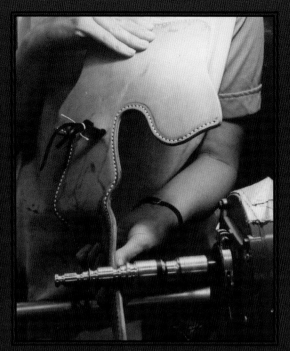

John (at left) overlooking the production of Cobra rifle slings, one of the many leather products produced for firearms by Bianchi Gunleather and later Bianchi International. "The Cobra slings were designed at Bianchi and became the most popular and most copied rifle sling in the world," says John. "Everybody in the rifle sling business makes a copy of the Cobra to this day. It is estimated that millions have been produced worldwide. Our product innovations at the time were so prolific that we couldn't afford to file for patents on every design, and many of our products were quickly copied by other makers. And that continues to this day."

This is an edge burnisher, which is used to smooth and blend the edges of two pieces of leather bonded together in making a lined holster or any leather product that consisted of a front piece and a lining. "Tools like this were not commercially available. Almost every piece of equipment in our plant was internally engineered, designed and custom made in our machine shop," notes Bianchi.

This was one of the company's steps toward assembly line efficiency, with employees assigned to do special tasks. This station was for attaching snaps to retention straps on a variety of products.

pedal driven racers. Everything we did raised morale because it didn't cost anything and everyone had a great time."

Aside from the fun side of operations, John also instituted an employee program for improving work conditions and manufacturing. "The employees on the line knew what they were doing and often they would make very important suggestions or observations, and we made this a formal process. It was called SAC, Suggestion Action Committee, and it consisted of a formalized program where you could turn in a suggestion with your name, job position, etc. Within a day of turning it in, somebody from management had to personally walk out into the plant to Joe's workbench, and everybody would be looking because someone from management was coming to talk to one of the workers. The manager would tell that person, 'Thank you for the suggestion, it is being considered and within ten days you'll get a preliminary evaluation of how the suggestion action committee rates your suggestion.' Nobody in a shirt and tie had ever spoken to that person, and now someone from management had read their suggestion and taken the time to personally thank them. All of a sudden that worker feels like a million bucks."

John made the entire process into a monthly event. "At the end of the month all of the suggestions would be evaluated and given points based on the impact it has on the company…health, safety, quality, productivity, and if the suggestion only affected your team of workers you got lesser points than one that had an affect on the whole company. And you could save the points or you could cash them in. In the lunchroom one whole wall was a big glass cabinet with prizes. There were color televisions, AM/FM radios, sporting goods, items just for the women, electric tools, all kinds of things. And they could cash points in or save them up for something really big like a color TV. When we had the awards ceremony every month we'd take a long lunch break and everyone would gather on the production floor. Each person would be called by name up onto a little platform to get their picture taken and receive a certificate for their suggestion. This seems so simple, but to factory workers who might have never been recognized for anything in their life, getting a certificate with their name hand written in calligraphy and co-signed by both the general manager and the president and having their picture taken meant a lot. They could take it home and show their family. Small things pay big rewards."

An important event that Bianchi International had each year was Family Day, which encouraged the workers to bring their spouses and children in to see exactly where they worked and what they did, and who their co-workers were. "Not done in industry," says John.

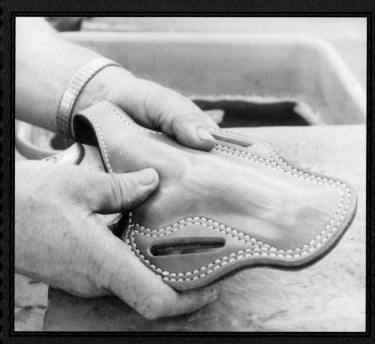

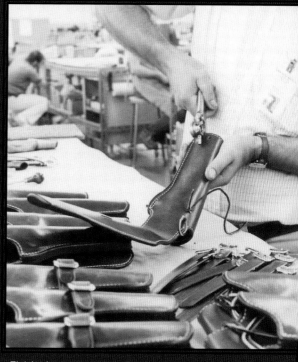

This is wet forming, used to shape holsters over a cast aluminum gun model. This ensured that every holster was properly formed and fitted to the specific gun it was made to fit. "Historically this was only done by hand and as volume increased we came up with the idea of using 3-inch thick surgical rubber pads to initially make the first impression in the leather, which was then finish formed by hand," explains Bianchi. "Neil Perkins first came up with the idea when we had Safari Ltd."

Holsters were pre-wetted before being formed for a specific gun. "We put a little dish washing soap in the water to accelerate the penetration of the leather and soften it before being hand fitted," says Bianchi. "We still use this technique today at Frontier Gunleather."

Finished western style belt holsters being hole punched for rawhide tie down thongs. "The use of tie downs was a 20th century practice which was seldom seen in the Old West," says Bianchi.

A high speed polishing wheel with a horsehair brush is used to finish off edges and polish the holster. This is a technique that has been employed by holster makers for over 150 years.

In the process of making holsters more efficiently, a die-cutting station was used to cut out holster blanks, thereby eliminating hand cutting. The end result was the same quality but with far better precision than traditional hand cutting from a pattern with a hand held knife.

This was one of many special steps used to make police security-type holsters. In this application a cylinder cutout is being made for a revolver holster.

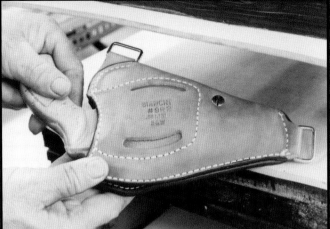

This is the Bianchi No. 9 upside down shoulder holster for the Chiefs Special. The design was based on the famous Berns-Martin holster dating back to the 1930s.

X15 shoulder holsters being prepared for oiling, finishing, and harness assembly. On average Bianchi turned out nearly 1,000 every month and the holster remained in production at Bianchi International for more than thirty years. It is still manufactured today under the Bianchi name by BAE Systems, which owns both Bianchi International and Safariland.

Shown is a small portion of the arsenal of cast aluminum gun models used in wet forming holsters. "Wet forming was a traditional way of shaping a holster, but we didn't want to have an inventory of real guns sitting on shelves. The cast aluminum models could be easily stored and were not subject to damage or rust from being exposed to moisture during the wet forming process," says Bianchi. "In the Old West, form fitting holsters was unheard of. It didn't really come into practical use until the 1950s."

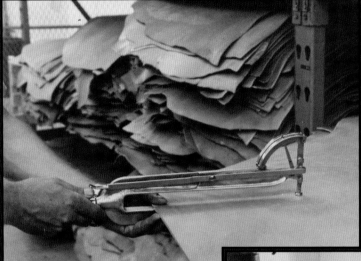

Measuring device used to determine the thickness of a hide from the center to the edge. The thickness of leather is measured in ounces per square foot. Different thicknesses are used for different parts of a holster from the pouch to thinner leather used for lining.

A shoemaker's sanding drum was used to sand and blend the main seams similar to the sole of a shoe.

In this process, cartridge slides are being hand looped for .38 caliber slides worn on a belt. "We had thousands of .38 caliber aluminum slugs that were used for forming cartridge loops," explains Bianchi. "In police circles at the time .38 caliber was the prevailing cartridge. We developed high speed production techniques for law enforcement holsters that had never been achieved in the industry, without compromising quality."

Preparing wet fit holsters to go into the drying chamber at Bianchi International. "We would dry up to 1,000 products at a time in the drying chamber. It was a conveyor belt that went through the drying oven. They would load wet holsters at one end and an hour later, take dried holsters off the other," says Bianchi. "The drying time varied depending upon the size of the articles and we had various times and speeds for the conveyor belt system. "

With the advent of Bianchi's very popular western holsters, cowboy image, and advertising in the 1970s, John took on a very different appearance at trade shows. Not the clean cut salesman but the rough edged cowpoke everyone had come to expect. As his following grew, people would stand in line for an autographed promotional poster. This was during the great Histograph era at Bianchi.

"People go to work, an employee comes home, and the wife says, 'What did you do today?' He says, 'Well I work in the shop,' and she says 'But what do you do?' Sometimes that's hard to explain. Once the wife became a partner," and John emphasizes partner, "in what he was doing, saw the work he was doing, saw his co-workers, saw his working environment, the whole family became involved in the process. If he came home tired, or late, they knew what his environment was like. What did that cost? Nothing. What did it pay back? Enormous. Simple things that make a difference," John stresses. "Hardly a week went by that we didn't get a call from a management group or a university that had heard about our work environment and they wanted to come down and see how it worked."

"When groups came though, whether it was a fan club or a tourist group or whatever, we would have hosts from the factory, not management, but factory workers who were articulate and liked to meet people. Dressed for the occasion, they would give the tour of 'their factory'. Visitors enjoyed being on that level with the workers more than if the vice president of the company had taken them through the tour. They could ask the workers about their jobs and what they did, so everyone participated. What did it cost? Nothing. What did it pay back? Monumental, because everyone was proud to be a part of Bianchi, to be involved in what was going on."

While John Bianchi was still running the company, his last objective was to produce 1,440 units a day. That's one a minute around the clock. "Every minute of every day, somewhere in the world, someone was buying a Bianchi holster. The demand was that great by the late 1970s. By the time I left the company in 1992 (John sold Bianchi International in 1987 and contracted to manage it until 1990), we had produced over 20 million belts and holsters. Since that time they have produced another 20 million, so there are more than 40 million Bianchi brand belts and holsters worldwide."

The question most people were asking in the 1970s and 1980s was how Bianchi managed to combine high quality leatherwork with mass production. Holster making had always been a handcraft industry. "It was an industry that was dormant. For over a hundred years nobody had ever automated the manufacturing of holsters and gun belts. I had to figure out a way to shorten the process, take the handwork that might normally be done in ten minutes and get it done in ten seconds, for example. How do you do that?" asks John. "In my case necessity truly was the mother of invention," says Bianchi with a laugh. "I'm not an industrial engineer, but I had to become one by default. I had to create 'devices' that could replace handwork only, only if it could do the job better. I never replaced a hand operation unless it could be done better. So we had to break new

Before there was a Mag-Lite there was the Bianchi B-Lite, which evolved from the original Kel-Lite developed in the 1960s by a Los Angeles County Deputy Sheriff, Don Keller, a friend of John Bianchi's. As John recalls, when the demand for the Kel-Lite exceeded Keller's capabilities they began making the Bianchi B-Lite; the design forerunner of the Mag-Lite. The B-Lite was originally contracted out to Tony Maglica, who started making his own version, the Mag-Lite. The Bianchi B-Lite is virtually a collector's item today. Following a chain of events, the Mag-Lite became the most successful flashlight in the world and is manufactured today in many different configurations by the millions. But it all began with John Bianchi and Don Keller.

John Bianchi, Sr. (right) was the Chairman of the Board and the company's goodwill ambassador. He is shown here presenting an S&W .44 Magnum to Chuck Neeley, president and general manager of the Endicott-Johnson leather tannery, which supplied tens of thousands of hides, tanned to Bianchi specifications.

One of the great Bianchi promotional items was a bar room mirror for Bianchi Dealer display. They became cost prohibitive and were limited to perhaps two dozen presented only to major dealers throughout the country. Among Bianchi memorabilia the bar room mirror is one of the rarest pieces.

Cal Beauregard (left) a close friend of both the Bianchi family (pictured with John Bianchi, Sr.) and the author, was a Ford Motor Company executive and liaison for Ford to the Secret Service and White House motor pool. Cal and John still keep in touch to this day. Beauregard is also an avid gun collector.

turf. You couldn't go to a store and buy a piece of machinery to do this work. It didn't exist. We went and bought a motor and a hydraulic press and then went to our tool and die makers, and these were guys who could make anything, they were so clever, anything I could imagine they would make. The spirit at Bianchi was so incredible. They were brilliant people. We had that kind of talent and we made our own machinery. The work that we produced, the quality of the work we produced, had never been done before. It became like an automotive assembly line, everything moved from station to station. Snaps, for example. One person set snaps all day long and that's all he did, and when we were done setting up this process, refining it, Bianchi International was turning out one holster every minute!"

In 1978, John and Donna Bianchi suffered through the loss of their son, John, Jr., who was critically injured in an off-road motorcycle accident. As John explained it, his son survived the accident but was in a coma for a long time. "He suffered a brain injury which left him a little impaired and he was suffering from bouts of depression. One day he took his own life. He was fifteen." The picture of John and his son was taken on an outing near Lake Tahoe, California, in 1969.

## Tragedy and the End of a Relationship

Back in 1978, John and Donna Bianchi had suffered through the loss of their son, John Jr., and it had put a terrible strain on their marriage. Compounded by the constant work and travel of building the company, their relationship was beginning to unravel. "It really began to tear our marriage apart. We separated in 1988, though we continued to work together, but four years later our thirty-three year marriage finally came to an end.

"I had been traveling all over the world for the company. I was on airplanes all the time. It was a very dynamic environment," recalls John. But by 1991 he was beginning to see the wisdom in an old Vaudevillian saying, "Don't stay past midnight and leave while they're still applauding." In 1992 that's exactly what he did. "I left and spent a year traveling around the world."

Looking back on the events that led to the sale of Bianchi International, and though more than thirty years have passed since the loss of his son, John was having a difficult time discussing it as we sat and talked. "I haven't really spoken about it in twenty years," he says quietly, "but it's important to me that I do it now. It was a tragic set of

Donna Bianchi was President and CEO of Bianchi International. She was a brilliant administrative innovator and developed all financial and personnel systems for the company. She was one of the industry's forward thinking CEOs who brought the computer sciences into the company well ahead of many other larger manufacturers. "She was a tireless executive that often put in twelve to fourteen hours a day. She was also instrumental in helping develop the M12 (UM84) holster through her acquisition of Gregory Mountain Products, a premier manufacturer of nylon outdoor equipment specializing in expedition quality tents and backpacks. The acquisition of the Gregory Company accelerated Bianchi International's manufacturing capability not only for the UM84 project, but for a wide range of similar products." Despite her total commitment to the company, she also managed to raise four children. The Bianchi's daughter Hope is still with Bianchi International's division of BAE Systems.

circumstances. My son John was badly injured in an off-road motorcycle accident. He was a motocross rider, wore a helmet and protective gear, but the accident left him in a coma for a long time. Miraculously, he survived his injuries and came out of the coma against all odds, but a brain injury from the accident left him a little impaired and he was suffering from bouts of depression. In the year that he lost, his friends had all moved on, John felt very much alone. One day he took his own life. He was fifteen," John cuts his words off abruptly. "I've never told that story to anybody. For twenty years I couldn't mention his name," John admits, as his voice tones down to a hush. "So after 1978, I stayed and tried to manage the company under extremely difficult circumstances. I never really recovered from the loss."

John sold Bianchi International in 1987-88 and agreed to stay on and help run it, but that too took a terrible toll. "I sold the company to a man who turned out to be a ruthless financial investor. He was an absolute disaster as an owner. In that period he had bought a number of other companies, all through leveraged buyout financing, and as a result of inept management few of them survived the resulting turmoil. He didn't know how to deal with people and he just brutalized the company management team. He tried to come in heavy handed over the various presidents and general managers of these highly successful businesses. At Bianchi, he came in and abruptly terminated a number of key people, and unnecessarily tried to restructure the management team. Morale sank and he essentially compromised the integrity and the loyalty of everyone there. If it weren't for the internal core strengths that I had instilled in the company it too would have been destroyed, but he wasn't strong enough to undermine the foundation. It was one of the worst periods in my life having to deal with the effect it had on the employees and the compromise of integrity, and the hurt feelings. It was a terrible time. When I left in 1992, my employment contract had been prematurely terminated, which resulted in a major lawsuit for compensation that was settled out of court in my favor. We retained ownership of the factory building and real estate, which was placed in trust for my three daughters. After the frustration of the legal battles, I needed to catch my breath," and John stops to take a deep one and exhale the thoughts running through his head.

There were subsequent ownerships of the company and today, Bianchi International, as well as Safariland, is owned by BAE Systems, a global defense company that continues to produce the products pioneered by John Bianchi for nearly half a century. John's daughter Hope is still with the company. ✍

Following her graduation from Pepperdine University with a degree in business, Hope Bianchi Sjursen (center) came to work as a manufacturer's field representative in the 1970s. Today she fills a variety of corporate management positions with responsibility for numerous companies under the BAE Systems umbrella, including Bianchi International.

The legendary Bianchi International Management Team in 1980. From left to right back row: Ed Vaniman, Richard Nichols, Don Metzger, Donna Bianchi, Michael Bunny, John Bianchi (seated), Dennis Smith, John Bianchi, Sr., Lee Shrank, Paul Black, and Richard Gerfen.

John Bianchi's right hand man in product development was Richard Nichols, a very talented designer who led the design team in the three and a half year UM84 development project. He also conducted the initial field tests at Camp Pendleton Marine Base in California. Nichols was instrumental in the design and development of most of Bianchi International's products for over twenty years. He was also singularly responsible for launching the first Bianchi Cup competitions in 1979.

In 1976 Bianchi International commemorated the manufacturing of its 1 millionth holster with a limited edition .999 sterling silver coin presented to key employees, major dealers, and industry VIP's.

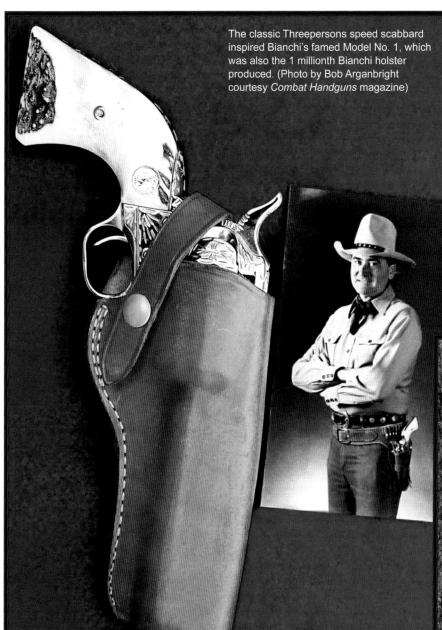

The classic Threepersons speed scabbard inspired Bianchi's famed Model No. 1, which was also the 1 millionth Bianchi holster produced. (Photo by Bob Arganbright courtesy *Combat Handguns* magazine)

The Cooper Combat with unusual Carl fly-off safety strap was the forerunner of the full steel lined Auto Draw holster. (Photo by Bob Arganbright courtesy *Combat Handguns* magazine)

Bianchi's purchase of the Berns-Martin Holster Company in April 1974 led to these break front duty and concealment holsters. (Photo by Bob Arganbright courtesy *Combat Handguns* magazine)

The Model 4501 Pocket Change Holster is constructed of Toughtek with nylon lining, carrying a vintage Colt Detective Special. Bianchi pioneered the pocket holster concept. (Photo by Bob Arganbright courtesy *Combat Handguns* magazine)

The traditional basketweave style Bianchi holster has been a staple of both law enforcement and civilian gun owners for decades. Pictured with the author's S&W K-22 Masterpiece is a thirty year old and in excellent condition Bianchi S&W K #5B holster.

Designed in the early 1980s, Bianchi's #5 Blackwidow has been a very successful holster. Because barrel length was no longer a factor, the innovative thumb breaksafety design was suitable for any number of Model 1911's, and was also adaptable for other semi-autos and revolvers. This was one of the first "minimalist" style concealed carry belt rigs, and more than a quarter of a century later there are over 130 size and model variations. Not only is the #5 Blackwidow still manufactured by Bianchi International, it is the lead off holster image on the current company website!

The innovative Bianchi X15 shoulder holster for the Model 1911 spawned many specialized variations for other sidearms. This twenty plus year old rig carrying a Smith & Wesson Classic Hunter is the Bianchi #X-2100 designed for the S&W Model 29. The holster was also known as the Phantom.

CHAPTER

# *The Secrets Of John Bianchi*

## The Master of Concealed Carry and the Philosophy of "Bianchi's Law"

Back in 1958 when John started as a patrolman with the Monrovia Police Department, there wasn't much in the way of concealed carry holsters. There were belt holsters for snub nose revolvers. What most detectives carried were old style shoulder holsters and an odd assortment of custom-made rigs done by saddle makers and small, local leather shops, but nothing in the way of mass produced quality concealment holsters. "It's not that there wasn't a need for them," says Bianchi, "it's just that no one was making them. The first thing I realized after I became a policeman was that there was a very limited selection of off-duty concealment-type holsters. There was no innovation. Holsters had remained unchanged from the 1930s to the 1950s. No innovation at all. People went into a gun store to buy a gun, and when it came to a holster the salesman or shop owner would go into the back room and rummage through a box to find a holster to fit the gun. You didn't say, 'I want a black one with basketweave and a thumb strap,' you took what he had. Holsters, outside of old style western rigs or military holsters, weren't that plentiful. There were old established holster companies but they had been making the same style rigs for decades. A holster was strictly a function item, like buying a cleaning kit. No particular name brand recognition or styling."

After John started making holsters for himself and his fellow officers and went into business in the late 1950s, he began to concentrate on the idea of concealed carry more than traditional open carry. There were a variety of standardized uniform duty holsters like the traditional Sam Browne rig (named after British General Sir Samuel Browne) which had been in use by police departments since World War I. There was not too much in the way of specialized holsters for undercover work, or for holsters designed for specific models of guns or for a particular style of concealed carry. "The Sam Browne was derived from a British sword belt, 2-1/4 inches wide with a rectangular double pronged brass buckle. The industry needed a little more creativity; a way to make holsters a little more stylish, a little more functional, and more practical. Police officers had been coming to me for years, saying, 'I like this gun but I've never been able to find a holster to fit it,' and I'd tell them, 'Let me borrow the gun for a few days.' I'd wet form a holster just for that gun; make a pattern, then when the next guy asked, I had a holster for that model gun. Pretty soon I had police departments from all over the Los Angeles area requesting specially made holsters for concealed carry."

When it became obvious that there were two needs, one for high-security uniformed belt holsters and one for more concealable, secure off-duty holsters, Bianchi became motivated to find better ways to make both, but for concealed carry there had been one motivating incident that occurred when he was a patrolman in Monrovia. "I was working the night shift. It was about three in the morning and I spotted this suspicious character walking along old Highway 66. I'm thinking, 'It's three o'clock, what's he doing walking along the side of the road in the dark?' So I stopped to question him. I didn't like his answers and I decided to take him in. Just about then the sergeant pulls up. He was an old timer who did things the way they were done in the 1930s. He says, 'What are you doing, kid?' I said, 'Well sergeant I've got this guy wandering around, he doesn't have any ID on him, doesn't know where he's been or where he's going and I think we ought to check him out. 'Oh, damn it,' he grumbles, 'all right, go ahead' and I start to handcuff him, and the sergeant

*"Beware of the man with one gun, because he probably knows how to use it."*
– John Bianchi

At the same time John was building his western persona with the sepia ads and histographs, he was also becoming the master of concealed carry and that led to yet another image of John Bianchi, as a suave man of mystery in the James Bond vein. This was part of a new series of ads that played up on his double world record for the most concealed guns in 1983 and 1993. This shot was from 1993.

This pair of ads from the 1990s continued to play up the secret agent theme and promote Bianchi's line of concealment holsters, including the X15 shoulder holster pictured in the ad by the sea.

In the early 1990s John had developed a new shoulder holster called Gun-Quick. The design was intended to adapt to any number of different semi-autos. All of the guns on the table could work with the fully adjustable Gun-Quick rig!

shouts, 'You don't need those! We never cuff those kinds of guys. We just put 'um in the back of the car and if they give us any trouble give 'um a wallop on the side of the head with a sap. You young kids always have to get those handcuffs out and go by the book!' I said, 'Sergeant, the book says I've got to put handcuffs on him.' He growls at me, but I cuff him anyway, pat the guy down, put him in the back of the patrol car and off we go. We get to the station and while I'm booking him, he's sitting on the waiting bench behind me. While I'm typing up the report I look into the window glass and I see the reflection of the guy sitting on the bench. He's wiggling all around, trying to get something out from under his shirt. I turned and slammed him to the floor and called for help. Under his shirt he had a 10-inch butcher knife strapped to his chest with an Ace bandage! It had gotten completely past the typical in-the-field pat down! And I thought, 'If this character could do that with a butcher knife, I could make a belly band with a little fastener and a soft leather holster for deep concealed carry.' Well, the thing caught on and I made a bunch of them. After that I began concentrating mainly on the designs of concealable holsters." John busts out

laughing, "I guess I owe my career to that guy!"

By the early 1960s, John had come out with a variety of hip holsters, ankle holsters, and cross draw secure holsters, and they were selling as fast as he could make them. "About that time, the Pasadena Police Academy called me and one of the instructors said, 'Everybody is talking about you and the concealed carry holsters you're making. How about coming over and giving us a demonstration?' So I did, and they were so fascinated they made me an instructor on weapons concealment. This was a challenge because I was still with the Monrovia Police Department, going to college on the GI Bill, and helping out my dad with his business and making holsters when I wasn't doing everything else. But I was really enjoying it. I thought it was really great. I developed this program for the Police Academy whereby I would conceal on me as many guns as I thought I could comfortably carry. I would be wearing a sports coat and I would lecture about how to achieve excellent concealment as a mental game, how everyone is different, and that a concealment holster that works for one person won't necessarily work for another because of that person's body configuration. Then I'd say, 'Well, let me give you a demonstration.' They knew something was coming up. I'd ask for two volunteers and say, 'Now, here are the rules: you're out on the street. Tell me, what's a reasonable length of time to frisk a suspect?' They'd say, '10 to 15 seconds.' Then I'd say, you two come up and frisk me. I'd stand hands against the wall, legs spread and the two of them would pat me down. They'd find guns that they never knew existed. They thought I'd have three or four hidden on me and I had a dozen. They'd lay out all the guns they found, then I'd turn them around to face the class and say 'let's give them a round of applause, they did a super job! These guys are professionals; they're highly trained and leave nothing to chance.' While all eyes were on them as they headed back to their seats, I'd pull the last gun loaded with blanks and fire two shots! Bang, bang! And it would bring the hall down every time. They never knew it was coming and I managed to pull it off for several years. It created a lot of interest. There were write-ups in newspapers and magazines about the whole concept of how to properly conceal a gun for law enforcement and at the same time what to look for when you're on the street and you're encountering a suspect with concealed firearms. So it was a very fertile field and a wonderful opportunity."

John studied all of the existing holster designs on the market, particularly shoulder holsters, and found one common problem with all of them: they were uncomfortable. "Even the legendary upside-down Berns-Martin shoulder holster, a very clever, well made holster, only used a 1-inch cotton webbing shoulder strap to support guns that were getting bigger and heavier," says John. "And the Berns-Martin only worked for small frame double action revolvers. It had to be a revolver because the concept of the retention device enclosed the triggerguard. The trend, however, was going toward semi-autos. So I introduced shoulder holsters for 1911 semi-autos using wide, 3-inch straps. Wow, what an idea. Everyone followed, everybody jumped on the bandwagon. After we hit the market, all of the detective novel writers started mentioning Bianchi shoulder holsters! Even Stacy Keach wore an X15 shoulder holster as Mike Hammer on TV. To this day I still get calls from people saying, 'Hey, I was reading this old novel and they talk about the character using a Bianchi holster.' And I'm never surprised because so many of them had done it."

Bianchi's concealed carry holster line became so successful that in 1975 he was able to purchase and incorporate the famous Berns-Martin company, founded in 1925, into Bianchi Gunleather. Over the years Bianchi came up with numerous devices for assisting not only concealed carry, but to quote John, "secure concealed carry." Among them were special spring and elastic closures, and the use of horizontal, vertical, and 45-degree canted shoulder holsters. "We did things that were totally unheard of that opened up the field for other manufacturers. As time went by the size of carry guns and their calibers continued to increase, and we needed to keep innovating in order to produce holsters that could conceal larger and larger guns rather than the small snub nose .38s that were used in the past. There was a dynamic, evolutionary change taking place."

In 1983 John Bianchi had set a world record for concealing 27 guns. This ad campaign helped nationalize his reputation as "The Master of Concealed Carry."

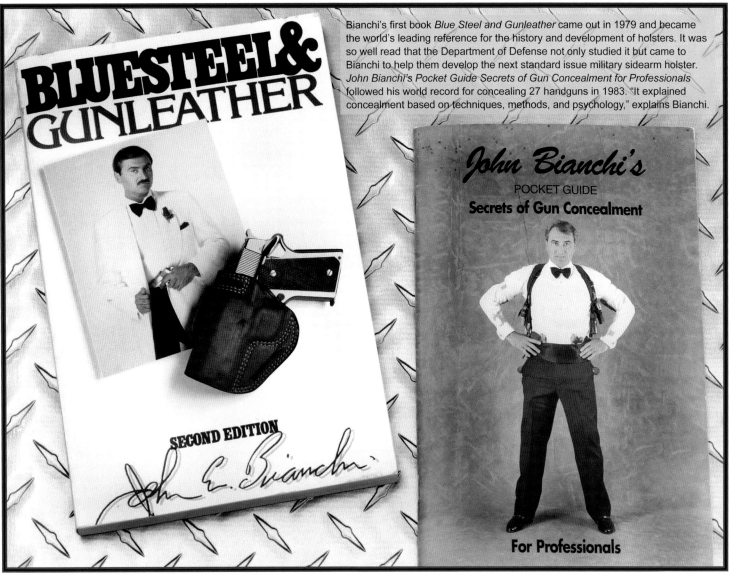

Bianchi's first book *Blue Steel and Gunleather* came out in 1979 and became the world's leading reference for the history and development of holsters. It was so well read that the Department of Defense not only studied it but came to Bianchi to help them develop the next standard issue military sidearm holster. *John Bianchi's Pocket Guide Secrets of Gun Concealment for Professionals* followed his world record for concealing 27 handguns in 1983. "It explained concealment based on techniques, methods, and psychology," explains Bianchi.

## The 1911, Forever Young

In the 1960s legendary shootist and firearms instructor Jeff Cooper helped resurrect interest in the old Colt Model 1911A1. "With few exceptions," says Bianchi, "by the 1960s the 1911 had been retired from general use. The military still used them, as did the Texas Rangers and some of the border states with Mexico, but most lawmen were carrying large frame revolvers. If you wanted to carry a 1911, at least concealed, you usually had to have a custom holster made."

"Cooper had his own school of shooting techniques based around the .45 Auto," says Bianchi, "and one day he called me wanting to discuss holster designs. It was still the early 1960s and I started making holsters for his top students, which were more progressive,

sturdier holsters for the 1911." Bianchi modified the No. 2 Speed Scabbard, used heavier leather, and added a safety strap. "That started a whole new generation of innovation in the design of holsters just for the 1911, including the original X15 shoulder holster, which used a spring clip to retain the gun. The spring clip was an inspiration I got from seeing how the Berns-Martin holsters were made."

### Clandestine Operations (Black Ops)

While John was consulting with law enforcement agencies, he was also occasionally contacted by the federal government to consult on concealed carry for agents in the field. On one occasion John was asked to meet with legendary former OSS (Office of Strategic Services) agent and CIA consultant Mitchell WerBell III to work on a project during the later part of the Vietnam War. "I had been contacted by WerBell to meet him at a hotel. When I walked into the room, the floor looked like it was covered in confetti. They had been practicing shooting into stacks of phone books using fully automatic weapons with high-tech silencers! The books were completely shot to pieces and there were spent shell casings everywhere. WerBell wanted me to outfit his operatives with devices to conceal these automatic weapons. There were three men who looked like professional assassins, and I imagine they were. What I had to do was not only show them how to conceal their guns but how to project a confident image that would not give away their concealment. They had to look natural in their environment and not like they were packing full automatic weapons with silencers," explains Bianchi.

WerBell had been initially contracted to oversee the development and manufacturing of silencers for the M-16 rifle. The project was known by the acronym SIONICS, which stood for "Studies in the Operational Negation of Insurgents and Counter-Subversion." For the mission in which Bianchi would become a consultant, the silencers had been adopted to the Ingram MAC-10 sub machine gun. MAC stood for Military Arms Corporation, which was part of an organization created by WerBell that comprised Quantum Ordnance Bankers (a group of investors) and SIONICS, the company created to manufacture the silencers.

"Later in his career, WerBell became more and more flamboyant and less prudent in his clandestine endeavors. Even that night he was standing on the balcony of the hotel room,

Revealing how he concealed 27 handguns, Bianchi explains that the technique was based on a combination of factors including the proper selection of appropriate revolvers and semi-auto pistols, holsters and simple concealment devices and apparatus. In this series of photos from 1983, John revealed how he layered guns and holsters, positioned them around his body and concealed smaller guns in pockets, and around his arms, legs, and ankles. He had on four shoulder holsters, 14 other holsters comprised of belt, inside the waistband, and ankle holsters, in addition to pocket holsters and guns held by elastic bands and Velcro. With his white dinner jacket buttoned not a single gun was obvious! "The most important element was practice and mind set, like a magician practicing an illusion."

In the July 1993 issue of *Guns & Ammo* John broke his previous world record by concealing 32 handguns!

In this 1993 *Guns & Ammo* article by writer Bill O'Brian, Bianchi revealed how he was able to put on the same white dinner jacket as he had in 1983, and with a series of the latest concealment holsters pack a record breaking 32 handguns on his person!

# HIDEOUT HOLSTERS

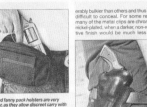

erably bulkier than others and thus more difficult to conceal. For some reason many of the metal clips are chrome or nickel-plated, when a darker, non-reflective finish would be much less eye-

for you depends on many factors including those outlined above.

**HOLSTER TYPES**

While the first handgun holsters are generally believed to have been mounted on saddles for horseback use, belt-mounted holsters inspired by belt-mounted knife and sword scabbards could not have been long in following. Today's concealment holsters include many designed to be worn on the belt or the trouser waistband.

For the most effective concealment under a jacket, the best position for a belt-mounted holster is in the area from the strong-side high to the small of the back. Crossdraw holsters, which place the gun on the hip opposite the shooting hand, can be more comfortable and accessible than other types in some circumstances but are often best avoided because the gun is very easily exposed in this position. Experiment with different holster types and positions to see which

*Belt and fanny pack holsters are very popular, as they allow discreet carry in any weather. This pack from Michaels of Oregon handles guns up to the size of this Ruger SP101 .357 Magnum revolver.*

*This type of holster, sometimes referred to as a "pancake" style, can be quite comfortable if properly designed and executed. However, it usually requires a jacket for good concealment. This particular model is the DeSantis Speed Scabbard; the gun is a Smith & Wesson Model 15 .38 Special with 4-inch barrel.*

works the best for you and your gun. For optimum concealment, choose a holster type that keeps the gun butt close to your body instead of sticking out to give its presence away.

Inside-the-pants holsters that place the gun and holster on the inside of the waistband are usually not as comfortable as holsters that go on the outside, but they do offer considerably better con-

*These 32 guns were all concealed on John Bianchi's person for the photos on the previous pages: (1) Star Firestar .40 S&W, (2) SIG P 228 9mm, (3) Davis P32 .32 ACP, (4) CZ 50 .32 ACP*, (5) Colt Detective Special .38, (6) S&W Model 60 .38, (7) Karsen 9mm, (8) S&W Model 6906 9mm, (9) FIE "Best" .25 ACP*, (10) S&W Bodyguard .38, (11) NAA .22 LR Mini-Revolver, (12) Colt Agent .38*, (13) S&W Ladysmith .38, (14) S&W Model 3953 DAO 9mm, (15) Seecamp .25 ACP, (16) S&W Model 3913 9mm, (17) FEG PMK-380 .380, (18) SIG P 220 .45, (19) S&W Model 640 9mm, (20) S&W Model 66 .357, (20) Colt 1991A1 .45, (22) Davis Derringer D22 .22 LR, (23) Sterling .25 ACP, (24) Colt Custom Commander .45, (25) Iver Johnson .22-.22 LR*, (26) SIG P 225 9mm, (27) Davis Derringer D25 .25 ACP, (28) Bersa Model 86 .380, (29) Taurus Model 85CH .38, (30) AMT DA Backup .380, (31) SIG P 230 .380, (32) Bauer .25 ACP*. Asterisks indicate makes or models not currently manufactured.

64 GUNS & AMMO JULY 1993

---

*Ankle holsters like this nylon Bianchi Ranger are popular with law enforcement for backup guns, but for a variety of reasons they are not the best choice for a primary defensive arm in most circumstances. The pistol shown here is a stainless steel Walther PPK.*

*The "paddle" style of holster is worn outside the pants with the large, stiff contoured paddle that fits inside the waistband and is contoured to the body. This type of holster, in this case a Safariland Model 518S holding a Beretta Model 92FS 9mm, can be worn either with or without a belt.*

cealment. Many attach to the belt using a metal or plastic spring clip, and most of these work pretty well. However, pay close attention to the clip's design when choosing this type of holster. Some are not secure enough to ensure that the holster is not drawn along with the gun in an emergency, and some clips are consid-

catching should a bit of the clip become exposed. Many times the individual shooter can remedy the situation with a bit of paint or electrician's tape. Other inside-the-pants holsters have leather loops that go around the belt, and some of these loops fasten with snaps to allow the holster to be attached or removed without unfastening the belt.

Holsters that are fully exposed on the outside of the belt are best reserved for the shorter-barreled handguns. One of

*To ensure proper concealment, care must be taken in the selection of both holster and clothing. This jacket is too short, revealing holster and related items on the belt when bending over or raising one's arms.*

position the gun outside the waistband but are held in place by a large, stiff "paddle" that fits inside the waistband and is contoured to the body. Paddle holsters can be worn either with or without a belt.

Speaking of belts, care must be taken in choosing a belt for concealed carry. Many gunbelts are a tipoff to a trained eye whether the gun itself is visible or not.

the most popular of these types is the "belt slide" or "pancake" style, which is usually worn behind the strong-side hip with the butt of the gun canted forward. Another design that is gaining in popularity is typified by Galco's "S.O.B." or small-of-the-back, holster. This type places the gun in a horizontal position at the small of the back. The "paddle" types

*continued on page 84*

## DIRECTORY

| | | | | |
|---|---|---|---|---|
| **ACE CASE CO.** Dept. GA 1530 Pleasant Ridge Ellisville, MO 63011 | **C&C GLOBAL** Dept. GA, P.O. Box 93216 Los Angeles, CA 90093 | **THE GUNFITTERS** Dept. GA, P.O. Box 426 Cambridge, WI 53523 | **LEATHERWOOD HOLSTERS** Dept. GA, Teel Road Winchendon, MA 01475 | **SEER INC.** Dept. GA P.O. Box 539687 Grand Prairie, TX 75053 |
| **AHERN ENTERPRISES** Dept. GA, P.O. Box 186 Commerce, GA 30529 | **CATHEY ENTERPRISES** Dept. GA, 3423 Main Drive Brownswood, TX 76801 | **GUNGEAR SUPPLY** Dept. GA, P.O. Box 361 New Castle, IN 47362 | **MICHAELS OF OREGON** Dept. GA P.O. Box 13010 Portland, OR 97213 | **TEX SHOEMAKER AND SONS** Dept. GA 714 W. Cienega Ave. San Dimas, CA 91773 |
| **AKER LEATHER PRODUCTS** Dept. GA, 2248 Main Street #6 Chula Vista, CA 91911 | **DESANTIS HOLSTER** Dept. GA, 149 Denton Ave. New Hyde Park, NY 11040 | **GUNRACER** Dept. GA, P.O. Box 660 Coarsegold, CA 93614 | **MIXSON LEATHERCRAFT** Dept. GA, 7435 W. 19th Court Hialeah, FL 33014 | **SHOOTING SYSTEMS** Dept. GA 1075 Headquarters Park Fenton, MO 63026 |
| **ALESSI** Dept. GA 2465 Niagara Falls Blvd. Amherst, NY 14228 | **DOCTOR CENTER** Dept. GA, 334 N. Euclid Ave. Ontario, CA 91764 | **ERNIE HILL SPEED LEATHER** Dept. GA, 4507 N. 195th Ave. Litchfield Park, AZ 85340 | **PACHMAYR LTD.** Dept. GA 1875 S. Monrovia Ave. Monrovia, CA 91016 | **SOUTHWIND SANCTIONS** Dept. GA P.O. Box 351 Miami, OK 74355 |
| **BAGMASTER MANUFACTURING** Dept. GA, 2731 Sutton Ave. St. Louis, MO 63143 | **EAGLE INDUSTRIES UNLIMITED** Dept. GA 400 Biltmore Drive, #530 Fenton, MO 63026 | **DOM HUME LEATHERGOODS** Dept. GA, P.O. Box 351 Miami, OK 74355 | **PISTOL PACKAGING** Dept. GA Hamel, MN 55340 | **SPEED SYSTEMS** Dept. GA P.O. Box 3952 Wilmington, NC 28406 |
| **BIANCHI INTERNATIONAL** Dept. GA, 100 Calle Cortez Temecula, CA 92390 | **EL PASO SADDLERY** Dept. GA, Box 27194 El Paso, TX 79906 | **HUNTER COMPANY** Dept. GA, 3300 W. 71st Ave. Westminster, CO 80030 | **RINGLER CUSTOM LEATHER** Dept. GA, P.O. Box 206 Cody, WY 82414 | **MILT SPARKS HOLSTERS** Dept. GA, 605 E. 44th St. Boise, ID 83714 |
| **TED BLOCKER HOLSTERS** Dept. GA, 5360 N.E. 112th Portland, OR 97220 | **GALCO INTERNATIONAL** Dept. GA 2019 W. Quail Ave. Phoenix, AZ 85027 | **JIM'S SPORTING GOODS** Dept. GA, 3260 Adams Ave. San Diego, CA 92116 | **SAFARILAND LTD.** Dept. GA, P.O. Box 51478 Ontario, CA 91761 | **STRONG HOLSTER CO.** Dept. GA 105 Maplewood Ave. Gloucester, MA 01930 |
| **BRAUER BROTHERS MFG. CO.** Dept. GA, 2020 Delmar St. Louis, MO 63103 | **GOSHEN ENTERPRISES** Dept. GA 1355 Lee Mountain Road Sedona, AZ 85007 | **KRAMER HANDGUN LEATHER** Dept. GA, 809 S. Jasper Street Tacoma, WA 98465 | **SAHARA INTERNATIONAL** Dept. GA, 522 Hampton Ave. West Palm Beach, FL 33409 | **TABLER MARKETING** Dept. GA 2554 Lincoln Blvd., #555 Marina del Rey, CA 90291 |
| **J. M. BUCHEIMER** Dept. GA, 721 N. 20th Street St. Louis, MO 63103 | **GOULD & GOODRICH LEATHER** Dept. GA, Box 1479 Lillington, NC 27546 | **THE LEATHER ARSENAL** Dept. GA, 27549 Middleton Rd. Middleton, ID 83644 | **SECOND CHANCE BODY ARMOR** Dept. GA, P.O. Box 578 7919 Gemini St. Central Lake, MI 49622 | **TRAILRIDER PRODUCTS** Dept. GA P.O. Box 2284 Littleton, CO 80161 |

GUNS & AMMO JULY 1993 65

---

## HIDEOUT HOLSTERS

continued from page 65

the gun's weight for a more comfortable feel. While I have not seen an accessory carrier specifically for tear gas or pepper spray, some of the magazine pouches are capable of holding one of these aerosol canisters for situations where less than lethal force is necessary.

*Inside-the-pants holsters like this one from Alessi are not as comfortable for extended wear as outside-the-pants styles, but they offer superior concealment. Most are held in place by a metal or plastic spring clip, though some have leather straps that go around the belt. This full-size Glock 17 9mm would be well concealed under the proper outer garments, although one of the compact Glock models might be a better choice for all-around concealed carry.*

handgun's barrel, the more likely the vertical, muzzle-downward carry will be preferable for concealment. Otherwise the choice of holster angle is largely a matter of personal preference.

The harnesses used with shoulder holsters range from very simple to very complex. The more complex designs with multiple adjustments can be difficult to fit comfortably without help from an experienced assistant. Some harnesses attach to the belt, which helps them to stay comfortably in place and aids in a smooth draw. Some other carriers for accessories like handcuffs or spare magazines on the side opposite the gun, and this helps to balance out

*An interesting alternative to conventional belt or shoulder carry is the wallet holster like this one from Galco. It holds a Beretta Model 950 .25 auto that can be fired without removing it from the holster.*

For those who spend a lot of time sitting, whether at a desk or behind the wheel of a car, shoulder holsters get in the way less than belt holsters and also offer easier access than all but the crossdraw types. Like most belt holsters, most of the time a shoulder holster requires some sort of jacket for concealment. However, some shooters have successfully concealed small handguns in a shoulder rig under a shirt. If this course is followed you must be certain that the shirt is opaque enough to prevent the gun and holster rig from showing through. A button under a necktie can be left open to allow quick access to the gun. Without a tie you can either unfasten a button when trouble is anticipated or simply rip the shirt open in an emergency. A special elastic shoulder holster for just this type of carry is available from Doctor Center, and other companies like Gould & Goodrich offer similar elastic under-the-shirt waistband rigs.

only very compact handguns. These types of holsters offer their own special problems when it comes to concealment—pants must be sufficiently roomy to avoid outlining the gun, and the holster must be mounted high enough so that it is not exposed while sitting. Drawing from an ankle holster requires a standing individual to bend over, crouch down or balance on one leg, and it's impossible to draw from while running. On the other hand, a good ankle holster is very fast and easy to access while sitting—or driving, which is particularly valuable given the current epidemic of car-jackings in many areas.

Specially designed fanny packs for carrying concealed firearms are currently very popular, and nearly every major holster maker offers at least one model. These offer their own particular advantages and drawbacks. In very hot weather or while jogging, they may be the only viable concealment option for

*Shoulder holsters like this nylon Ahern Tri-Speed model holding a Colt Double Eagle come in a wide variety of styles. Spare magazines or other gear carried on the off side help to balance the rig.*

Leg holsters are yet another alternative to conventional belt holsters. This category includes both ankle holsters and holsters that are worn higher on the calf. Their location limits them to using

some people, allowing the gun to "hide in plain sight." They are convenient and allow carrying other gear from a wallet to tear gas and handcuffs.

On the minus side, this carry system

84 GUNS & AMMO JULY 1993

---

is so popular that it can be a tipoff to many streetwise individuals. Also, an exposed fanny pack is vulnerable to snatching just like a purse. Various methods of design and construction for concealment presented John has frequently successfully concealed numerous handguns at once in order to demonstrate various concealed-carry techniques. In 1983, while associated with Bianchi International, he has posed for an ad campaign wearing an amazing 27 handguns concealed under formal dinner attire. Though he has since sold the company, he agreed to help us attempt a recreation of the famous occasion—and ended up breaking his own record!

We provided John with a wide assortment of both handguns and holsters of various makes and types to let him pick and choose the best combinations for concealment. Some improvisation was required, as when a holster from one manufacturer was mated to the offside of a shoulder holster harness from another maker to create a double shoulder rig. John brought his own elastic straps to conceal derringers and small auto pistols on his arms and thighs, and a North American Arms .22-caliber Mini-Revolver was suspended from a cord around his neck.

We kept count of the guns as they went on, and at 30 we decided to stop and get on with the photography. When the guns came off, however, we had somehow missed a couple and there were actually 32—not including the Glock 17 that he's holding in his hand! And the guns were not all tiny pocket pistols, either. They included a full-size Colt 1991A1 .45 auto, a Smith & Wesson 4-inch .357 Magnum and an Israeli copy of the Browning 9mm Hi-Power, to name a few. The total weight of all of the unloaded guns and holsters together amounted to a whopping 49 pounds! (The 27 guns used in the original ad weighed "only" 34 pounds.) Just for fun we also calculated the approximate retail value of all of the guns and came up with a total of \$12,000.

Admittedly, walking around carrying 49 pounds of concealed handguns is neither practical nor comfortable, and our sincere thanks go to John Bianchi for his patience and cooperation. But the fact that it can be done most certainly proves that there's a concealment holster for just about anyone.

*An interesting alternative... (continued)*

## ONE MAN—32 GUNS

For the color photos accompanying this article we enlisted the aid of holster guru John Bianchi, author of *Blue Steel & Gunleather*. In training law enforcement personnel John has frequently successfully concealed numerous handguns at once...

uled to be on newsstands this October.

A number of other unconventional concealment holster types are also available, and some of them are pretty imaginative. For instance, Seer Inc. makes a dummy pager that goes on the belt and a complete roundup and in-depth evaluation is in the works for the *Guns & Ammo 1994 Annual*, which is scheduled. Along these same lines, Leatherwood makes a holster that is entirely concealed inside the pants and is attached to a dummy pager, pager case or folding-knife sheath exposed on the belt. To draw, the belt accessory is pulled upward until the holstered gun's grip is exposed. Some makers like Tex Shoemaker offer wallet-style holsters to conceal a small handgun like the American Derringer High Standard double-action derringer in the hip pocket. Some are designed to remain in the

*Holsters need not be fancy to work well. This Galco Jak-Slide comfortably carries a SIG P 220 .45 auto using a minimum amount of leather.*

pocket when the gun is drawn, while with others the gun and holster are drawn together, and the gun need not be removed to fire. For the ladies, bra, garter and purse holsters are available.

So which holster is best for you? Like the choice of handgun, only you can say for sure, and it's wise to try several different types before making a final decision. John Bianchi pretty much sums it up with what he calls "Bianchi's Law" in his book *Blue Steel & Gunleather:* "While many different combinations of holster and gun are available, there will be one that is just right for each individual. Until the most certainly proves that there's a concealment holster for just about anyone.

---

which overlooked a marina and yacht basin filled with multi-million dollar boats, firing a silenced fully automatic machine pistol at styrofoam coffee cups he had thrown into the water. The cups were virtually disintegrating and he's shooting at them between these million dollar yachts. 'Nobody can hear it,' he said with a smile, and all I could hear was this hushed *burrrup, burrup* as he fired off short bursts from his luxury hotel suite balcony into the San Diego Yacht Basin! All of this was done under the auspices of the CIA, but conducted at a distance from which they could avow any accountability."

Bianchi's meetings with WerBell became as John describes them now, "more and more bizarre and less clandestine in nature. The lead intelligence agency WerBell was working with was reluctant to officially indemnify me or acknowledge the existence of this program in which I was participating. As WerBell's security and his contacts became more and more nefarious, I was becoming reluctant to participate. Because these agencies could not officially operate within the United States [the FBI could, the CIA could not], I continued to supply Mitch with equipment for several years without asking any questions. Mitch's operations eventually made headlines but no one ever connected Mitch or the agencies involved. He died in 1983 and his legendary exploits are well documented in the public domain."

John also worked for the Executive Protective Section of the State Department, the agents that travel with foreign dignitaries, the Secretary of Defense, Secretary of State, etc. He was contracted to make special briefcases that held secret communications and miniaturized tracking devices. "When events in the Middle East began to surface as an international terrorist threat, kidnappings of officials became a major concern of all intelligence agencies. At one point I was called upon to design and custom make men's trouser belts with concealed transmitting devices - antennas that ran the full length of the belt so they could be tracked. Tracking devices in shoes had become well known by then and were no longer effective or secure. The belt was a new idea and worked well for several years." John's work for the government was more of a patriotic contribution than a profit motivated business venture, often requiring more time to develop than what he charged for doing it.

Another operation in which John was called in to assist was during the Iranian occupation of the U.S. Embassy in Tehran. He was called in without being told what the operation was. Late in 1979 he arrived at a Special Forces training facility that was located in the high security stockade of a military base. "The mission called for the design and training in the use of special carry equipment for 1911 Government Model .45 Autos that had been modified for the Delta Force team. This was the U.S. Army's elite special operations group, highly trained and on the cutting edge of every conceivable tactical method, procedure, and weapon's system. I was asked to outfit a unit that was on constant alert and which could be dispatched to any part of the world and any environmental condition at any time. They literally had an 'open checkbook' to accomplish whatever mission they were assigned and to acquire whatever they needed with little checks and balances. The policy enabled this group to be incredibly effective with quick response capabilities while avoiding 'red tape.' The operatives were the most courageous, highly-trained, and competent military force I was ever associated with."

John was asked to equip a special team with handgun carry equipment for an undisclosed mission. "My work was done in secrecy, and though I had my suspicions as to the objective, I never learned of the actual mission or where it was to take place until the ill-fated Iranian rescue mission was announced worldwide by radio and television on April 25, 1980. At that time I was attending an international conference of top corporate executives in Madrid, Spain. Dr. Henry Kissinger was the guest speaker at this event, and I was honored to be recognized by Dr. Kissinger and called back stage for a personal meeting. It was later in the day I learned that the rescue mission led by U.S. Army Col. Charlie Beckwith, with whom I had consulted on training and equipping his Delta Force operatives, had failed due to a combination of elements: a massive dust storm hampering helicopter operations, and a breakdown of communications and logistical coordination in the desert. This resulted in one of our own helicopters crashing and the death of several brave Special Forces soldiers who answered the call of duty. I realized these were some of the men I had helped train and equip and my heart just sank. It had a very depressing and emotional effect on me. I was in a state of shock and disappointment. Years later, Col. Beckwith was reluctant to write a book about this exploit after the classified restrictions were lifted. He was a highly decorated officer but humble and never sought public recognition. After much effort, I finally convinced him to write the story of the mission in his own words rather than wait and have someone else, who wasn't there, tell the story. The book, *Delta Force – The Army's Elite Counterterrorist Unit*, was published in 1983. I remained in contact with Col. Beckwith for many years after the tragic events of 1980."

John continued to consult with the government on concealment and "sanitizing" equipment for use in the field. "Sanitized meant no markings that could be traced back to a manufacturer or country of origin."

## The Detonics Connection

The first mass-produced (as opposed to custom built) compact 1911-based .45 Auto was the Detonics. It evolved, in part, from the custom built compact 1911s handcrafted by Southern California gunsmith Armand Swenson. His work had received good reviews in several gun magazines by the late 1960s. Swenson was also the inventor of the 1911 ambidextrous safety, among other innovations adopted for the Detonics and later 1911-style .45 Autos. What became the basis for the original Detonics was a custom compact 1911 designed by Pat Yates, who worked for EXCOA (Explosives Corporation of

All of the improvements that John Bianchi had suggested for the Detonics Combat Master were incorporated into the gun by 1980 when Bianchi received the first example bearing serial number JEB-1. Bianchi not only carried the gun but used it on the cover of the Second Edition of his best selling book *Blue Steel & Gunleather* and in the Bianchi ad "Wolf in Sheep's Clothing". Among the features suggested by Bianchi were the bobbed hammer, Armand Swenson ambidextrous safety, checkered backstrap, beveled magazine well, and rubber combat grips. The guide rod and heavy duty double recoil spring had already been adopted, as had the use of stainless steel for the frame and slide. One of the Combat Master's distinguishing characteristics was the rear slide contour and forward mounting of the adjustable rear sight. The Combat Master weighed 30 oz. empty, measured 6-5/8 inches in overall length, 4-1/2 inches in height with a 3-1/2 inch barrel. Capacity was 6+1.

In 1990 John began the design for a new type of concealed carry rig. "I had done just about every kind of leather holster imaginable over the years. What I came up with was an injection molded holster with a spring loaded device to secure the gun. It was fully adjustable for a variety of different semi-autos. It was very concealable, very fast on the draw. I called it Gun-Quick. I licensed the design to my old partner Neil Perkins at Safariland. I not only designed the rig, I designed the packaging, did the marketing, and even appeared in the ads. It was the first time I ever designed a holster that was marketed by a competitor! It was a big hit and I collected royalties on it for seventeen years."

America in Issaquah, Washington). He had built his earliest examples in the late 1960s by modifying old GI model 1911s.

In 1974, several former EXCOA managers established Detonics Firearms Industries on the outskirts of Seattle, Washington. Within a year, they purchased the manufacturing rights to co-worker Pat Yates' compact 1911 design. After a few engineering improvements and modifications to his original concept, and tooling for investment cast frames and slides, the first Detonics Combat Masters were introduced around 1976. These were followed by the stainless steel version that became the hallmark of early Detonics semi-autos. The company hit its stride when a Detonics was chosen for the backup gun carried in a leg holster by Don Johnson as Miami Police detective Sonny Crockett in the 1984-1989 television series *Miami Vice*. Crockett's leg holster was based on an original Bianchi design.

The original Detonics Firearms Industries never quite made enough money to get ahead and was acquired by communications mogul Bruce McCaw in 1987. It emerged as the New Detonics Manufacturing Corporation from 1988 through 1992, and then quietly faded out of sight until resurrected in 2004 as Detonics USA. Currently, the fourth iteration of Detonics USA, headquartered in Millstadt, Illinois, produces the latest version of the Combat Master. The original guns, built in Washington, and bearing the "*Detonics .45 Seattle, WA.*" inscription on the frame, have become collectible reminders of a time long before compact 1911 .45 Autos were considered *de rigueur* among firearms manufacturers.

John Bianchi's brief but influential involvement with the original Bellevue, Washington, company came about a few

**Modern Weapons Delivery Systems**

Stealth was a good definition for the Bianchi Gun-Quick rig. Designed to work with a variety of different semi-auto pistols, John designed a unique stainless steel coil spring encased in a tubular plastic sleeve, to function as a retention system that could be adjusted for different pistols. The spring kept the pistol tightly in the holster, but by simply grasping the grips and pulling the gun up slightly and away from the muzzle enclosure it could be quickly drawn. It re-holstered just as fast by inserting the gun under the spring and then into the muzzle enclosure. The design was unlike anything that had been done before. Constructed of space age materials it projected a long term life cycle for durability and ease of use. In a video made for the Gun-Quick, Bianchi was able to draw and re-holster in three seconds.

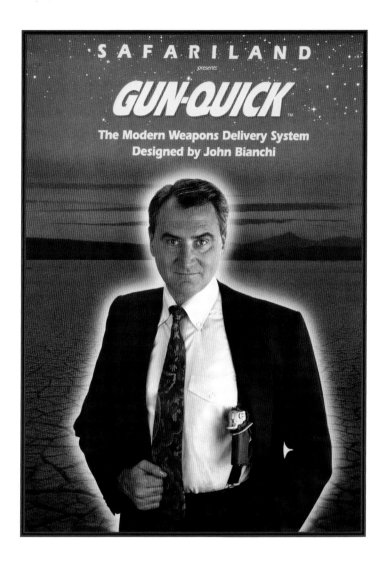

years after the Detonics was introduced. As the first production compact 1911 .45 Auto, the Detonics had an immediate following among concealed carry aficionados who favored the stopping power of the venerable .45 ACP cartridge.

"They were already in development and had a number of guns out on the street, but not in any great quantities," explains Bianchi. "It was in the late 1970s, maybe 1979, when I met one of the owners at a show who wanted to discuss the gun's features. He had a prototype to show me and said something to the effect of, 'You're on the cutting edge of all the concealment holsters. You know what the market is looking for in the way of compact guns and compact holsters and we're working on refining the Detonics.' What he wanted was my suggestion for any changes to the example they had brought to the show. Over the course of the three-day event we had several meetings during quiet periods at the Bianchi booth and we talked about what features I felt a compact .45 Auto should embody. I don't remember the exact details, but I rattled off a few items, some of which they were already

working on, so I don't profess to take credit for them, but he was writing down everything I said. I told him an ambidextrous safety was essential and I gave him the history of my experience with Armand Swenson, who made the first 1911 ambidextrous safety for me because I'm left-handed. At the time, in the late 1960s, Armand and I had been shooting with Jeff Cooper and Ray Chapman in Big Bear, California. I then suggested they modify the gun with a beveled magazine well, and modify the grip safety, although they ended up eliminating it altogether. Then I said it needed to have rubber combat grips, and I suggested that the backstrap be checkered or knurled to provide a better gripping surface since the grip frame had been shortened to accommodate a six-round magazine. When the improved gun came out they put a diamond pattern on the backstrap, which worked out well because you ended up with both horizontal and vertical gripping surfaces. They were already successfully working with stainless steel, and I said that was a very good idea. Looking at the prototype, I suggested that the ejection port needed to be relieved, which in fact reaffirmed what they were already planning to do, and then, I added, it's got to have

a bobbed hammer.

"It was a very clever gun, and I was intrigued by it, so about six months later I get a call and they tell me they've got a gun for me and 'hope you like it.' It arrives and it had every feature I had suggested. In retrospect the only critical analysis I would have of the gun now is that the slide needed more pronounced serrations because it is a hard gun to cycle due to the heavy double recoil spring and guide rod design. It also could have used a more pronounced slide stop."

Thirty years after receiving the gun and almost a quarter century after John Bianchi stopped carrying the specially inscribed Combat Master, he joined the author for an afternoon "shoot" both in the studio and on the test range. After a thorough take down and cleaning, the 30-year old .45 Auto was loaded with Federal American Eagle 230gr. FMJ ammo and test fired. Bianchi and the author used a B-27 silhouette target at a combat distance of 21 feet (seven-yards) and rapid fired the gun using a two hand Weaver stance. After adjusting the rear sight, shots grouped under two-inches in the X and 10. With the exception of one stove pipe out of 50 rounds the gun performed flawlessly. Bianchi was surprised by how manageable the recoil was, having remembered it as having quite a kick. "I'd have to describe the recoil as 'user friendly' considering its size and caliber. At over two pounds when loaded, it's a pretty hefty gun and that probably helps mitigate some of the recoil. Firing it for the first time in 25 years I was pleasantly surprised. The tolerances are very good, the slide was tight, the trigger, for a factory gun, is very acceptable, and comparing it to today's .45 Auto compacts I still like it very much. It remains a very credible gun."

## Concealed Carry and Duty Rigs

While Bianchi was focusing on concealment, he was also looking for ways to improve duty holsters for law enforcement. That gave birth to a whole host of Bianchi Gunleather break front holsters, the first being the Model 27. Similar to the old Berns-Martin front draw Bianchi had admired, it was more secure and better made, becoming one of the most popular police duty holsters of the 1970s. "We sold tens of thousands of Model 27 holsters over the years," says Bianchi. "Then we came out with the Auto Draw, which was a break front designed for a semi-auto." Bianchi and company spent over $100,000 developing the Auto Draw security holster. Former police officer and noted author, columnist, and firearms instructor Massad Ayoob carried his duty gun in an Auto Draw for much of the 1980s. "It saved the life of a friend of mine," wrote Ayoob in a 2008 issue of *Guns* magazine, "when it kept his murderous assailant from snatching his .45 auto out of his uniform holster after he was ambushed and knocked unconscious." In the 1970s Bianchi also introduced the No. 3 Pistol Pocket, an inside-the-waistband holster with a leather ridge to keep the holster mouth open, (a design often seen today) and secure one-way snaps for the wide leather loop that fastened it to the belt. A thumb-break safety snap proved convenient, fast, and acceptable to police departments. "Cops and detectives bought them in droves," wrote Ayoob.

"In the 1970s we took the market by storm with holsters for every type and size gun for law enforcement, undercover concealment, civilian, and even military use," says Bianchi. But for John, the operative word was probably "concealment." By the 1980s not only did he offer the most extensive line of concealment rigs on the market, he held the world record for the most concealed handguns.

"As we developed new holsters I would come up with techniques and ways to conceal them and I would practice carrying as many guns as possible. The first time I went for a record was in 1983 and I had 27 guns on me, everything from Derringers to a Colt Python. They were concealed so that I could stand and chat and move around, but I had guns everywhere, up and down my legs, around my waist, in multiple shoulder holsters, strapped to my arms, around my neck, down my back, and all within reach."

On March 24, 1993, Bianchi and the staff of *Guns & Ammo* magazine set out to break the previous record. The guns ranged from .22 Derringers to half a dozen medium PPK-sized semi-autos, .38 and .357 magnum revolvers, and multiple 9mm and .45 ACP semi-autos, all concealed under a formal white dinner jacket and dress slacks. The photo session was for the July 1993, issue and Bianchi had no idea how many guns he would end up concealing.

"There are two aspects to gun concealment," says Bianchi. "One is mechanically doing it, and the other is mental preparation. It's like being a magician. Part of a magician's technique for creating illusions, 'the hand is quicker than the eye,' is in believing in what you are doing. You have to master the mental preparation…that is, to comfortably carry and conceal a handgun and provide quick and easy access in an emergency. Everything you do must look and feel natural even though you may have a gun up your sleeve!"

The first time he had done this, the total was 27 guns, "But," John laments, "that had been ten years earlier, I had been twenty, maybe twenty-five pounds lighter, so I had to really get myself in the right frame of mind. Every time we added a gun I had to think about it, had to envision where it would go, how it would work, what do I have to adjust…if I move the Python an inch or two to the left then I can twist a PPK around it butt forward…and it was like a domino theory. The most important thing was that they had to all be concealed and I had to be able to move about naturally. *Guns & Ammo* was supplying all of the holsters and guns, so I didn't have any of the little devices I'd used the first time. There were witnesses, cameras, people recording it because they not only wanted to see the end result; they wanted to see how I would do it! I had two helpers to move guns and holsters around on me. They had about 50 different guns, every conceivable type of concealment holster from all different manufacturers and I looked at everything and thought, 'Boy, you bit off more than you can chew, big guy' but I started to put on holsters and guns. I started at my ankles and worked my way up, thighs, waist, pockets, arms, back, neck, and it went on and on. My hope was that I could duplicate the 27 guns from before but no one was counting. When I was ready I came out of the dressing room and they started taking photos as I walked and turned around. I was carrying more than 32 pounds of guns on me. After the photos were done I started pulling guns. They were coming from my arms, my ankles, behind my back, out of my pockets, and now they're counting them. When everything was on the table the total number was 32 guns! I was amazed. I had no idea we were going to establish a new record. That was the last time I did it."

The secret to concealed carry, according to John Bianchi, is the proper psychological state of mind. "First you must maintain a positive mental attitude. Secondly, you must constantly visualize yourself armed and concealed, and third, practice, practice, practice. Avoid the temptation to become trapped by your pre-conceived notions about what make and model gun and rig you *think* you would like to carry," cautions Bianchi. "Your favorite handgun may be a 6-inch S&W .357 magnum, but your personal body dimensions and weight distribution might make that impractical. You must work diligently to select the right combination that suits your particular limitations. Remember that the best concealed gun is worthless unless you can access it with reasonable ease and moderate speed."

Through years of dynamic innovation, Bianchi has had a profound effect on revolutionizing gun carry methods and procedures world wide. Every holster made today bears the original Bianchi design influence! John considered the 1990s a continuous learning curve because so many breakthroughs were being made in holster technology. "Holster makers were constantly learning how to do it better, something that we had done successfully for years and there was a continual evolutionary cycle. The basics, however, always prevailed. A holster had to be comfortable whether you were standing, sitting, or moving, it had to keep the gun in place and it had to allow ease of draw. People would go to a movie and see a holster, and say, 'Oh I've got to have one like James Bond or Dirty Harry, or like Bruce Willis used in his last film', never realizing whether or not the holster is practical. What looks good on the screen doesn't always work when you're really carrying a gun. I call it Bianchi's law of concealed carry: one gun, one holster, one carry method, and master it. Once you embrace this philosophy you eliminate the risk of confusion and uncertainty of using holsters of different makes, multiple guns, barrel lengths, and calibers. In an emergency situation, you must instinctively grasp one familiar pistol, knowing exactly where and how it is holstered. This is all part of the subconscious mental conditioning necessary to accomplish your highest potential in defensive combat shooting.

"Beware of the man with one gun, because he probably knows how to use it." ∅

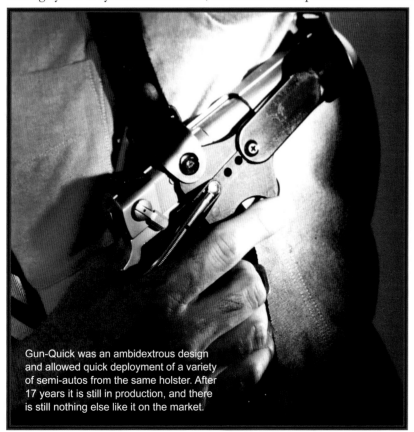

Gun-Quick was an ambidextrous design and allowed quick deployment of a variety of semi-autos from the same holster. After 17 years it is still in production, and there is still nothing else like it on the market.

Safariland introduces

# GUN-QUICK

**The Modern Weapons Delivery System**

The unique design of GUN-QUICK allows a smooth, quick-draw in one easy motion.

**1.** Make certain that pistol safety is engaged and muzzle is pointed in a safe direction. Grasp pistol grip firmly with trigger finger extended and clear of trigger guard.

**2.** Draw pistol against retention spring (using approximately 15 lbs. pressure) allowing muzzle to fall free. Avoid jerking motion or use of excessive force to draw pistol.

**3.** Retention spring will roll smoothly off hammer (or grip tang) freeing the pistol.

# CHAPTER

## The Military Connection

### The M12 UM84 – The World's Most Successful Holster

The military has been a major part of John Bianchi's life. From National Guard Reservist at age fifteen in 1953 to active duty at age seventeen with the U.S. Army, he worked his way up through the ranks from an active duty private in 1955 to the rank of Major General in the California State Military Reserve, and was called back to active duty for two years following the attacks of September 11, 2001. But General Bianchi the soldier, Dr. Bianchi the administrator (he holds a Ph.D in Business Management), and John Bianchi the legendary maker of holsters all have one thing in common; dedication to doing the best possible job in every situation. As fate would have it, Bianchi's military experience would not only create the bedrock for his systematic work ethic, but in the 1980s he would be tasked with creating the first universal holster in history for the U.S. government, the M12 (UM84) sidearm holster for the Beretta Model 92F pistol.

In January 1985, after much deliberation and testing, it would be announced that the Beretta would succeed the venerable Colt Model 1911A1 as America's standard issue military sidearm. In addition to a new gun, the military would also have a new holster. During the early trials to determine a replacement for the 1911A1, a separate fact finding team had been established within the Department of Defense to look into new holster designs.

Up to this point in time, all branches of service had been relying primarily on the old M1916 holster, which had evolved from the original Model 1912 holster in use since the Model 1911 had been adopted. Although a proven general purpose holster, as author Gene Gangarosa Jr. wrote in his 1994 book, *Modern Beretta Firearms*, the M1916 had many disadvantages. "For one, the M1916 is made of leather, and more modern synthetic materials now available offer much easier cleaning and maintenance methods. Holsters made from new ballistic nylon synthetics are much less expensive than leather ones, a strong consideration when ordering half a million or more at a time. Also, when worn as issued, the M1916 holster hangs too low on the web belt for comfortable carry; moreover, it cambers the pistol away from the body, hindering concealment and increasing the likelihood of snagging the holster. Still another problem is that like the M1911-type pistol itself, the M1916 holster is poorly suited to left-handed use," observed Gangarosa.

There was already one replacement in the system, unofficially, the Bianchi Model 66 holster, which went into production in 1970. It was not only innovative in its design, it was the first commercially manufactured ambidextrous holster. Although the M66 was not officially adopted by the U.S. military, many thousands were acquired and placed into service during the Vietnam War and afterward through individual units, including the Navy SEALS. There were, however, several problems. The M66 was leather (lacking sufficient durability for amphibious operations), it was costly to manufacture, and most importantly, would not fit the Beretta Model 92F pistol, the most likely successor to the M1911Al.

"One day in 1981, the phone rang and it was the Department of Defense," says John raising his eyebrows with a look of puzzlement. "The caller said, 'You've probably heard

*"The handgun and its holster form a team; if they are poorly matched, the functioning of the team will be impaired, with possibly fatal results."*

– Author Gene Gangarosa Jr.
*Modern Beretta Firearms*

Major General John E. Bianchi's battle dress camouflage jacket with the M12 (UM84) General Officer's version of the holster and belt made in black leather, and General Officer's special Beretta Compact (4.25 in. barrel) Model 92F. The Special General Officer's Compact Model 92F (serial No. D34825Z) was presented to General Bianchi by Beretta in 1988.

"The Nighthawk Knife was developed concurrently with the M12 to incorporate a number of features, not only in the knife but in the carrying system. Eventually we submitted it for military approval, but it became a staple item in the Bianchi International catalog. The knife was unique in that it had a brass hilt with two holes. The handle was hollow so you could keep survival items inside it and was capped off with a tiny compass in the buttcap. In a survival situation you could taper a tree branch or a piece of wood to make a pole and insert one end into the handle, then use the two holes in the hilt to lash the knife to the pole and make a spear. You could use a parachute cord or a piece of wire to tie the knife, so it was possible to use it for a number of different needs. The blade had saw teeth on top to make it more versatile. The sheath had a nylon liner that prevented the blade from ever cutting into the stitching. It also had an attached sharpening stone riveted to the back of the sheath, which had never been done before in the history of knife making. You also had a small case with a plastic box to hold a signal mirror, a cigarette lighter, some wicks, a razor blade, needle, and thread. Also housed in the back of the sheath was a larger, professional compass and measuring device to read a map. The sheath also incorporated the same universal mount as the M12 holster so it could be carried on a GI web belt or a conventional belt. It was the ideal survival knife. It was manufactured for about seven or eight years."

that the government is looking to replace the 1911 pistol and we haven't made a decision on what that will be, but we need to concurrently come up with a new design for the holster. We read your book [*Bluesteel & Gunleather*, 1978] and we are convinced that you are the final authority on holster design.' I was very flattered to hear they had read my book at the Department of Defense, and then they really threw me a curve. The caller asked if they could send a team of acquisition people out to Bianchi International to visit and get some ideas on how to design a new military holster. Boy, they hit my ego button and I was flattered. It was something that was pent up in me for years. I wanted to develop the next generation of military holsters. It was long overdue and needed, and I honestly felt that there was no one more dedicated or qualified to do it than I, based on my military experience, my police experience, and my manufacturing experience."

Bianchi, who at that time was a Lt. Col. in the Military Reserve, said he would welcome a visit and offer whatever advice he could. The next thing he knew a team of three government researchers was on his doorstep. "I had to bury my military involvement. They knew I was a reserve officer, but I could never risk trying to influence anybody with my military status. So that had to be absolutely off the table and I religiously stuck to that principle."

When the DoD team arrived they were carrying a copy of *Bluesteel & Gunleather*. "They sat down in my office and started going through the book from one page to another saying, 'this is fascinating, and this is fascinating, absolutely fascinating,' and then they dropped the big question, 'What should the new holster consist of?' Well, I just ran off at the mouth. I said, 'That's a big question and it's a dynamic challenge, and just off the cuff I haven't given it much thought aside from the fact that it has been a passion of mine.' But now we were talking about hands-on nitty-gritty and we have to get down to specifics, so I started off with the statistics I already knew. First of all I said, 'Thirteen percent of the military is left handed and there are no left-handed holsters, so it has to be ambidextrous to minimize the inventory items. We don't want a left-hand holster and a right-hand holster, so one holster needs to be interchangeable.' They looked at me and said, 'That makes sense.' And then I told them, 'It needs to appeal to Army, Air Force, Marines, Navy, and Coast Guard, so that means it needs to be environmentally balanced, suitable for extreme cold, extreme heat, humidity, dust, salt water, everything.' They looked at each other again and said they'd never even thought about that. Well, that heated up the discussion and the creative juices started to flow. I explained that additionally, it needs to be conducive to paratrooper use. The current design in use requires the pistol to be tied to the paratrooper's leg with a Cavalry strap dating back to the 1890s. And the holster was still being carried by a brass wire prong on a web belt. I said, 'That carry method with the brass prong has to go. It has to be more secure, it has to ride higher on the hip.' So we talked about the holster needing to protect the gun against environmental factors, as well as abrasion, rolling on it, and falling on it. It had to be chemically and biologically adaptive; it had to be able to be cleaned very quickly in the event of exposure to chemical, biological, or even nuclear contamination without harm to the material. If it is leather and it gets wet, it takes forever to dry. Troops are in the field, and can't have a wet holster, so that ruled out leather. Now we're getting

**1981** **UNIVERSAL MILITARY HOLSTER DEVELOPMENT** **1984**

This storyboard was developed at Bianchi International in 1980-81, and used in the marketing brochure, documenting the various stages of development in the M12 (UM84) holster over a period of three years. The display board shows every variation in the holster's development process, the trial and error, and the evolution of the belt mounting device. It shows the different materials that were tested in development and final versions of the M12 (UM84).

into a field I knew very little about at the time, synthetic materials. We talked for three days, and they jotted down everything that I said. I'm just talking, not realizing they're hanging on my every word as if I'm the foremost authority in the world. So, at the end of three days, they toured the plant, saw what our capability was, thanked me, and left. And I kind of forgot about it."

About six months later, John gets an RFQ (Request for Quotation) in the mail to design the holster. "They had sent it out to five different government qualified makers of military supplies, not holster makers necessarily, but companies that made canteen covers, and web belts, and to Bianchi International. I looked at the RFQ, and it's this thick," John holds his thumb and index finger about an inch apart, "and it has 64 points

of compliance! Did I say all that? Everything I had suggested they put in the RFQ! Now it was back to haunt me. I looked at it and thought, 'Nobody could do all of these things, that's just too much in one product.' Then my competitive juices started to flow and my ego got in the way of common sense. They asked for a quote for the design and creation of a prototype. We got together our team of accountants, production managers, and designers, and worked out a design timeframe of 18 months and while figuring out what it was going to cost…" John lets out a deep breath, "…$200,000. Then we got to talking about it, and realizing that maybe we needed to shave this a little, and we ended up quoting $180,000. We sent in the bid and two months later we get a call; we'd won the bid. I thought, 'Gee, that's great. Wonder what the other bids were?' I called and they said, 'Well, it doesn't go public for another ten days, and then its common knowledge and you can look at it.' When we saw the other bids we were flabbergasted. One was $6,000; another was $2,500; the next highest bid was $12,000, and we had bid $180,000! Later we were told they determined these other people had no idea what they were getting into and what they were bidding on. 'It was obvious that you folks had given it a lot of thought

# The TOTAL FORCE Concept

BIANCHI'S AMBIDEXTROUS UNIVERSAL NATO MILITARY HOLSTER SYSTEM
## UM-84

---

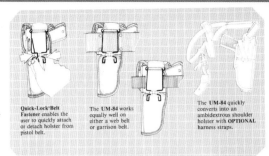

The **TOTAL FORCE** Concept and the new 9mm NATO service pistol require a universal military holster system suited for all services and all situations.

Bianchi International's **UM-84** Ambidextrous Universal Military Holster is that new *TOTAL FORCE* holster.

- The **UM-84** holster's omnidirectional wear capabilities provide the soldier with unlimited military application. Worn on the hip, leg, or shoulder, the UM-84 easily converts from left to right hand draw.
- The **UM-84** easily converts to a shoulder holster.

**Quick-Lock Belt Fastener** enables the user to quickly attach or detach pistol holster from pistol belt.

The **UM-84** works equally well on either a web belt or garrison belt.

The **UM-84** quickly converts into an ambidextrous shoulder holster with **OPTIONAL** harness straps.

BIANCHI'S AMBIDEXTROUS UNIVERSAL NATO MILITARY HOLSTER SYSTEM
## UM-84

Right-hand cross draw    Right hip for right-hand draw    Left hip for left-hand draw    Left-hand shoulder    Right-hand shoulder    Optional Hip Extender with leg straps

**Three years of intensive research and development** have resulted in the design of the Bianchi Model #UM-84, a universal, multi-purpose, military holster system for NATO forces. This is a new, high-technology, ambidextrous hip holster which can be quickly converted to an ambidextrous cross-draw hip holster or ambidextrous shoulder holster, thus providing six possible methods of wear. It is designed to fit a wide variety of NATO pistols.

The Model #UM-84 is a state-of-the-art holster employing a combination of space-age materials, including a special, non-absorbant closed-cell polyfoam core with a ballistic nylon outer facing. This type of construction provides excellent padded protection for the weapon never before achieved. The all new **Quick-Lock™ belt fastener** enables the user to quickly attach or detach the holster from the pistol belt and to convert the holster from right to left hand

in seconds. The safety fastener on the flap is a simple, fail-safe design which operates silently and smoothly under all conditions.

The UM-84 holster was designed to provide the greatest degree of comfort and security for modern military purposes. The holster is positioned on the web pistol belt at the optimum center of gravity. This results in added security during vigorous field activity.

The **UM-84 holster's omnidirectional wear capabilities** provide virtually unlimited military applications for ground, airborne, aircrew,

armored and security personnel. The smart, attractive styling is based on the "form follows function" concept. Its abrasion-resistant construction, coupled with its universal application, makes this rugged holster the state-of-the-art for military handguns.

**BIANCHI INTERNATIONAL™**

---

Bianchi International's UM84 brochure showed the developmental sequences of the holster from 1981 to 1984. "It was the most demanding, most expensive holster development project in history," says Bianchi. "It is still in general use to this day." This was also a commercial sales brochure. When Bianchi sold the patent rights to the U.S. government, he retained the commercial sales and manufacturing rights. "We made them on a small scale for other governments as well, but the U.S. also delivered a lot to other countries on a Military Foreign Aid Program, equipping allied forces with holsters.

---

In 1986, this DuPont brochure featured a section on their role in the UM84's development. "We told them what elements we needed, and they formulated the materials to meet all of the environmental demands."

The literature detailed the use of DuPont's Hytrel® in place of leather in the manufacturing of the holster. It was used for the forward fold as a one-piece construction component that also provided for the belt mounting device and flexible nylon cleaning rod.

---

## Engineering Design
### WITH DUPONT POLYMERS

Bearing Materials: Choosing the Right Type of "Delrin" (Pg. 4)

**DUPONT**

---

**DURABILITY A MAJOR CRITERION AS "HYTREL" REPLACES LEATHER IN BIANCHI-DESIGNED PISTOL CARRIER**

TEMECULA, CALIFORNIA

Quick-Lock™ fasteners snap into ammunition pouch to be used with pistol belt.

## A HOLSTER FOR THE MILITARY'S NEW 9 MM SIDE ARM
BY LES BECKA

and understand what the challenge is, they told us. Within six weeks we were awarded the contract for the design, and we were to begin work within 30 days."

John had decided not to wait for the money and started working on preliminary designs. They were two months into the project and they still hadn't heard a word from Washington. "There were three of us working full time on this project. I headed up the team and we had our own R&D department, supplemented by direct access to our own in-house tool and die department and machine tool department, so we didn't have to farm out any of the developmental work. We could do everything in-house up to making the designs for the injection molded pieces. We're six months into it when we finally get a phone call. 'Bad news, Congress cut all developmental funds. We thought you ought to know. You can continue with development if you want. There's no guarantee when you'll be paid.' Once again ego got in the way of common sense. If it were any other public company they would have stopped development right there. Stockholders wouldn't have put up with it. Well, I was the principal stock holder," John says with a laugh, "so there was no one to say 'stop development,' and I decided to proceed full bore right on through. Luckily, about six months later the funds were reinstated and we began getting progress payments as we worked. But the job really posed some enormous challenges. Not so much the government's requirements but my requirements, because I knew the military had been using the same holster for 70 years, and if this new one is going to be around as long, I want it to be fail-safe. If my name is on it, it's got to be primo. As we worked and reworked the design, we came to the realization that we needed space age materials that we were not familiar with or accustomed to working with. At the time, my wife Donna was president of Bianchi International; I was chairman of the board, a position my dad had held until he retired. Donna was really the genius behind the administration. She handled finance, human resources, and sales, while I was handling legal, product development, and marketing. She was very resourceful and when we needed to find a new material for manufacturing the military holster, she found a company in San Diego, Gregory Mountain Products, which worked with expedition quality nylon materials. She came in and told me, 'The company is for sale,' and I said, 'Well, we don't want to buy a company just to make the holster,' and she said, 'Well, its got other attributes; they make high-tech backpacks and tents for mountaineering expeditions. It's a premier company.' She was adamant. I said, 'How are we going to pay for it?' She answered, 'Don't worry, I'll take care of it,' and she did. We bought the company, brought its skilled workers in-house, and integrated them into Bianchi International. Now we had the design and the technology to build the new military holster."

Another 18 months passed and Bianchi's team was still struggling with the nuances of complying with all of the features that had to work together. Being ambidextrous, the mounting mechanism had to be transferable from one side to the other. "We didn't want clips on both sides of the holster because that would interfere with your hands, scratch your hands, snag on things. We needed a quick fix for that problem, but at every level of development we had to submit parts for testing against chemical, biological, nuclear exposure, salt water, atmospheric conditions, humidity, heat, cold, and it went on and on."

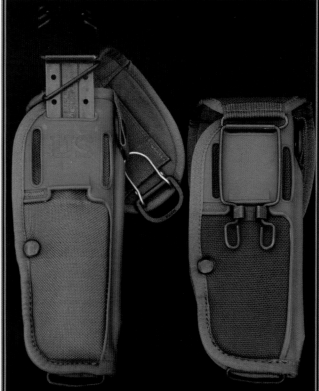

Shown are left- and right-hand holster configurations detailing how the clip device, designed by John Bianchi, worked to allow a quick switch from right to left hand mounting. As John had researched the percentages of right and left-handed soldiers in the military, he knew that only thirteen percent were left-handed, but nevertheless the new holster had to be ambidextrous in order to minimize inventory items and make one holster universally adaptable. Releasing and squeezing the retaining pins allowed the entire mechanism, including the holster flap, to be pulled out of the retainer, which is part of the holster's synthetic wraparound. The opposite side of the holster had the same retainer, so all one needed to do was to push the clip through the slit and lock it into place. "It could be done in a matter of seconds," says Bianchi.

In 1983, Bianchi Director of Product Development, Richard Nichols, went to the U.S. Marine base at Camp Pendleton, California, where volunteers tested the final prototype of the M12 in its various configurations from belt mount to shoulder holster. At the time, the Model 1911A1 .45 Auto was still the U.S. Military's standard sidearm, but the holster was designed to carry either the 1911 or new Beretta 92F (M9), which Bianchi knew was very likely to emerge as the victor in the government pistol trials.

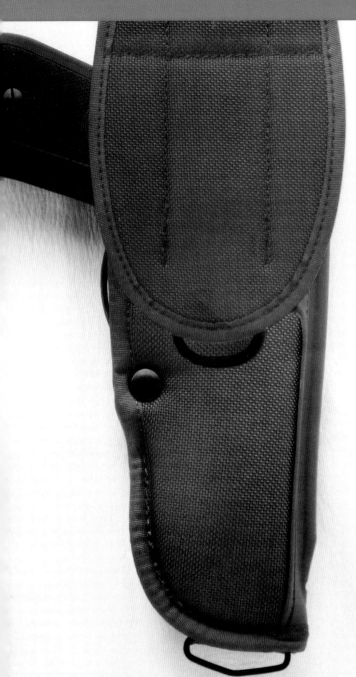

# THE BIANCHI UM-84
## Quietly, it is making every other military holster in the world obsolete.

The Bianchi International UM84 sales brochure outlined the development of the holster for the military and described the various civilian versions available. Bianchi International produced around 70,000 M12 (UM84) holsters between 1984 and 1994. The UM84 is still manufactured for the civilian market, and the M12 remains the U.S. military's primary sidearm holster for all branches of service and in all combat zones after more than 25 years. From all reports, its service record remains impeccable. The longevity of the M12 is testament to the highly dedicated individuals at Bianchi International who worked as a tightly knit team and relentlessly pursued perfection. "This went beyond the profit motivation and truly became a labor of love," says Bianchi. "Our goal was to design a holster that would be in service for the foreseeable future, and we achieved that goal."

### AMERICA SELECTED THE UM-84 HOLSTER FOR ITS NEW BERETTA SIDE ARM. NOW DRAW YOUR OWN CONCLUSIONS.

☐ Quiet. Lightweight. Tough. Comfortable. Ambidextrous. Attractively styled. The first truly versatile systematized military holster in history. Procurement efficient. User efficient. Cost efficient.

No wonder the U.S. Armed Forces are buying hundreds of thousands of Bianchi's UM-84 holster specially configured for their new Beretta 92F 9mm side arm.

Designated the M-12, the U.S. version of the UM-84 holster is the first new standard issue U.S. military holster since the introduction of the 1909 model originally designed for mounted cavalry troops. And it represents a quantum leap forward in holster technology.

This same technology, these same materials and craftsmanship that meet the same rigid military specifications are available to you right now in three different models of the UM-84 holster accommodating 23 different 9mm NATO pistols.

**Procure one holster for every holster job.**
☐ The unprecedented versatility of the UM-84 springs from its unique modular design. The holster is ambidextrous and can be converted from right- to left-handed use in seconds. It can be worn with or without flap on either a web belt or a garrison belt in either a side-draw or cross-draw position. Attachment is easy, fast and secure with a special quick-lock feature. Just as quickly, it converts to an ambidextrous shoulder holster. With optional accessories *it can be worn in 14 different ways*. So it's the only 9mm side arm holster you need to buy. Whether it is used in the field, airborne, in tanks or any other military situation. Modular design means other economies, too. For example, the holster is maintainable by replacing subassemblies. So you can stock spare parts instead of complete holsters for replacement purposes.

Easy on the user, easy on the weapon, easy on the budget.
☐ The UM-84 employs leading edge-technology materials and manufacturing techniques to advance the state of the art of side arm holsters. The holster features a tough ballistic nylon outer facing over a core made of special non-absorbent closed cell polyfoam plus other advanced synthetics. The result is an abrasion resistant holster that is silent in use, is easy and quick to draw from, does not crack like leather, is 20% lighter, is non-reflective and will function in environments ranging from -60°F to +200°F. Equally important, the design and the materials provide an order of impact and moisture protection and security for the weapon never before offered by a holster. So the economies of this all-climate, all-use holster also extend to the side arm it houses.

But the versatility of this new universal holster doesn't stop there. It is available in six different colors to coordinate with just about any military garb. It incorporates - we thought of everything - features like an integral flexible cleaning rod for weapon cleaning in the field. And a positive hook-type flap closure that eliminates entirely the telltale snap- or snap fasteners and the inherent unreliability of conventional military stud fasteners.

**The UM-84 Holster System packs the features you want.**
☐ The UM-84 was developed and is manufactured by Bianchi International, the world's largest builder of handgun holsters. Special production equipment and techniques make Bianchi uniquely qualified to deliver large quantities of these holsters on schedule. Most important, development is complete and paid for entirely at Bianchi's expense, the requisite manufacturing capacity is in place and the resulting economies will be quickly apparent from our quotation. We firmly believe that for 9mm NATO handgun holsters there is only one conclusion you can draw: Bianchi UM-84. Contact Bianchi today.

**MAINTAINABLE**
Use mild soap and warm water to clean and air dry. Replace subassemblies instead of entire holster for increased cost effectiveness.

The M-12 configuration of the UM-84 holsters. Selected as the U.S. Armed Forces hip holster.

**CLOSED-CELL POLYFOAM CORE**

**D-RING FLAP CLOSURE**

**HOLSTER INSERT TUBE**

**QUICK-LOCK™ BELT FASTENER**

For fast, positive, secure attachment to web belt with no belt threading and optimum center of gravity positioning. It is quickly removed and installed on opposite side for right- or left-handed holster use in seconds.

**AMBIDEXTROUS**
Converts in seconds from right hand to left hand.

**REMOVABLE, REVERSIBLE FLAP**

For right, left or flapless holster.

**METAL HARDWARE**
Only tough stainless steel with black non-reflective coatings.

**MODERN DESIGN**
Excellent weapon protection coupled with full weapon accessibility. Minimum interference with weapon in motorized vehicles, aircraft. Optimum weight balance. High ride eliminates need for tie-down. Silent. Secure. Up to 20% lighter than leather. Operates in environmental extremes from -60°F to +200°F.

**PLASTIC PANEL**
Made of resilient lightweight, almost indestructible polymer.

**MIL SPEC NYLON CLEANING ROD**

Built into holster for field cleaning of the side arm. Round tap tip is designed to accept standard bore brush.

**GARRISON BELT SLOTS**
On both sides for ambidextrous use. Can be used with or without belt fastener.

**RETENTION GROMMET**
Positions pistol for weapon retention, reinforces holster stitching.

**BALLISTIC CLOTH FACING** Lightweight but extremely tough material once used in bullet-proof vests. It has proven virtually impervious to rigorous military environments.

**STITCHING**
Strong, long-wearing multifilament nylon.

**DOUBLE-REINFORCED FOLDS**
For long field life in the harshest conditions.

**OPTIONAL SHOULDER HARNESSES**
For fast conversion to ambidextrous shoulder use. Fully adjustable, one-size fits-all design. Features integral magazine pouch.

**OPTIONAL HIP EXTENDER WITH LEG STRAPS**
Lets wearer UM-84 on leg. Holster locks into place on extender quickly, securely with Quick-Lock™ belt fastener.

### THE BIANCHI UM-84
A state-of-the-art holster system for today's armed forces.

U.S. and foreign patents pending.

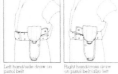

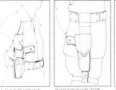

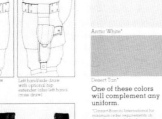

Dr. Ugo Beretta, (right) president of Fabbrica d' Armi Pietro Beretta, and John Bianchi have known each other for more than 25 years. On January 9, 2010 they met at NRA Director Alan Cors' "tank farm" in Virginia. Among Cors' military memorabilia was this very early example of the M12 (UM84) holster and M9 Beretta pistol, which Bianchi and Beretta are holding. Both men were Cors' "guests of honor" at his military museum collection. Cors has over 200 armored vehicles, both foreign and domestic, among what is regarded as one of the most significant private collections of military armaments in the world.

Bianchi got to the point where the holster was designed except for a simple but functional fastening mechanism. "We had designed fastening mechanisms for a variety of holsters, but this was a unique situation. It had to be safe, it had to be secure, it had to be simple and interchangeable from left to right in seconds by an untrained individual, in the dark! It bugged me night and day," the frustration of the events lingering in his voice as John came to his moment of revelation. "It literally put the completion of the project on hold. We hadn't been able to come up with this device. One day I left the plant and I'm on my way home, coming over the hill on the way to Palm Springs and it hit me like a bolt of lightning. Whammo! There it was. I saw it in my mind's eye. I rushed into the house, got a coat hanger and a beer can and I fabricated a working model. It was Friday night and I couldn't wait to get back to the plant on Monday and give it to the engineers. I called them all over the weekend, which I never, never did, and I said, 'I got it, I got it!' The next week they made the first prototype by hand out of sheetmetal and a spring wire clip. We put it together and got ready to submit it for approval. By this time the government had decided on the Beretta and the company sent us some guns so we could design the holster to fit perfectly. Coincidentally, the Beretta's

measurements were close enough to the Model 1911A1 still in use, that the new holster would actually fit either gun!

"During the design process I came up with another idea. The fold of the holster was a natural place to put a flexible cleaning rod. They didn't ask for it, but I decided to just do it. We designed a flexible nylon cleaning rod and put it in a channel along the line of the fold. They loved it, but they didn't want the cleaning rod. The holster already exceeded all of their expectations, but the budget was tight and there was nothing left to cover the cost of the cleaning rod. I said, 'It's got a cleaning rod and it's going to stay.' At this point we were already 30 months into the project and I'd put in so much time and energy that I wanted the holster to have the cleaning rod. It was a .12 cent item. I said, 'I'll give you the 12 cents, I'm not taking it off.' This was a friendly, working relationship, it was not confrontational. The rod stayed and they paid off the balance of the design fee, which gave us a lot of breathing space. Up to then we were really running tight. The design fee had been $180,000 plus separate payments for the patent rights and prototyping of one complete holster."

Having bought and paid for the design, DoD went shopping for a manufacturer. There were other holster makers who would ultimately bid on manufacturing it, but Bianchi knew none would be able to achieve the level of sophistication that he had designed into the holster. "They put it out for bid and we won that too. Not by price alone. There were some lower bidders, but the samples they submitted didn't qualify. So the first big package was for 30,000 holsters. This was in 1984, and that is where the designation UM84 originated. It stood for Universal Military and the first year of manufacture, 1984. By January of 1985, the formal announcement had been made that the Beretta would replace the Colt Model 1911A1. The first run of holsters was field tested and evaluated by our own troops. It had to be accepted by all the services. It had to fit their uniform requirements and nuances. The response was terrific. We had a few more follow-on contracts during which time other competitors, who were not holster makers, watched very closely. It took them a couple of years to develop comparable technology to make dead ringers for the original Bianchi design, and finally some of the low-end bidders started getting contracts." Today, every country in the world has adopted the same concept. "The last I heard there were more than 300,000 in use," says John with a great deal of pride.

Bianchi International produced around 70,000 M12 holsters between 1984 and 1994. The primary material combat versions are made from DuPont Hytrel®, and the holsters are produced in a number of finish variations, including standard green, camouflage, and desert camouflage. They are also crafted in black leather for General Officers holsters. The ambidextrous belt fastener and flap make the holster universally acceptable. It can also be easily refitted with a Military Chest Harness (M13) to convert it to a shoulder holster, and adapted for a tactical mount with a (M1425) Hip Extender.

The UM84 for the civilian market was offered in other variations to accommodate not only the 1911A1 and Beretta 92F, but in models for the Browning High Power, Steyr

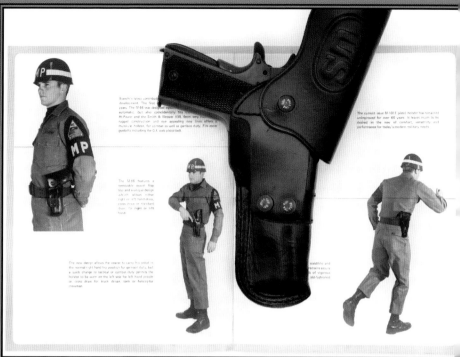

Pictured is a vintage Bianchi catalog for the M-66 holster. It was a military aftermarket product developed for the Model 1911 and Bianchi's first ambidextrous military holster. "That goes back to the Vietnam War when there was a need for a high-tech holster for the 1911. We sold it directly to the military on an individual and joint basis, but it was never officially adopted or issued by the military. Units had discretionary funds like Special Forces and they could purchase commercial equipment," explains Bianchi. "We sold the M66 as a civilian holster. We had it in the catalogs for about ten years." The flap could either be unsnapped or, since it was snapped from both sides, rotated up to draw the gun. "The flap could also be removed entirely making the holster easier for more concealed carry use." (1911 courtesy Dr. John Wells; M-66 holster courtesy J.C. Devine Inc. Auctioneers)

Col. Bianchi is shown giving a field briefing to senior military officers in 1986, at which time he was commanding officer of the 4th Infantry Brigade in the California State Military Reserve.

Col. Bianchi, Commander of the 4th Infantry Brigade, is shown presenting a cased Beretta 92F to newly promoted Deputy Commander Col. James Carr, a highly decorated career officer with over 30 years of service.

GB, Walther P-38, and other large framed automatic pistols with barrel lengths of up to five inches. Another, smaller UM84II was produced to fit smaller pistols in the four-inch barrel range such as the S&W 9mm pistols, the Beretta compact models, the SIG P226, and Colt Officer's Model. A third version, the UM84III was developed for the H&K P7 pistols.[1]

"My design philosophy has always been to take the time to design it right so it will stand the test of time, become a classic and never go obsolete. It doesn't always work out that way, but I go in with that mindset, to make it timeless. For the most part, everything I have designed, or some variation of it, is in the current Bianchi International catalog. My design concepts, with or without patents, have completely and thoroughly revolutionized holster design and performance universally all over the world," says Bianchi. In support of that statement, the No. 1 and No .2 holsters designed by John Bianchi over 50 years ago are still made today.

As for the M12 it became the most successful military holster ever devised and is still in use more than 25 years later, while Bianchi International continues to offer civilian UM84 versions in a variety of configurations and colors for the Beretta 92FS and other models.

Looking back on the development of the M12 (UM84), Bianchi admits that it was the most demanding, expensive design project in the history of the company, but over the years M12 technology led to the development of the Bianchi Ranger line of synthetic holsters, belts and accessories, and the Bianchi AccuMold Elite police duty gear in use today. To summarize the significance of the M12, Gene Gangarosa Jr. wrote, "Bianchi's development of the M12 military holster has proven a model of efficiency and private initiative that would make Adam Smith, the 18th century proponent of capitalism, proud. John Bianchi's vision, business acumen and initiative have shown how a business can and should work to identify a need and then fulfill it propitiously."[2]

The longevity of the M12 is testament to the highly dedicated individuals at Bianchi International who worked as a tightly knit team and relentlessly pursued perfection. "This went beyond the profit motivation and truly became a labor of love," says Bianchi. "Our goal was to design a holster that would be in service for the foreseeable future, and we achieved that goal." ✄

[1] *Modern Beretta Firearms* by Gene Gangarosa Jr., 1994.

[2] ibid

By 1989, Gen. Bianchi was Commander of Southern Area Command, encompassing all of Southern California. "I had troops stationed from Central California to the Mexican border, which required constant travel."

Col. Bianchi was promoted to Brigadier General in 1988 and was appointed Deputy Commanding General of the California State Military Reserve.

Deputy Commanding General John E. Bianchi conducting field inspections in the late 1980s.

In 1989, Brigadier General Bianchi was promoted to Major General and appointed Commanding General of the California Military Reserve. He served in this post until he retired in 1997, and was recalled to duty following the attacks on September 11, 2001. Gen. Bianchi was once again appointed to his former post as Commanding General. During his career, Gen. Bianchi served as Inspector General of the State Military Department, Commander of the 3rd Infantry Brigade, Commander of the 4th Infantry Brigade, Commander of the Southern Area Command, Deputy Commanding General, and ultimately Commanding General of the California State Reserve. He retired a second time in 2004.

John Bianchi receiving a commendation and gold medallion from one of the directors of the U.S. Marshal's Commission on which Bianchi served as a member of the Board of Directors for the 200th anniversary of the U.S. Marshal's Service.

While serving on the U.S. Marshal's Commission, John was present during the presentation in the Oval Office of a cased commemorative U.S. Marshal's Winchester rifle and S&W revolver to President George H.W. Bush. Among those in the photo are Bianchi (far left) President Bush (center) Winthrop Rockefeller (behind President Bush), Washington insider Herb Bryant, (fourth from left), Attorney General William French Smith, K. Michael Moore (holding book) who became director of the U.S. Marshal's Service Office in 1989, other members of the U.S. Marshal's Bicentennial Commission, and Secret Service agents in background.

Best wishes to Brig. Gen. John E. Bianchi, a capable Doctor, true patriot and fine American,
Strom Thurmond, U.S. Senator-S.C.

The second retirement in August 2004 brought a conclusion to John Bianchi's military career spanning five decades.

When Bianchi was on the U.S. Marshal's Bicentennial Commission he met with South Carolina Senator Strom Thurmond in Washington, D.C. "He was a great supporter of the military and I was honored to be accepted as one of his acquaintances. He used to call me 'General John'. He was a former Major General with the South Carolina National Guard."

## STATE OF CALIFORNIA
### THE MILITARY DEPARTMENT OF THE STATE OF CALIFORNIA

## CERTIFICATE OF RETIREMENT

TO ALL WHO SHALL SEE THESE PRESENTS, GREETINGS:

THIS IS TO CERTIFY THAT

**Major General John E. Bianchi**

HAVING SERVED CALIFORNIA FAITHFULLY AND HONORABLY,
WAS RETIRED FROM THE

## CALIFORNIA STATE MILITARY RESERVE

ON THE 19TH DAY OF AUGUST
TWO THOUSAND AND FOUR

HQ, OTAG, SACRAMENTO ,CA
SSN 569-44-8767
S.O. #4-232-R-01 DTD 19 AUGUST 2004

MG THOMAS W. ERES
THE ADJUTANT GENERAL

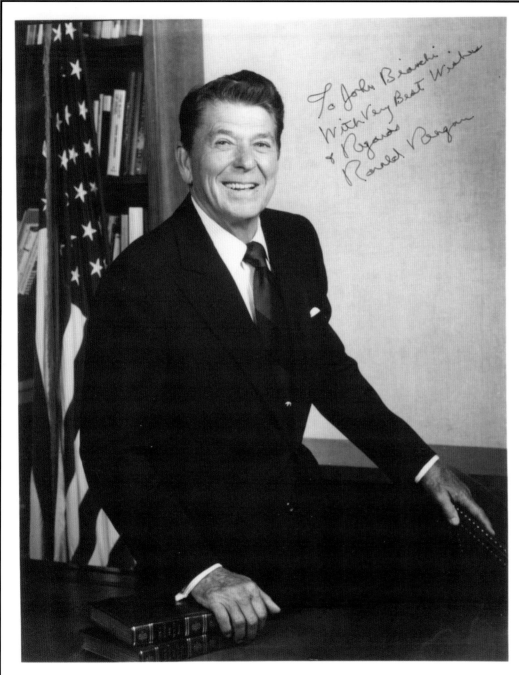

Autographed photo from President Reagan to John Bianchi.

To John Bianchi

Autographed photo from President George H.W. Bush and First Lady Barbara
Bush to John Bianchi in thanks for his service on the U.S. Marshal's Commission.

## CHAPTER

# Going West - Bianchi Cowboy Gun Belts, TV, and Movies

## The Stars and Their Tales

Back in the 1960s, John Bianchi was making belts and holsters used by many of the production companies filming TV and movie Westerns. "It's hard to say that in this or that episode of *Gunsmoke* or another show if I made the holster that an actor is wearing because many of the principal actors' gun belts were made by Arvo Ojala, whom I knew very well. There's a famous picture of all the Warner Bros. Western actors taken together, and Arvo made most of their rigs, while we supplied stock holsters for the rest of the actors."

Bianchi recalls that Arvo came down from Washington in the early 1950s and began working as a gun coach for the TV actors. "He could do such fascinating tricks, so when they saw how good he was with a gun the studios said, 'Hey, we have to incorporate that into our series.' You couldn't buy holsters like Arvo was wearing, so he started making the quick draw metal-lined holsters for the stars of the shows as well as teaching them how to fast draw. The originals, going back to the 1940s, were made by Wild West performer and movie stuntman Rod Redwing, who made the holster for Alan Ladd in *Shane*. I knew Rod; he'd come into Arvo's shop and visit. Rod was like a magician, he'd fast draw from holsters he made with metal liners. He used spring-loaded corset stays from women's old corsets to keep the holster open, creating a cavity that allowed the cylinder to turn freely while still holstered. Rod would cock the gun in the holster before drawing it, and that's what the fast draw was based on, being able to thumb the gun in the holster, no live ammo of course, strictly blanks. Rod was the first one to do this, and his designs inspired Arvo to take it to the next level in the 1950s and 1960s with more refined, heavy duty holsters.

"Rod did a trick that we could never figure out. He used to have a throwing knife, and at a distance of about 30 feet he would pull the knife, throw it, draw the gun, shoot it, put a hole in the target and the knife point would go in the bullet hole! Rod was originally a stuntman as far back as *Gone with the Wind*. In one scene he plays a Union soldier walking up the staircase at Tara. Vivian Leigh (Scarlett O'Hara) shoots him and he tumbles backwards down the stairs. That was Rod Redwing. I learned a lot of holster making techniques from both Rod and Arvo. They were great influences on me. Rod's stuff he kind of made for himself, and they always had a kind of rustic look, even the holster he made for *Shane*. Arvo, on the other hand, made his own style of holster and he provided great inspiration.

"I was doing small concealment holsters at the time, and I had limited capability because I was working out of my garage. Arvo was working on a larger scale. He had die-cutting machines, he had the dies, he had blanks to cut out the steel liners for the holsters, and he had some great leather crafters from Mexico and Guatemala. They were great workers. Arvo focused on one thing, making the Arvo Ojala Hollywood metal lined holster and gun belt. We make a similar one today at Frontier Gunleather, inspired by Arvo, and I give him full credit for it. All the principal Western TV stars of the 1950s and 1960s used Arvo's holsters.

"Andy Anderson came along in the early 1960s. He used to work for Arvo, and finally

"*Tomorrow is the most important thing in life. Comes into us at midnight very clean. It's perfect when it arrives and puts itself in our hands. It hopes we've learned something from yesterday.*"

– John Wayne

Charcoal portrait of John Wayne and John Bianchi done by acclaimed Southern California artist Paul Gleason. It was a gift to Bianchi from Gleason, who knew of his close association with Wayne. "It was based on a photo of 'The Duke' and me with some other people on one of his film locales. In the portrait I am depicted as being right-handed, and I am actually left-handed," says Bianchi.

This is John Bianchi's signature outfit. The gun belt and Colt .45 Peacemaker (serial No. 272452) were worn in countless ads and personal appearances. The silver hatband on his signature hat is an original Bohlin piece that John once had on display in the Frontier Museum with film star Leo Carrillo's Bohlin saddle that was used in the annual Rose Parade. Carrillo, who played sidekick Pancho to Duncan Renaldo's Cisco Kid in the 1950-56 television series, was a respected conservationist. The Leo Carrillo State Park, west of Malibu, California, on the Pacific Coast Highway, was named in his honor. John acquired the Carrillo saddles and complete silver mounted chaps, vest and silver accoutrements that Carrillo and his wife wore in the Rose Parade during the 1940s and 1950s. They are now in the Autry National Center Museum in Los Angeles.

John's famous silver mounted double gun rig is another often worn in ads and this famous poster done in 1996. This is still the most popular poster for John to autograph, and over 10,000 have been printed!

went out on his own. The Andy Anderson Walk and Draw rig became equally famous in TV and movies in the late 1960s and 1970s. Andy actually started out as a saddle maker. He did really good leather work. When he left Arvo, he opened up a shop across the street on Lankershim Boulevard in North Hollywood. Their shops were almost facing each other and they became serious competitors. Alfonso Pineda also had his shop in North Hollywood, and he had worked for Arvo as well before going out on his own. I think everyone learned a lot from Arvo, but he was a hard guy to work for. He designed the fast draw holster, perfected the style, and streamlined it. No frills, just purely fast draw and functional, that design is still in use today.

"I remember one day Arvo called me. He was hard to understand. He spoke very quickly with a Swedish dialect, and the older he got the harder it was to understand him. 'What's-the-fastest-you-ever-made-a-holster,' he ran the whole question together, and I stopped to think about it. I said back, 'What kind of holster?' He fired back, 'gunbelt like me.' I'd never thought about it in those terms back then, and he says, '45 minutes. Whole thing from start to finish and I delivered it to the studio.' I said, 'How did that happen?' He answers back, 'Well, they're shooting a Western and they break for lunch and the director calls me and says they're going to start shooting again at 1:30 and they need a new holster for the principal and it has to be done a certain way. So, 45 minutes. I got in my car, drove it over there and delivered it!' That's the kind of guy Arvo was. The fastest

Pictured are four custom guns that were presented to John Bianchi over the years: an engraved Uberti Schofield (serial No. 5818) from the late Val Forgett, Sr. (President of Navy Arms Co.), an engraved Uberti Bird's Head .45 (serial No. 142368), also from Forgett, a SAA from the original U.S.F.A. Co. (Serial No. JEB37) made in the mid-1970s, and a fully engraved .22 caliber Colt Scout (serial No. G191758) along with an accompanying scaled down, hand tooled holster and belt made by Bianchi.

I was ever able to make one of his rigs was three hours!"

During the 1960s and for years after, John became friends with many top Western actors of the golden age of movies and B&W television, including Kelo Henderson from *26 Men*, Hugh O'Brian, James Arness, and John Wayne. "These were fast times. Everybody was on a tight schedule and I can't say we became friends at the time; it was later on at a banquet or the Golden Boot Awards, and programs like that where we would interact and really get to know each other. Everybody knew my reputation and if they needed something special they always came to me. I actually proposed the John Wayne Commemorative Gun Belt and Holster. Back at the museum in Temecula we

had a John Wayne showcase that was seven feet high, ten feet long, with his costumes, boots, guns, spurs, the works, even his eye patch from *True Grit*."

Years later Bianchi is still in touch with Hugh O'Brian, James Arness, and the Wayne family. There is even a new Hugh O'Brian-Wyatt Earp Buntline holster set (two holsters, one for the Buntline and one for the 4-3/4 inch barreled Colt from the TV show) with the guns specially produced by Colt's and bearing Hugh O'Brian's signature on the backstraps. O'Brian's 4-3/4 inch TV gun, incidentally, did not have a front sight, though the Colt Single Action in the new commemorative set does. John still continues lifelong friendships with actor Michael Dante, actor/producer/director Patrick Curtis, and many others, including O'Brian and James Arness.

John's adult cowboy persona began in the late 1960s. By then Bianchi was already a world leader in modern holster design and technology, but there was another aspect of

Notes, letters and photos from John Wayne to John Bianchi, including "The Duke's" hand written notes to John on a new holster he was ordering. The picture below shows Michael Wayne, sculptor David Manuel, John Bianchi, and Patrick Wayne at the unveiling of Manuel's "The Shootist" bronze in 1984. The piece was a tribute to John Wayne and his last film. Bianchi was the master of ceremonies at the Los Angeles unveiling. The artist's proof of the Limited Edition series of 35 bronzes was presented to Bianchi by the Wayne family in appreciation of his long relationship with their father.

six guns. The only authentic 19th century model Bianchi was making at the time was his copy of the flap holster used throughout the Civil War. Then in 1969, something unexpected happened.

"I had just come back from a hunting trip and I had a 10-day growth of beard. I was anxious to get back to the factory and see what was going on, so I went to the office as is. When I walked in everyone went wild. 'Hey boss, you really look wild, let's get your picture,' so someone snapped a shot and said, 'Don't shave your beard off, I've got an idea.' The next day they did some trial shots with me wearing one of our Western belts and holsters. We had no idea what we were going to do with them but the advertising guys looked them over." John breaks into a laugh, "One of them said, 'There might be a pony in there,'" alluding to the punch line of an old joke. As it turned out it was more than a pony.

"They did more test shots and came up with our first Western ad. I had a lot of apprehension because we didn't know if the market was ready for anything provocative. Not that the picture was provocative, it was the innuendo of the ad copy. It was simply me in Western garb holding a couple of holsters and a bandoleer. The headline was 'Everybody's After John Bianchi's Hide.' It was done in sepia tone to give it an old look. We had no idea what the response would be, but it clicked with the public. There were no plans of ever going beyond that first ad, but we started getting calls like, 'When's the next one coming out?' So we had to figure what to do next."

In 1970 it was still quite unusual for the CEO of a company to appear in the company's ads. "It just wasn't done," says John, "but the response was amazing, we were getting more calls for catalogs and even copies of the ad. When dealers started calling in with suggestions for the next ad I said, 'The next one? There is no next one.' But the demand became so great and there was so much enthusiasm that we decided to do another one and take it a little farther than the first ad. This was our first serious location photo shoot. It was photographed in the desert with me wearing Western clothing and chaps, one of our gun belts and holsters, and a second Colt Single Action stuffed behind my gun belt. So there I stood looking like I'd just come off the trail, leaning on the south end of a north facing mule that was loaded down with Bianchi holsters and belts. The ad was done in sepia tone again and this time the headline read, 'Bianchi's Not Sitting on His Ass!' We thought we were going to get a lot of static for that one…but we didn't. The response was terrific and that launched it. From that point on it was, 'What are you going to do next?' and the requests just kept coming. We ended up doing an entire series of 10 ads that ran for years."

During this same period, Bianchi Leather was doing a lot of contract work for the movie and TV studios, making Buscadero (extra fancy) rigs, but they weren't in the Bianchi Leather catalog, yet. Most of the gunleather Bianchi was making back then was for police and detective shows. "During the sixties, seventies, and eighties we made all of the Sam Browne outfits worn in movie and TV police shows. We made thousands of them for prop houses and studio rental houses, and for costume houses we made

holster making that he sought to explore. His very first belt holster in 1958, the No. 1, had been designed for the venerable 1873 Colt Peacemaker. It was a simple homage to his childhood and the very first holster he had made. By 1963 the John Bianchi Combat Action Holsters product line had two Western holsters and a version of the Civil War Cavalry flap holster. The original No. 1 Lawman was a basic TV and movie style rig with exposed triggerguard, while the later Model 1880 Gunfighter Special was based on early 20th century "Buscadero" style fast draw belt holsters made for Colts and other Western

everything from Civil War gun belts to shoulder holsters." Bianchi leather was on camera more than any other, but, laments John, "We didn't have the time to deal one-on-one with individual shows, actors, or producers to make the 'hero' holsters for a show, so we made standard rigs for everyone else: the extras and background actors. On balance it didn't amount to a lot of dollars relative to the overall scope of the business, but we flooded that market so just about everyone was wearing a Bianchi rig."

At the same time another interesting situation was developing. The sepia ads had been so successful, that the demand from the public was like Oliver Twist asking, "Please, sir, I want some more." And John figured out how to serve up something very special. "We decided to take the idea of the ads to the next level and create promotional posters for the dealers. I called them 'Histographs' because they were done to look like historical photos from the Old West. We did the first one in 1973 and did one every two years through 1981 using props and costumes from my own collection. We did 'The Wild Bunch' first. It was photographed at a little Western style steakhouse saloon in Fallbrook, California, near the Bianchi plant. It had been there for many, many years and was a perfect backdrop. It looked like a movie set. For the most part we used company employees, except for the bartender from the saloon, who was the perfect image of a Western era barkeep. Like the first sepia ad, we never had any plans to do another Histograph after the first one. Well," John laughs, "forget it! Again the response was phenomenal. We never dreamed there would be such a widespread demand. Originally we had made them for dealers only, every dealer got one to frame in his shop and then the customers started coming in and wanting to buy them. Now the dealers started buying extra copies from us and selling them to their customers. All of a sudden we had another business making posters!"

The Wild Bunch had been such a success that John and his ad team had to start working up an idea for another. Luck had been their best friend on the first Histograph, everything had fallen into place, the idea, the costumes, and the location. Now, like a movie, they had to start with an idea and then figure out how to make it work. And they had to top The Wild Bunch! "It took about two years to get a vision and really study it. It had to be really good, and more over it had to be historically accurate. We couldn't afford to do anything hokey. We ended up doing five Histographs, and the most famous, elaborate, and costly was the 'Cavalry Troopers', which was shot in Monument Valley."

John took an entire crew to the very locale where John Ford had made so many memorable John Wayne Westerns. "I think we had 24 people up there, the actors, support team and photographer. We had to plan it for the right time of year for the weather and sun to be right. The brightness in Monument Valley is so intense you've really got to have a professional film crew to work there. It was after summer and we were there for the better part of a week."

When the crew was ready to head out, John made reservations at Gouldings Lodge, the legendary hotel where John Ford and his crew had stayed while they were filming the epic John Wayne Westerns like *She Wore A Yellow Ribbon* and *Fort Apache*. All that

A presentation to John Bianchi from Michael Wayne and the Wayne family for John arraigning the Colt John Wayne Commemorative program in 1983. "The Colt factory presented me with an identical piece in appreciation for putting the program together. I foolishly included the Colt presentation piece in the transfer of Frontier Museum assets to the Autry, thinking it would eventually go into the John Bianchi wing at the museum, which never materialized. While 'The Duke' was alive," recalls Bianchi, "he was talking to Colt about a tribute gun. Discussions resulted with Wayne becoming frustrated with the slow progress, and he lost interest. After his death, Michael Wayne asked me to represent the Wayne family and get the program back on track, which was accomplished after two years of effort."

was missing for the photo shoot was an American Indian and an Indian pony. As John recalls, that was not supposed to be a problem, "The manager at Gouldings Lodge said, 'Oh we've got Indians up here and horses too…' so we went without an Indian and a horse. When we got there we found one Indian kid and he wouldn't pose in a breechcloth, 'Oh no, gotta have pants, gotta have pants…' and one tired old horse. It was on a reservation and we had to borrow the horse from a sheep herder. We had Phil Spangenberger as our advisor on costuming, guns, and everything we needed to make the shot look historically correct. Phil was also in the picture as the Cavalry Sergeant to my right. We had six of Phil's cowboy reenactment friends, sculptor Dave Manuel (portraying Frederic Remington), the Indian, the horse, a Gatling gun from Stembridge studio rental, and two Cavalry tents in the background. We waited until the lighting was just right in the background, with the shadows across Monument Valley and a deep blue sky with clouds. We had huge reflectors, like they use in the movies, to get everyone evenly lighted, and the photographer used an 8x10 view camera. It was an enormous operation for one picture. The final shot we used looked incredible. The first thing people said when they saw it was, 'Boy, that must have been an expensive backdrop. How did you superimpose all that stuff?' And we'd tell them, 'No, we went there, that's really Monument Valley and we hauled all that stuff up there.' They couldn't believe it. Boy, that was something."

Bianchi had also started building sets and a studio in the Temecula warehouse. "We built a studio with high ceilings and we had all the props we were acquiring for the Western museum that we would open in 1982. So we had our own sets, props, even a chuck wagon, and we could do just about anything that you could do on a Western movie set."

The five Histographs were "The Wild Bunch" shot in 1973, "The Last of the Lawmen" in 1975, "Los Bandidos" in 1977, "The Troopers", shot in Monument Valley in 1979, and "The Cowboys", done in 1981. The posters were printed on heavy stock and measured approximately 24x36 inches. Each has, over the years, become highly collectible. "There would have been another Histograph in 1983 but by then we had opened the Western museum in Temecula next to the factory and it was all consuming of time, resources and money. It exhausted me but those Histograph images were the inspiration that launched the Single Action Shooting Society (SASS)," says Bianchi.

In 1987, John was to play a major "starring" role in the history of the real U.S. Marshals. Both John and *Gunsmoke* star James Arness (who had become the embodiment of a U.S. Marshal for two generations) had been asked to serve on the U.S. Marshals Bicentennial Commission in Washington, D.C. by the first Bush Administration. The Commission also consisted of Nicholas Katzenbach, Winthrop P. Rockefeller, William French Smith, James R.

Shown at right and on pages 87-91 is a Western image series of sepia toned ads for a national campaign that forever immortalized the John Bianchi image in the minds of millions of police, military, and sportsmen worldwide. The first ad was released in 1970. "All of the ad headlines were based on a double entendre with a touch of risqué humor like the infamous 'Bianchi's Not Sitting on His Ass'. We launched this campaign with a bit of apprehension but the response was so great we couldn't get new ads out fast enough!"

# Everybody's after John Bianchi's hide!

And for good reason! It's what he does with fine leathers that sets Bianchi apart from all other holster makers. John's a pro in the leather business. He has designed and created some of the most sought-after rigs on the market today. Everything from fast draw beauties to sophisticated special rigs for law enforcement agencies. John's a shooter, former police officer and an expert in his field. He knows what you need in a holster. That's why sportsmen everywhere are after Bianchi's quality-crafted hide. Send $1 today for your copy of Bianchi's new 36-page catalog for 1970. Features everything in holsters & leather accessories for the shooter and law man.

*Mr. Dealer: Bianchi leather goods are sold only through franchised dealers from coast to coast. Write today for free confidential dealer info and latest catalog.*

**BIANCHI** LEATHER PRODUCTS, INC.
*(PRONOUNCED BE-YANKEE)*
212 West Foothill Boulevard, Dept. GW-8, Monrovia, Calif. 91016

PREPARED FOR NATIONAL ADVERTISING MEDIA

## Bianchi...Wanted by Lawmen Everywhere!

Lawmen have put the arm on Bianchi because they know they're getting quality leathers that are a cut above all the rest. From sophisticated concealment holsters like the 9R Special Agent and X-15 to sensibly styled Sam Browne rigs and accessories. Bianchi has duty holsters for every need and function: the all new break-front 2800 Judge; the popular Border Patrol models; Speed and Cross-Draw rigs. All made with your comfort and safety in mind.

Remember, when you buy Bianchi, you're buying a lifetime of service as well as a product that could be a life saver! Bianchi . . . always on the good side of the Law! It's been that way for over 50 years!*

*Send $1 for full color '76 Catalog.*

## Bianchi's Not Sitting on His Ass!

On the contrary: He's bustin' it! Bianchi (the one on the right) is going all out to bring you the finest quality leather goods money can buy. He won't take any short cuts in quality just to speed up delivery.

Bianchi may have a computer up front in the office. But back in the leather shop, every Bianchi belt and holster is still made the slow, old-fashioned way, bench-made by hand. Our older friends and customers don't mind the wait . . . they know they're getting quality goods that are head and shoulders above all the rest. Nobody makes holsters and belts better than Bianchi — police and sportsman's first choice for over 50 years.*

So drop Bianchi a line today and ask for the new 1975 color catalog. It's worth two bucks, but it's only a dollar to you if you mention this ad.

SEND $1 FOR '75 CATALOG — First of its kind. Full-color from cover to cover. Get yours from Bianchi today! *Successors to Berns-Martin, founded in 1925.

## Bianchi rustles up the best in leather!

No bull . . . Bianchi starts out with the best top-grade hides he can rustle up. Then he herds together into one top quality line, *everything* in gether into one top quality line, *everything* in holsters and leather accessories for the sportsman, lawman, and the military. Bianchi's got to have the best hides to complement the innovative designs and functional styling that set his line of leather goods apart from and ahead of all others on the market. For that extra special holster and gun belt combo, look to the leader in leather. *If you can afford the best . . . you'll buy Bianchi!* Send $1 today for giant Bianchi Leather Catalog.

• DEALERS INQUIRE — *Bianchi Leather Products are sold exclusively through franchised dealers from coast to coast. Write today for information.*

## BIANCHI
(pronounced Be-Yankee)
RANCHO CALIFORNIA, TEMECULA, CALIF. 92390

*\*scene shot within 1 mile of new Bianchi plant in historic Butterfield country.*

## Bianchi Stops Fooling Around
### (When It Comes To Making Fine Leather)

When you buy Bianchi, you're buying the finest leather both sides of the Pecos . . . bar none! Bianchi is the world's largest holster maker. There's a reason for it. Bianchi leather has the personal touch no machine can match. We make our holsters the slow, old-fashioned way, by hand, from the finest double shoulder cut cowhide; lock stitched with waxed linen cord and full welted seams. All our holsters are form fitted for the exact gun they're to carry and hand rubbed with the finest oils and waxes to insure long leather life. Whether you're a hunter, shooter or law enforcement officer Bianchi has the widest range of belts, holsters and accessories to satisfy your every need. At Bianchi we stop fooling around when it comes to fine leather!*

*Send $1 for full color '76 Catalog.*

*MR. DEALER: Bianchi leather goods are sold only through franchised dealers around the world. Write for free confidential dealership information. Bianchi Leather Products, Inc., 100 Calle Cortez, Temecula, CA. 92390. Dealer inquiries invited.*

## BIANCHI LEATHER PRODUCTS, INC.
100 Calle Cortez, Dept. ___
Temecula, CA. 92390
(Pronounced Be-Yankee)*Successors to Berns-Martin, founded in 1925.
ENCLOSED IS $1 FOR YOUR 1976 FULL COLOR CATALOG OF BELTS & HOLSTERS.

Name _____
Address _____
City _____ State _____ Zip _____

## Bianchi's hell-bent for leather!

Bianchi's drivin' hard! Delivering quality, design, and service. Makin' sure all his franchised dealers get a wagon load of profits by sellin' the best there is in leather holsters and accessories. Bianchi (he's the one in the hat) won't settle for anything less than the finest top-grade leather for his products. And while you're selling the best there is, Bianchi's makin' sure you get a full profit margin on every sale. Count on Bianchi to deliver. Just as fast as that famous painstaking craftsmanship will allow. Get on the Bianchi team and start headin' for profits! WRITE TODAY FOR GIANT BIANCHI LEATHER CATALOG AND CONFIDENTIAL DEALER INFO.

*Bianchi Leather Products are sold exclusively through selected franchised dealers from coast to coast and in many foreign countries.*

## BIANCHI

(pronounced Be-Yankee)

RANCHO CALIFORNIA, TEMECULA, CALIF. 92390

*scene shot within 1 mile of new Bianchi plant in historic Butterfield country.*

## Bianchi's on the Wagon!

The #1 Selling Holster in the World Today is BIANCHI, and He's Headin' for your Local Dealer with a Wagon Load of the Best Quality Belts, Holsters and Shooting Accessories Money can Buy. More than One Million Police Officers, the Military, and Shooters like you will buy BIANCHI in 1982. Dealers inquire!

 **Get the whole Bianchi Gunleather® story by sending $1.00 today for a 64 page, full color 1982 pocket catalog. Then buy the best — BIANCHI!**

## BIANCHI GUNLEATHER®

*"The world standard by which all gunleather is judged."*

100 Calle Cortez • Dept.      • Temecula, CA 92390

# Reach for Bianchi!

There are a lot of city-slicker outfits that come on strong with special deals, new-fangled designs and exaggerated claims. But when you come right down to good ol' craftsmanship, quality, and the best service around, nobody beats Bianchi Gunleather. A lot of holster brands might even look like a Bianchi -- that's because his designs and styling are the most imitated in the business. But only Bianchi (that's him on the phone) has the years of know-how to put together the type of holster you look for. If you can afford the best, and you certainly deserve the best, then "Reach for Bianchi."

By the way, that varmint in the cell is goin' about it all wrong -- ol' John makes the best security holsters you can get!

**Photograph taken inside the Bianchi Gunleather plant, in historical Temecula, California.**

**For Reader Service Information See Ad Index.**

See the complete Bianchi line at your nearest franchised Bianchi dealer. He has the rig to meet the demands of the toughest hombre.

## Write
**Today for our Full-Color Catalog**
Send $1.00 to:

## BIANCHI
### GUNLEATHER™

100 CALLE CORTEZ DEPT.
TEMECULA, CALIFORNIA 92390

## Bianchi respects competition!

Why shouldn't he. Imitation's the sincerest form of flattery. And Bianchi's sure been flattered by a lot of people in the leather business! But Bianchi's top quality line of holsters and leather accessories just can't be duplicated. Bianchi's the acknowledged leader in leather . . . years of experience as a shooter, former police officer, and leading leather authority has taught him what *you* need in a holster. That's why it's Boothill for competition when Bianchi's in town. *If you can afford the best . . . you'll buy Bianchi!* Send $1.00 today for giant Bianchi Leather Catalog.

*DEALERS INQUIRE* — *Bianchi Leather Products are sold exclusively through franchised dealers from coast to coast. Write today for information.*

## BIANCHI
(pronounced Be-Yankee)

RANCHO CALIFORNIA, TEMECULA, CALIF. 92390

*scene shot within 1 mile of new Bianchi plant in historic Butterfield country.*

Photograph taken at the FRONTIER MUSEUM, Historical Center, Temecula, CA

# Bianchi's worth fightin' over!

These are some pretty tough words, but the fact remains Bianchi is the best darn gunleather you'll ever draw a six-iron from.

Bianchi remains the absolute leader year after year in developing the finest quality leather money can buy. Bianchi's complete line of leather products is designed and produced for sportsmen, police and military worldwide. Bianchi boasts well over 3,000 variations of hand-crafted belts, holsters and slings — all from the best cut prime leather available. But don't just take the word of these wranglers here in this picture — get on down and see the complete Bianchi line at your nearest authorized Bianchi dealer. You'll be fightin' for more Bianchi gunleather just as soon as you strap on that first rig.

Send $1.00 for complete full color 1983 pocket edition catalog to:

# BIANCHI GUNLEATHER®

"The world standard by which all gunleather is judged."
100 Calle Cortez, Dept.      Temecula, CA 92390

After the wraps were on the "Bianchi's Worth Fightin' Over!" ad, Ken Dodd who was the brilliant art and advertising director responsible for the creation and production of most of the company ads, posters, and Histographs throughout the 1970s and 1980s, got to sit in John's seat on the set, which was the actual bar in the Frontier Museum. "Ken went on to start his own successful advertising agency and we still keep in touch."

Pictured is a trio of presentation guns given to John Bianchi for his various accomplishments in the firearms industry. At top, a factory engraved Colt Single Action Centennial serial number (PC 1277) presented by the Gun Owners of America Campaign Committee, a Colt Python (serial No. V59739) that John received for being second runner up in the 1980 Outstanding American Handgun Award Foundation for career achievement, and a nickel Colt Mark IV Series Government .45 Auto (serial No. SS 2357) with his likeness scrimshawed on the left grip panel and John Wayne's on the right, presented by gunsmith Michael Ottmer.

Thompson (Governor of Illinois), Judge Constance Baker Motley, J.W. Marriott, Gene Autry, Dr. Gerald W. Lynch (president of the John Jay College of Criminal Justice), Barney Klinger, and Dr. James Q. Wilson.

"At the time there was an apparent void in the U.S. Marshals' history," says Bianchi. "There was a lot of written material, but nothing substantial or symbolic to represent the U.S. Marshals had ever been done. And this was 1987, on the eve of the 200th anniversary."

The U.S. Marshals are America's oldest federal law enforcement agency, established by President George Washington following passage of the First Judiciary Act of September 24, 1789. Washington personally appointed the first 13 U.S. Marshals. Washington

knew that building a strong country depended not only on the laws that define the government but also on the quality of the individuals who serve it. Wrote our first President of their importance:

*"Impressed with a conviction that the due administration of justice is the firmest pillar of good Government, I have considered the first arrangement of the Judicial department as essential to the happiness of our Country, and to the stability of its political system; hence the selection of the fittest characters to expound the laws, and dispense justice, has been an invariable object of my anxious concern."*[1]

The first U.S. Marshal to fall in the line of duty was Robert Forsyth who was murdered on January 11, 1794 while attempting to serve court papers. To date, more than 200 U.S. Marshals have been killed in the line of duty.

To commemorate the legacy of the U.S. Marshals, a statue was commissioned by John Bianchi. Acclaimed painter and sculptor David Manuel, who had done the famous sculpture of John Wayne, was hired to do the piece. John first became acquainted with Dave Manuel in the late 1970s when the sculptor was exhibiting his work at one of Wally Beinfeld's gun shows in Las Vegas. "I was absolutely overwhelmed by the quality and brilliance of his Western and wildlife art figures. It was obvious that he was more than a sculptor, he was gifted. He had the capacity to put life into bronze. I bought some of his work; we became friends and kept in touch over the years. When John Wayne died, I thought to myself, 'What greater tribute to him could there be than to have a bronze statue commissioned?' I already had it in my mind's eye; I knew what the body language would be. I had a lot of his costumes and had known 'Duke' for many years, so I got together with the Wayne family and I commissioned Dave to do the bronze. We produced a limited edition of two-hundred and fifty, twenty-eight inch tall pieces to be offered in two phases, one-hundred and twenty-five at one price and the second set at $1,000 more, with a portion of the proceeds going to the John Wayne Cancer Foundation. Seven of the bronzes went to each of the Wayne children, plus two more for promotional purposes to Michael Wayne; Dave kept ten and I kept ten. The rest sold out pretty fast. We then did three large bronzes, one of which was placed in the lobby of the Bianchi Museum when it opened. The second one went to Winchester in New Haven, and the third to the John Wayne Cancer Clinic." The three bronzes were "Heroic scale," which on average are eight-feet high, roughly life size plus 10 percent. "They were just so well done. I knew Dave was the perfect person to do the U.S. Marshals bronze. I had all of the necessary costumes in my museum and did the original pose for Dave to photograph."

The ten-foot tall work of art, valued at over $300,000 and titled "Frontier Marshal", portrays a confident, dignified Marshal holding his 10 gallon hat and what appear to be court papers in one hand, while the other hand rests on his gun belt, brushing back his long duster coat just far enough to reveal the U.S. Marshal's badge on his vest. "The pose was intended to personify the stature of the U.S. Marshals as dedicated and evenhanded," explains Bianchi. "There's just a hint of John Wayne in the face, and certainly in the posture of the Frontier Marshal's stance."

The Heroic size sculpture was nearly ten feet tall with the base. Artist Dave Manuel is shown working on some of the final details.

(Left to right) William E. Hall, former Director of the Marshals Service; K.M. Moore, former Director of the Marshals Service; John Bianchi, member of U.S. Marshals foundation Board of Directors; Stanley E. Morris, former Director of the Marshals Service; and artist Dave Manuel participated in the ceremony that dedicated the U.S. Marshals National Memorial. The program included the unveiling of the bronze sculpture. (Bianchi collection)

This is the artist proof first bronze cast of the limited edition Frontier Marshal statues. Today it is displayed in John Bianchi's home. Above it are pictures of John and Nikki Bianchi with the Heroic bronze, which sits at the entrance of the U.S. Marshal's Virginia headquarters.

Renowned sculptor Dave Manuel is shown with the finished clay model for the U.S. Marshal's Bicentennial statue prior to casting in bronze. John Bianchi posed for the work to establish the body language Manuel would use to depict the quintessential image of a Frontier U.S. Marshal.

John Bianchi commissioned a limited edition of 21-½ inch tall Frontier Marshal bronze statues to be sold to help raise funds for the Bicentennial Commission Memorial.

Former Marshals Service Director Stanley E. Morris said, "The frontier era in which the Marshals Service gained such renown occurred in about the halfway point of our 200 plus year history. The sculpture thus seems a fitting symbol of the dedication of Marshals and their Deputies during those two centuries, and reminds us of the self-sacrifice and dangers so often associated with upholding the law."

It took Manuel six months to create the bronze, which was unveiled on November 8, 1989 in Oklahoma City, Oklahoma, to honor U.S. Marshals who have died in the line of duty. Today it stands outside the U.S. Marshals headquarters in Virginia, just across the river from Washington, D.C.

## Back to the Beginning

After he left Bianchi International in 1992, John admits he was pretty much burned out. "The one thing I had decided to do was keep the Western image I'd established through the series of sepia ads and the Histographs." Almost immediately there was a stream of requests for him to make custom holsters. "The phone never stopped ringing; 'John, when are you going to get back in the business?' they'd ask, and I'd say, 'Probably never.' 'Well, maybe you could just do this for me. I've got a special project coming up. Maybe you could make me a holster?' 'I'm out of the business, I don't even have a shop,' I'd tell them, but the phone kept ringing. Slowly but surely I got back into the operation, set up a small shop outside of Palm Springs, California, where I had moved, and put out a small catalog of just Western holsters. And it started all over again. Orders began pouring in!"

The non-compete clause with Bianchi International had long expired, and John made use of the technology he'd developed over the years, only scaled down into a small, compact operation. "I had little time-saving jigs and fixtures that could turn out high-quality stuff really fast. But it was still mostly a handmade operation." John had all of the Western holster and belt patterns he had developed since the 1950s, which were exactly what his new clientele wanted.

It wasn't business as usual; it was instead an unusual business, with John starting over as a holster maker specializing strictly in Western holsters. It was a return to his first love. There was also a new love in his life, Nicolette Fontana, the matriarch of the Fontana family and great granddaughter of Marco J. Fontana, who had established the city of Fontana, California, in the 1860s. In 1868, he founded the Fontana food empire which evolved into the The California Fruit Canners Association, consisting of worldwide distribution of canned fruits and vegetables, pasta, and macaroni products, and ultimately into the Del Monte Corporation.

The San Francisco-based operation consisted of several city blocks of manufacturing facilities, some of which still stand today, although the original waterfront building did not survive the 1906 San Francisco earthquake. The company rebuilt the cannery along Fisherman's Wharf, and over the last century accomplished many notable industrial and cultural achievements. Today "The Cannery" is noted for its many boutique shops and restaurants.

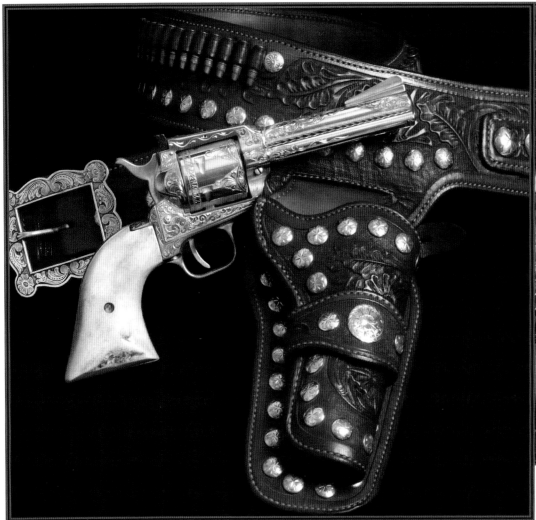

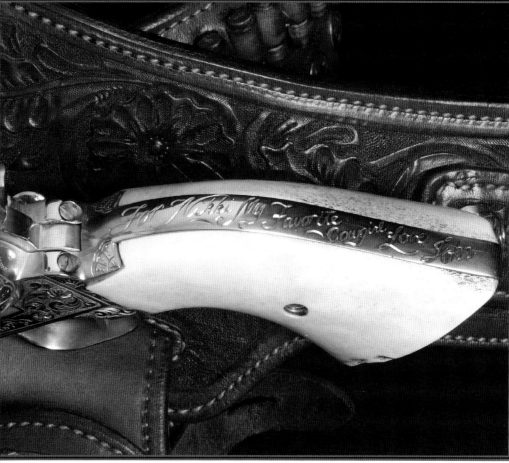

Special Colt factory engraved .22 caliber Scout (serial No. L 20229) that John had made for his wife Nikki, along with a custom holster and belt he handcrafted to go with it. The gun is inscribed: *For Nikki My Favorite Cowgirl*.

John is fond of saying that Nikki grew up in Central California on a 6,000 acre agricultural ranch managed by her father. An accomplished horse woman and breeder, Nikki was the owner of the Stock Horse Triumph Champion, which won the 1981 Cow Palace championship. John and Nikki were married in 1997, but even this was somewhat unconventional.

John says he met Nikki in November 1988, but admits that she can probably remember the hour and the date. "It was actually Thanksgiving 1988," says Nikki. John and Nikki dated for several years. She was a noted Palm Springs, California, interior designer, and later designed the Bianchi's current 6,500 square foot Tuscan-style villa in Rancho Mirage, California. "After we were together for nine years she says to me one day in April 1997, 'We're having brunch on Sunday April 6, at the Ritz-Carlton in Rancho Mirage and I've invited the family.' I said, 'That's nice.' And then she added, 'Send your beige suit to the cleaners.' So as the week goes on I find out we're getting married! I

guess you could say we had an arranged marriage," says John with a big laugh, "because she arranged it!"

Over the years John and Nikki became friends with many of the greatest Western film stars of the 20th century, and many of those friendships continue to this day. In the 1990s it wasn't unusual to see a picture of John or Nikki with stars like George Montgomery, Sue Ane Langdon, Robert and Keith Carradine, or Roy Rogers. It was the end of an era, and like John's wondrous childhood in the 1940s and 1950s, something no one will ever experience again. ✐

[1] Article: *The Marshals Monitor*, September 24, 2004, U.S. Department of Justice.

In 1972 John decided to take the idea of the sepia toned ads to the next level and create promotional posters for the dealers. "I called them 'Histographs' because they were done to look like historical photos from the Old West. We did the first one in 1973 and did one every two years through 1981 using props and costumes from my own collection. We did 'The Wild Bunch' first. It was photographed at a little Western style steakhouse saloon in Fallbrook, California, near the Bianchi plant, that had been there for many, many years. It was a perfect backdrop, it looked like a movie set." The first Histograph was so popular there was an overwhelming demand to do more. "We ended up doing five Histographs through 1981, and the most famous and elaborate was the 'Cavalry Troopers' shot in Monument Valley where John Ford filmed the great John Wayne Westerns *She Wore A Yellow Ribbon* and *Fort Apache*." The five Histographs were "The Wild Bunch" shot in 1973, "The Last of the Lawmen" in 1975, "Los Bandidos" in 1977, "The Troopers", shot in Monument Valley in 1979, and "The Cowboys", done in 1981. The posters were printed on heavy stock and measured approximately 24x36 inches. Each has, over the years, become highly collectible.

*"Last of the Lawmen"* *wear*
**BIANCHI LEATHER**

"The Last of the Lawmen" is a salute to the lawmen of the Old West, posed in front of the historic (then 125-year old) Butterfield Overland Stage Station located near Temecula, California.

CANTINA

"*Los Bandidos*"
*wear*
**BIANCHI LEATHER**

And starring John Bianchi as Pancho Villa, "Los Bandidos" depicts Villa (John Bianchi) and the Bandidos in
a strategy meeting at Rosa's Cantina prior to the raid on Columbus, New Mexico, March 9, 1916.

"The Wild Bunch"
*wears*
BIANCHI LEATHER

"The Wild Bunch" accurately and historically portrays characters that conquered the Old West…authentic clothing, hats, boots, gun belts, rifles, and pistols are accurate to the last detail.

*"The Troopers"*
*wear*
**BIANCHI LEATHER**

"The Troopers" is a small cavalry patrol in the northern regions of Old Arizona accompanied by famous Western artist Frederic Remington and an Apache scout. Remington was portrayed in this Histograph by renowned sculptor and artist David Manuel. The sergeant is noted Western historian and author Phil Spangenberger, who was responsible for assembling the historically accurate characters and equipment. This Histograph was shot in Monument Valley.

"The Cowboys" wear
**BIANCHI LEATHER**

"The Cowboys" depicts the year 1881 and a small group of Texas cowboys, camped in front of a chuck
wagon and pondering the long dusty Chisholm Trail from Ft. Worth to Abilene.

A complete set of Aldo Uberti miniature Colt revolvers and a Winchester 1866 Yellow Boy carbine presented to John Bianchi by Uberti over the years. "The earliest examples date back to the 1970's," says Bianchi of the framed miniature collection, which hangs on his home office wall.

This is not what it appears to be. Yes, it is a saddle stand, saddle, rifle and scabbard, and holster with a Single Action revolver, but all in miniature scale to correspond with the finely handcrafted revolver and rifle miniatures that were done by the great Aldo Uberti. Bianchi made the entire saddle and all accessories in scale to the guns! The hand tooled holster is only 3-3/4 inches in length.

Throughout his career, John Bianchi has received many awards and accolades. Among his most prized are those received for his service on the U.S. Marshals Bicentennial Commission. Also shown are the Bianchi 50th Anniversary medallion from 2008 (far left), special cast Bianchi belt buckles in brass and sterling silver, and a pin commemorating his star on the Palm Springs Walk of Stars.

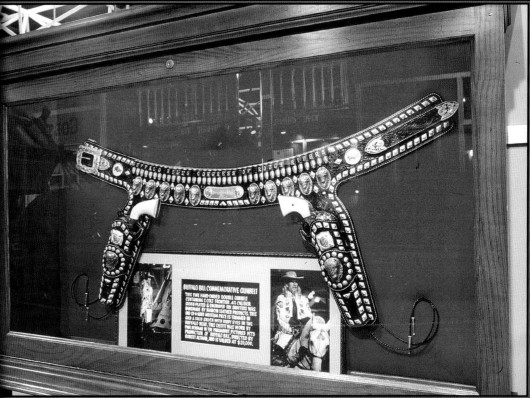

For the 1975 Paul Newman film *Buffalo Bill and the Indians*, John was commissioned to make two gun belts, a standard leather rig, a deluxe silver mounted double rig for two 7-1/2 inch Colts, and a matching pants belt with hand engraved sterling silver buckle. "This was the most elaborate and valuable gun belt ever produced," explains Bianchi. "In 1975, it was valued at $25,000." Newman only wore the deluxe rig in one scene when Buffalo Bill performed for the President in the film. "The scene was filmed at night on an Indian reservation near Calgary, Canada, and it was so cold we couldn't get the sticky backed foam lining we needed to size the belt to Newman's 29-inch waist to adhere. We finally used foam rubber to cinch it up for the scene!" Newman wore the decorative pants belt in quite a few scenes as well as the regular leather gun belt. Bianchi designed the deluxe gun belt and all of the custom silver. The complete set was handcrafted by Richard Nichols who was also Bianchi's Director of Product Development. "Richard was a master craftsman." The silver was produced by Diablo Silver in Grass Valley, California. After the film all of the rigs were returned and stored until being displayed in the Frontier Museum beginning in 1982. The current estimated value is approximately $75,000 and the holsters and belts now reside in the Autry Museum in Los Angeles.

Arvo Ojala was one of John Bianchi's early influences. In the 1950's and 1960's the Warner Bros. Westerns were king of the airwaves. From right to left, John Russell, Wade Preston, James Garner, Ty Hardin, Jack Kelly, Peter Brown, and Will Hutchins. All were students of Arvo Ojala and used Ojala's quick draw holsters with their Colt Single Actions. Note the black powder stains on Peter Brown's trousers, at the base of his holster, the result of a few blanks going off before he cleared leather!

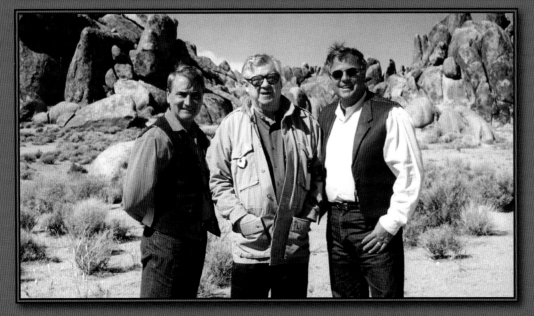

In this 1979 photo, John is pictured with his friend, film director Burt Kennedy (center) and Dave Snowden (Chief of Police, Beverly Hills, California). "These are old friends on location at the legendary movie location Alabama Hills near Lone Pine, California. Numerous epic films were shot at this location, dating back to *Gunga Din*. Burt Kennedy was a great friend and we enjoyed many Hollywood parties at his home."

Edged out of his first acting role in 1959 by a newcomer, this was John's first publicity photo. He lost the part to Clint Eastwood!

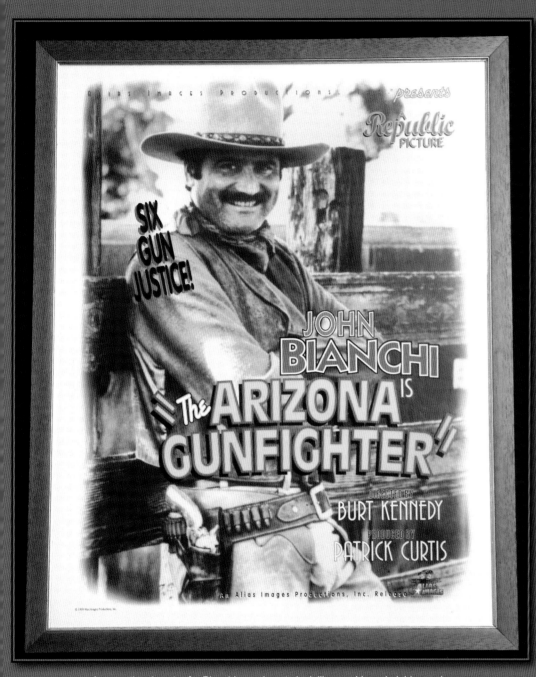

A promotional poster for Bianchi was done to look like an old movie lobby card with John Bianchi as the star of his own Western. The inside joke is that the credits for director and producer are real life director Burt Kennedy and legendary filmmaker, producer, and actor Patrick Curtis, both close friends of John Bianchi.

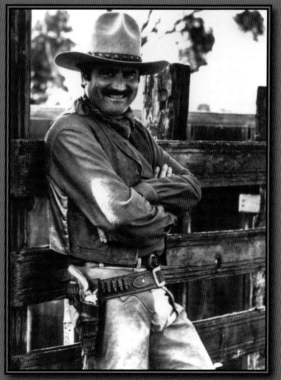

Original shot for this Bianchi promotional photo was reversed to have the gun belt on the right, even though Bianchi is left-handed. The mirror image has become well known leading to the opinion that Bianchi is right-handed! "Thousands of these 8x10 glossy photos have been autographed for fans worldwide whenever we were on location at shows and events. I signed every one of them left-handed!"

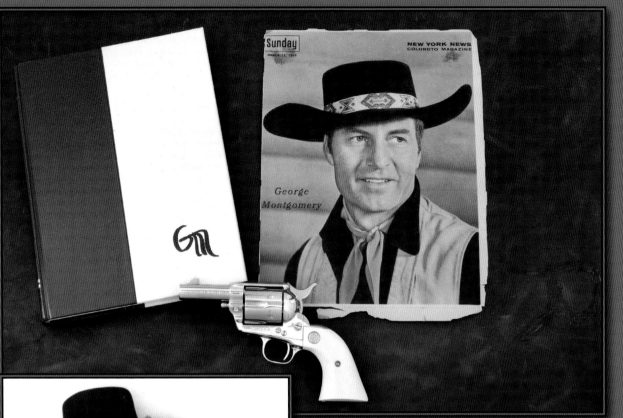

John and film star George Montgomery were friends for over 20 years. John not only knew him as an actor, but as an artist and sculptor. "George was always an artisan. He had handcrafted the most elegant furniture since the 1940s. He started sculpting in the 1970s and became a world renowned sculptor in his later years. He had a book published of his film career and art in 1981 titled *The Years of George Montgomery*. His career spanned five decades and 80 films. He was also a visionary in the collecting of fine art." Among the pictures shown are Montgomery in color and B&W stills from *Cimarron City*, and one of his favorite buckskin outfits, which he used for promotional photos. The last shot is with John at his home in the early 1990s. Montgomery and Bianchi both have stars on the Palm Springs Walk of Stars. "George was a great friend and real gentleman who shared many memorable trips, dinners, special events, and quiet times together either in his sculpting studio or my leather shop. Nikki and I along with George and his lady, Ann Lindbergh, were very close friends. George passed away December 12, 2000. Patrick Curtis, Wally Beinfeld, and I were with George when he died, and Nikki carried his ashes on her lap when we flew to Montana with Ann for his internment. His passing was a great loss to all who knew and loved him."

Early Western Wild West Show performer and film star Monte Montana (aka Monty Montana and Montie Montana) became friends with John in the 1970s. Montana lived in Palm Springs and was one of the honored guests at the opening of the Frontier Museum in 1982.

John and James Drury at the 2010 Tulsa show. (photo by Zach Fjestad)

John made a gun rig for James Drury that the actor still has.

During the 25 year run of the Golden Boot Awards, John became friends with many famous Western stars including Will Hutchins, who starred in the TV Western series *Sugarfoot*.

Slim Pickens donated one of his guns for Bianchi's Frontier Museum "Reel Cowboys" display.

TV actor Dick Jones was a terrific trick rider. John became friends with Jones through his participation in the Golden Boot Awards. Jones and Bianchi still keep in touch.

Bruce Boxleitner was an established actor in Westerns before his famous turn in science fiction with *Babylon 5*. "Every living actor who was involved with Westerns was honored during the quarter century of the Golden Boot Awards," says Bianchi, who served on the board.

Robert Fuller was another Western TV
star who became acquainted with John
through the Golden Boot Awards.

"Dale Robertson was quite a colorful guy," says Bianchi.
"The last time we had dinner with him was in 2000. He was
from Oklahoma and he raised horses there after he retired
from acting. I made a gun belt for him and he gave me a
fantastic Western belt buckle. It was made by Al Shelton
and usually given to customers of Robertson's Haymaker
Farm that spent $100,000 or more for one of his horses."

Kelo Henderson, who starred in one of the earliest TV Westerns, *26 Men*, about the Arizona Rangers, has been one of John's best friends for more than 25 years. "His show was one of the very first Westerns on TV. Kelo and his wife Gail live in Ridgecrest. He was a real *pistolero* and fast draw artist. Kelo was a genuine Arizona cowboy and went back to ranching after his film career." John made a special double fast draw rig for Henderson to replace a worn out Ojala rig. Henderson is shown wearing it in a 2000 photo.

John and Hugh O'Brian first met casually in the 1970s and got reacquainted for a new project that continues the Wyatt Earp legend in the 21st century. With O'Brian's continuing celebrity as Wyatt Earp, he teamed up with Bianchi's Frontier Gunleather and Colt to produce a Hugh O'Brian Wyatt Earp cased set of revolvers and matching holster rig based on the guns from *The Life and Legend of Wyatt Earp*. The guns and holster were unveiled at the 2010 Shot Show in Las Vegas. Bianchi had the original holsters and guns from the series in his Frontier Museum in the early 1980s. They are now in the Autry Museum.

Film and TV star Michael Dante is another long time friend of John and Nikki. His film career spans five decades and he continues to make public appearances and does a weekly celebrity radio show. "Michael and his wife Mary Jane live in Rancho Mirage, California, and we see each other frequently." Dante had many memorable movie roles and co-starred with Audie Murphy and other notables in the 1950s and starred in *Winterhawk*, where he played an Indian so convincingly that for years movie producers thought he was an American Indian. "One of the things about Michael in Westerns was that he was an excellent horseman. He was a Big League ball player before he was discovered by band leader Jimmy Dorsey."

Western film star Monte Hale was introduced to John by Gene Autry. "He was one of the easiest going guys I'd ever met. He was liked by all who knew him and we became good friends." Hale was also instrumental in helping establish the Autry Museum.

Gene Autry became acquainted with John Bianchi at one of the many Western events both attended. When Autry decided to build a Western museum he first came to John to become more familiar with the organizational process in establishing and operating a museum. "When I informed him it had taken 25 years of intense collecting to amass the collection in the Frontier Museum, he replied, 'I don't have that much time left.' And the rest is history," says Bianchi with a shrug. "My collection became the basis for the Autry National Center, without which there would be no Autry Museum today."

"I knew John Russell after his TV series, *Lawman*. I knew Peter Brown, who played his deputy, better on and off over the years, especially during the Golden Boot Awards in Hollywood."

James Arness has been associated with Bianchi since the Golden Boot Awards foundation honored the *Gunsmoke* star in the early 1980s. They both served on the U.S. Marshals Bicentennial Commission in Washington, D.C., and most recently have collaborated on a *Gunsmoke* Matt Dillon commemorative gun belt being offered by Bianchi's Frontier Gunleather. "He is a very soft spoken man's man and a good friend of John Wayne, who recommended him for the role of Matt Dillon in the award winning TV series. James Arness also graciously wrote the introduction to this book, for which I am deeply indebted."

"Rod Redwing was originally a stuntman as far back as *Gone with the Wind*. I learned a lot of holster making techniques from both Rod and Arvo. Rod made the holster worn by Alan Ladd in *Shane*, among others. He also did all of the close-up gun work and fast draws for Ladd. Rod was like a magician. He would cock the gun in the holster before drawing it, and that's what the fast draw was based on, being able to thumb the gun in the holster, no live ammo of course, strictly blanks."

"I first met Clayton Moore at the Golden Boot Awards in Hollywood and last visited with him at a celebrity party, at Patrick Curtis' home in 1996. Patrick was a longtime friend of Moore and his daughter Dawn and he recently wrote an article on Clayton for a 2010 issue of *Guns of the Old West* magazine. Patrick told me that Clayton was a great admirer of mine."

"Ben Cooper and I first became acquainted in 1969 when I made a fast draw rig for him when he was doing pre-production work on the series called *The Freebooters*, which unfortunately never materialized. But we became good friends due to our mutual fascination with guns and holsters. Ben is a great personality with a terrific sense of humor. He has been a wonderful master of ceremonies at the Golden Boot Awards and other Western events. We recently attended a Western celebration in Barstow, California, known as the Hullabaloo, which was disappointing, but we used the time to reminisce about the golden days of TV and movie Westerns and the many characters we knew from that period. Ben had recently lost his beloved wife Pamela of many years and he was still in a recovery mode but showed great spirit. One of his most memorable films was *Johnny Guitar*. He also played opposite Audie Murphy in several of his films. In one, Ben's character was killed by another old friend, actor Michael Dante."

LEFT TO RIGHT, STANDING:
REX ALLEN, TOM TYLER, RAY CORRIGAN, ALLAN "ROCKY" LANE, MONTE HALE, GEORGE CHEESBORO, AND KERMIT MAYNARD.
LEFT TO RIGHT, KNEELING:
TOM KEENE, ROY ROGERS, WILLIAM FARNUM, AND JACK HOLT.

*"John"*
*I hair all gone but me*
*Thanks for the Badge*
*Monte Hale*

GENE AUTRY WESTERN HERITAGE MUSEUM
Los Angeles, California

A photo to John from famous Western film stars Hoot Gibson, Monte Hale, and Bill Boyd, and another group shot signed by Monte Hale. "Monte made 18 films. He was a great guy and I was honored by him always referring to me as his 'good friend' over the years. Monte was a great story teller and frequently sent me assorted mementoes from his film career. He was well liked by all who knew him, and we were saddened by his passing in 2009."

*Hoot*
*To John Bianchi*
*My Buddie from*
*away back*
*Monte Hale*
*1939*
*Hoppy*

## AUTRY MUSEUM of WESTERN HERITAGE
Los Angeles, California
Hoot Gibson, Monte Hale, William "Hopalong Cassidy" Boyd

John and famous Hollywood leather crafter Bob Brown. "Bob made belts, saddles, holsters and other Western accoutrements for the film industry in the 1940's and 1950's. He made John Wayne and Montgomery Clift's holsters for *Red River*. He is credited with designing the first Hopalong Cassidy double gun belt for William Boyd in the 1940s. This was the first black rig with white lacing worn by 'B' Western film stars. Bob and I shared a common law enforcement background in Los Angeles County and knew each other for more than 40 years."

"Jock Mahoney was a friend of Western performer and trick shooter Joe Bowman and me. He loved to visit the Frontier Museum where he would reminisce for hours about the golden age of Western films and TV. He gave me one of his fringed shirts and we put it on exhibit in the museum. In his prime he was an incredible athlete, stuntman, and horseman. His physical agility was legend. The passing of the years did not treat him kindly. Jock was killed in an automobile accident in the mid-1980s."

A party at John's house in January 1996, following the unveiling reception for actor Pierce Lyden's star on the Palm Springs Walk of Stars. Lyden was one of Western film history's perennial "bad guys" and had the cinematic privilege of killing off many of his contemporaries! In the photo with John are (from left to right) Kelo Henderson, TV Western bad man Chris Alcaide, Pierce Lyden, film director Burt Kennedy, George Montgomery, character actor House Peters, John, and well known Western character actor Paul Harper, who appeared in almost every Sam Peckinpah film.

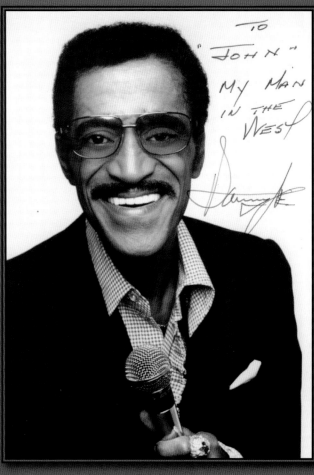

"Buddy Hackett was a very funny man but a very serious gun collector. He was a friend of Wally Beinfeld's, the great Las Vegas gun show promoter for 45 years. I made many holsters for Buddy but he never really wore them, he just liked to have them. He used to drive his vintage Rolls-Royce from L.A. to our Temecula factory for years just to hang out and watch holsters being made. His range of emotions went from incredibly funny to deadly serious when we talked about things that were close to his heart." Hackett appeared in an episode of *The Rifleman* during the show's second season, playing a serious role as badman Daniel "Pop" Malackie, in an episode titled *Bloodlines*. Hackett also appeared in an episode titled *The Clarence Bibs Story*. (Photo courtesy Doug Abbott collection)

"One of our best friends over the years has been actress Sue Ane Langdon, shown here in a photo from her film *Cheyenne Social Club*, co-starring Henry Fonda, Glenn Ford, and Hope Lange. Sue Ane and George Montgomery presented me with my star on the Palm Springs Walk of Stars in April 1997. Sue Ane is a beautiful actress with a long career, a wonderful personality, and comic sense of humor. She lives in Woodland Hills, California, and raises Arabian horses today."

"Sammy Davis Jr. was one of the fastest guns I have ever met. He was a gun enthusiast and enjoyed the fast draw era of the 1950s and 1960s. Jerry Lewis and a number of other Hollywood stars who were not necessarily connected with Westerns also enjoyed practicing fast draw. I made a lot of assorted holsters for Sammy from Western rigs to concealed carry. On one occasion he flew my wife and I to the opening of his show at Harrah's in Reno and treated us to a lavish weekend including a private back stage reception. He delighted in cooking Italian dishes in his private kitchen at the various hotels where he was headlining. I admired his talent and multifaceted range of humor and music."

A longtime friend of John and Nikki Bianchi was Western film legend Roy Rogers. John made a special Buscadero gun belt for Roy to commemorate his career. "I knew Roy, Dale, and their family for over 20 years. On one occasion Roy and Dale hosted Nikki and I at a luncheon at their home in Apple Valley. I liked Roy; he was very down to earth and sincere. He was most appreciative of the special commemorative gun belt I personally designed and made for him. We often talked about the old days of TV Westerns and longed for the return of the great Westerns of the 1940s and 1950s, but it was a bygone era and we knew it would never return. When Roy died Nikki and I were among a small group of invited friends and relatives at a private internment ceremony held in Apple Valley. We still keep in touch with Roy and Dale's daughter, Cheryl Rodgers-Barnett and her husband Larry."

"Western actor Morgan Woodward, with whom I became acquainted during the great years of the Golden Boot Awards in Hollywood, played a wide variety of supporting roles in Western films and dramas. He enjoys the Western image and still attends many Western functions. A little known fact is that Morgan is also a car enthusiast and private pilot."

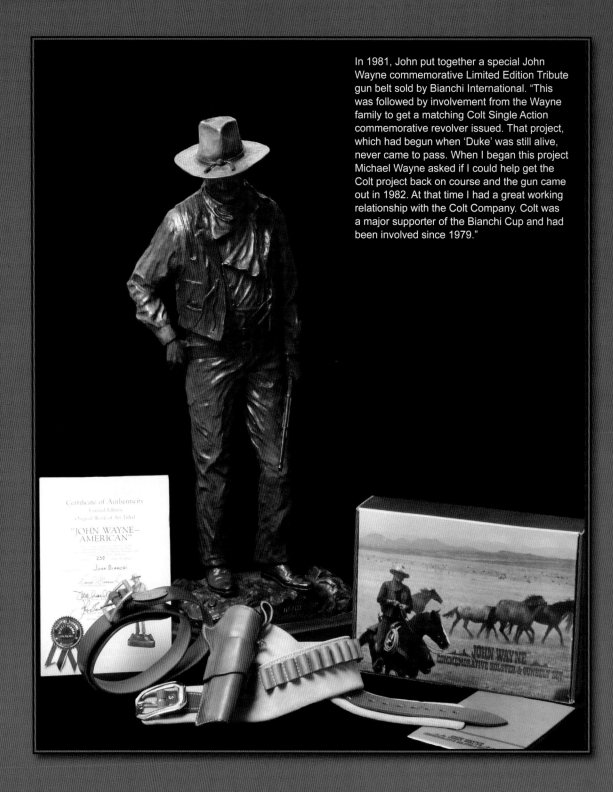

In 1981, John put together a special John Wayne commemorative Limited Edition Tribute gun belt sold by Bianchi International. "This was followed by involvement from the Wayne family to get a matching Colt Single Action commemorative revolver issued. That project, which had begun when 'Duke' was still alive, never came to pass. When I began this project Michael Wayne asked if I could help get the Colt project back on course and the gun came out in 1982. At that time I had a great working relationship with the Colt Company. Colt was a major supporter of the Bianchi Cup and had been involved since 1979."

In 1996, John made a special holster rig for actor Bobby Carradine (center). This photo was taken during the presentation with John, Keith, and Bobby Carradine.

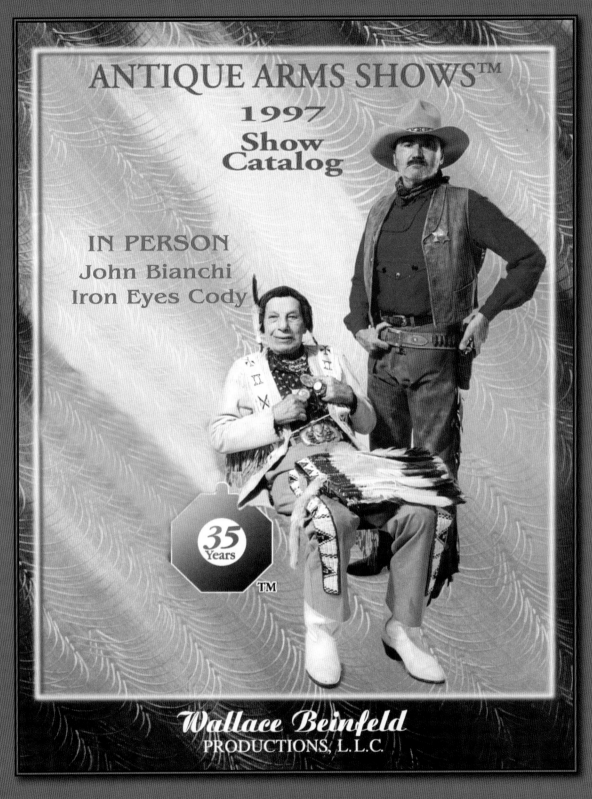

ANTIQUE ARMS SHOWS™
1997 Show Catalog

IN PERSON
John Bianchi
Iron Eyes Cody

35 Years ™

*Wallace Beinfeld*
PRODUCTIONS, L.L.C.

In 1997, Wally Beinfeld's Antique Arms show featured appearances by John Bianchi and Iron Eyes Cody.

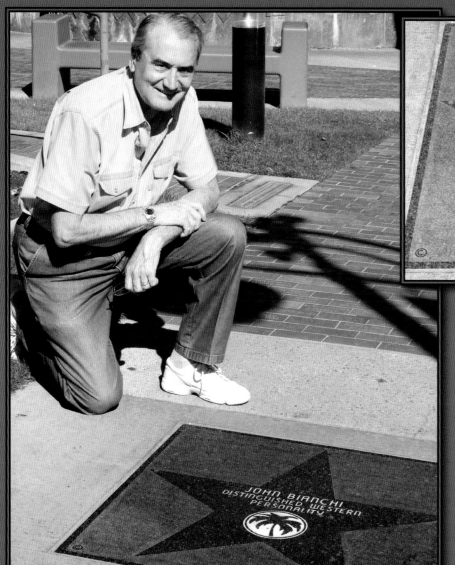

In April 1997, John was given his own star on the Palm Springs Walk of Stars joining some of Hollywood's most legendary actors, directors, and filmmakers. "To be given a star you either had to live in the Desert area, have performed here, made a film, be in show business, or be a notable personality." So many film stars lived in Palm Springs and the surrounding desert area that this was really like a second Beverly Hills for celebrities. Actors who received stars included Bob Hope, Gene Autry, Monte Hale, George Montgomery, Ronald Reagan, Ginger Rogers, Sue Ane Langdon, Roy Rogers, Randolph Scott, Alan Ladd, Frank Sinatra, Marilyn Monroe, Elizabeth Taylor, Dinah Shore, Elvis Presley, film directors Burt Kennedy and Patrick Curtis, among others totaling over 150 personalities. Actress Sue Ane Langdon presented John with his star.

Photographed by the author in 2009 at John's Rancho Mirage home, Bianchi stands behind the famous leather director's chair in which he sat signing autographs at shows for over 30 years. To John's right is one of the scale model stagecoaches from the Frontier Museum. "Famous model maker James Means built two scale models of the full size Wells, Fargo & Co. stage we had in the museum. He also made copies of the Wells, Fargo & Co. stages for all the banks. Those stagecoaches are highly valued works of art today."

John with longtime friend, actor Vince Lucchesi, who is best remembered for his recurring role as Captain Jerry Fuchs on the award winning television series *Hill Street Blues*.

"Film star Ruth Terry started out as a big band singer in the 1930's and became a contract actress to Republic Pictures, Columbia, and 20th Century Fox. She appeared in many films including Westerns with Gene Autry. She has been a friend and neighbor for over 25 years. Ruth is almost 90 and still keeps active," says Bianchi.

CHAPTER

*Putting History in its Place*

Creation of the Bianchi Museum and Gene Autry Western Heritage Museum

The Frontier Museum, which opened in April 1982, encompassed 25,000 square feet under one roof on a two-acre site adjacent to the Bianchi International facility. The architectural design was done by a former Disney architect. The Museum consisted of the display floor, administrative offices, research library, gift shop, and storage and curatorial department.

In the midst of building an empire based on making belts and holsters, John's love of the Old West began to manifest itself not only in his advertising and the line of Western holsters being produced, but in the vast inventory of props, clothing, guns and holsters he was amassing. By the early 1970s John had new aspirations. He wanted to build a Western museum.

"The seeds were planted at an early age," says Bianchi, recalling his teenage years growing up in Monrovia. "When I was a kid there was a museum in Arcadia, California, called the Pony Express Museum, and it was across the street from the Santa Anita Race Track. It was started in the 1920s by William Parker Lyon of Lyons Van and Storage. In retrospect, by the 1950s it was a junkyard, but for a kid who loved the Old West going through this huge collection was like Disneyland. It was probably a two-acre lot that included wagons, a train,

a ghost town village, and just thousands and thousands of artifacts from the Old West. Guns so numerous you couldn't count them; furnishings, clothing, anything having to do with the Old West, Parker Lyon collected them. I used to ride the red streetcar for ten cents from Monrovia to Arcadia in the 1940s and go and play on the train or the stagecoach and just get absorbed in this rich collection of Western stuff."

Many of the guns in Lyon's collection were historic pieces with provenance, others were just old guns. But to Bianchi they were an inspiration that would resurface decades later. "Even back then I had thought to myself, 'Maybe, one day I'll have a collection and I won't put it in a junk pile like this, I'll do it right. Well, I buried that thought deep in my psyche and much later as I began acquiring examples of American Western history, the guns, artifacts, clothing, I went to a collector's show and this old timer said, 'What do you collect, young

THE OLD WEST LINGERS IN THE HEARTS
AND IMAGINATION OF EVERY AMERICAN.
IT WAS A BRIEF AND COLORFUL ERA IN
HISTORY BETWEEN THE END OF THE CIVIL
WAR AND THE TURN OF THE CENTURY.
IT WAS A TIME OF HIGH HOPE AND PROMISE.
GREAT RISK AND HARDSHIP.
IT BROUGHT OUT THE BEST AND THE WORST IN MEN.
IT WAS THE TIME OF COWBOYS,
INDIANS, OUTLAWS AND LAWMEN.
IT WAS THE DAY OF THE GUNFIGHTER!

A VAST AND EXCITING ADVENTURE.....
AND THEN IT WAS OVER AS QUICKLY AS IT BEGAN.
THE SPIRIT OF THE OLD WEST LIVES
ON TODAY IN FACT AND IN LEGEND.

JOHN E. BIANCHI
FRONTIER MUSEUM
DEDICATED SPRING 1982

The Museum Dedication plaque in the entrance was intended to convey the message that what visitors were about to see was a part of our American history, a page of the past torn out and recreated for all to appreciate. That plaque is now mounted to a wall on Bianchi's patio in Palm Desert, California.

man?' and I told him I had some guns and some old hats, spurs, this and that, and he said, 'That's not a collection, that's an accumulation. If you want to be a real collector you need to have two things, focus and discipline.' So I'm listening and he goes on to say, 'You need to focus your area of interest so narrow that you can really get deeply involved in it rather than spreading your resources over a wide area. And then you have to discipline yourself to stay within that focus, and always go for the best.' Then he asked me what I was most interested in, and I said, gunfighters I guess, and we discussed it and we determined that my interests were the gunfighters, the outlaws and the lawmen, and related elements. So I took that to heart, took a look at my 'accumulation' of stuff and began to focus just on top quality pieces that had to do with gunfighters, outlaws and lawmen. I started collecting this stuff long before it became the popular investment quality venue it is today, so I got a leg up and a head start and I gathered it up like it was going out of style. Back then you could buy a nice first generation Colt Single Action for $300 to $600.

"Eventually word got out that there was this guy in California who had an interest in artifacts from the Frontier period, so I rarely had to look for any of it, people would call me. Elsie

When visitors entered the museum they were met by this bronze statue of John Wayne done by sculptor Dave Manuel. This was one of three: the second was done for the Winchester Corporate offices in New Haven, Connecticut, the third for the John Wayne Cancer Clinic. "When the Frontier Museum was sold, the Autry people did not want the John Wayne statue. I offered to give it to them and they still refused it. After storing it for a year I took it to the Kruse car auction in Scottsdale, Arizona, and it was auctioned off for $185,000. I smiled when I cashed the check!"

Hillier, my secretary at that time, grew very adept at sorting out the phone calls and only giving me the ones when there was substance and quality involved. Elsie's husband, Russ, was one of the characters in "The Lawmen" Histograph. He was to the far right holding a rifle and wearing the top hat."

In the late 1970s John had a feature write up in the *Los Angeles Times*. "It was about a half page and it showed my conference room table, which was just covered from one end to the other with historical guns, holsters, and such, and it said that '…some day John Bianchi hopes to open his own museum.' Well that opened up a floodgate nationwide and stuff flowed in. Families who had inherited old artifacts like Tom Mix's hat in the original Stetson box, Buffalo Bill memorabilia, so much that I could hardly react to it fast enough. One day my financial officer said to me, 'Boss, I hate to tell you this, but you know you probably have about two million dollars worth of guns in the conference room and it's really not secure.' I thought, oh boy, what do we do? So I called our in-house construction crew. They looked it over and came up with a fix. They pulled the drywall away from the outside wall, which was six-inch concrete, removed the inside walls and the drop ceiling, enclosed the entire conference room with a welded steel cage, put up new drywall, a new ceiling, added a heavy steel door and turned it into a vault! And that was our depository for a long time until we built the museum."

Probably the most fascinating pieces that came John Bianchi's way as he was gathering his collection together came from one man. "He was the grandson of Buffalo Bill's attorney," and John smiles like there's a punch line coming before he explains that when Buffalo Bill's show ended, the lawyer ended up with a lot of Cody's things. "I heard all of this as second hand information, and all I knew was that he used to live near me in Fallbrook, California, and now he lived in Palm Desert. So I put Elsie on it and she tracked this guy down…," and John pauses to make another point, "…this was long before the Internet or databases, she was just that good. He lived off Highway 74 in a retirement mobile home park. I called him and said we used to be neighbors in Fallbrook and I was sorry we never had a chance to meet, but I understand you are the grandson of Buffalo Bill's lawyer. He said he was and that if I wanted

to come over I was welcome. I can't tell you how many times I drove past his house coming to my house in the desert over Highway 74. We got acquainted and he took me into his carport where he pulled down these old steamer trunks. When he opened them my heart jumped. I didn't need any verification; here was Buffalo Bill's fringed jacket that he had worn in so many of the old photos and cabinet cards. Here was his original Stetson hat, one of the two saddles…the first one went to the Cody Museum in Wyoming…that he used in his show. There was a Winchester, a Sharps, and things that had never circulated since Buffalo Bill had died! We made a deal and I purchased everything. It was enough that I had to pay him off over time but it was a treasure trove. Today those items are almost priceless."

John has a hundred similar stories of people who came to him with guns and items that

The view from the museum lobby overlooking the main floor.
The John Wayne exhibit was the first display visitors saw.

had belonged to famous people, and many of them proved to be authentic. "There was a rancher in Temecula who lived just a few miles from the Museum, and like so many visitors he was emotionally overwhelmed by the quality and the feeling of the Museum. He asked to see me and said he had Buffalo Bill's shotgun. I thought, I've heard this story a few times before, but he said the next time he came to town he would bring it by. A little while later he brings in this double barreled shotgun and it was obvious it was really old. It was grimy, not rusted, just really dirty, but I could still tell it was a high quality piece. I said, can I buy it, and he replied that he was moving and didn't want it, so the Museum could have it. I figured it would be a nice shotgun even if it wasn't Buffalo Bill's, so I gave it to the boys in the curatorial department to clean up. As they were wiping down the rib between the barrels they found the inscription, *For The Honorable William F. Cody.* I immediately called my friends at the Cody Museum and gave them the maker's name and serial number. They said, 'We've got the mate to it here. You have the 12 gauge and we have the 20 gauge.' It was unbelievable. In two

years I had acquired absolutely authentic pieces originally owned by Buffalo Bill from people who were right where I lived."

John recalls another instance where someone called and said they had an old scrapbook they wanted me to have. "I asked what was in it and they said it was an old museum. A couple of weeks later they drop it off. The next day I come to work and Elsie hands me this package. In it is a very old photo album and on top of the cover in gold leaf it reads *Pony Express Museum, Arcadia, California. W. Parker Lyon.* I open it and my heart is just pounding. They had torn the museum down ages ago and most of the contents had gone to Harrah's in Reno. I'm turning the pages in this album and reliving my youth. Here are pictures of the old smoke stack train, the stagecoach, the wagons, all of the guns, everything that I had seen as a kid! A few years later Greg Martin published a book on the Pony Express Museum that had many of the same photos that were in the scrapbook. It's funny how things come full circle. I don't believe in coincidence, but I do believe in fate."

The Bianchi Frontier Museum was a masterpiece, inside and out. "We built a 25,000 square foot building on two acres adjacent to the plant. We hired an architectural designer from Disney to design the building, which turned out to be a real showpiece. We had set an opening date for the Museum about 18 months after we broke ground. I did a masterful marketing plan that was tied to the completion of Interstate 15, which the offices and Museum would face. At the time it was a two-lane highway, but the plan was for the new freeway to run right past us as it connected San Diego with Riverside, and there would be an off-ramp. The projection was 45,000 cars a day passing by. We did our calculations on what percentage of travelers we could attract to the Museum, pay an entry fee, and thereby support its operation. We completed the Museum on time against all odds, the building, the interior displays, most of which our own in-house staff completed after the original contractors couldn't get it done, got all the literature and brochures printed, and opened on time in April 1982, but the 15 Freeway was now years behind schedule. The traffic flow that we were banking on as critical to the success of the Museum never materialized, at least not in time for the Museum to be a financial success."

Success, of course, is often measured in more than dollars. What John Bianchi achieved with the Frontier Museum far outstripped the actual cost. "In conceptualizing with our advisors and consultants on the Museum I said that I wanted to do something that has never been done before; I want to put priceless artifacts on exhibit that are within reach of the viewers, but because of the atmosphere they wouldn't dream of disturbing it, touching it. Obviously guns had to be secured under glass, but other things, coaches, horses, buffalo, walk-in buildings like a general store, a saloon, even campsites, needed to all be as interactive as possible. I didn't want barriers between the viewers and the artifacts, I wanted there to be an emotional interaction. It was recommended that I consult with a behavioral psychologist. The challenge was how to modify human behavior to suit a given set of circumstances? This is a science that has been used for years in the design and planning of restaurants. For example, colors and lighting. Subdued lighting lowers the level of conversations. What we had to do was create a unique atmosphere, so that when you walked in you knew you were in a different world. The psychologist said this could be achieved through the appropriate use of sounds, colors, textures, and lighting. It had to be an almost magical balance between those four dynamics. Our design team determined that a combination of soft lighting, soundtracks, and background sounds, like horses, the clinking of wagons, people talking in stores, the sounds of the roulette wheel and honky-tonk piano in the saloon, would all convey the message that when you walked in you were in a special place. Parents would take one look down at their kids and they understood they would have to behave. It was surprising how many families came back, time and time again to view the experience. And they would stay for hours."

John had spared no expense in building extraordinary exhibits. "In order to have characters that looked more like real people than mannequins dressed in Western clothing, I researched exhibits from around the world in an effort to recreate the prominent figures of the Old West as close as possible to their original appearance. To accomplish this we had to go beyond the usual type of mannequin used in most museums and have special individual heads crafted, and in order to pose them, incorporate prosthesis technology for arms, legs, and hands, so that when an outlaw was holding a gun his individual fingers were where they should be. His stance and posture were totally lifelike. We made a list and came up with sixty-five figures

The remarkable interior of the Museum was actually built by Bianchi employees. "Everyone rose to the occasion after we terminated the original exhibit contractor because they were so far behind schedule. We had our own in-house construction crew for the factory and everyone volunteered their time to get it done. The result was far beyond my wildest expectations. This was our Museum built with the pride and dedication of the employees. The talent they exhibited was overwhelming."

John Bianchi on opening day in April 1982 with Michael Wayne (far right) and Western historian, author, and film consultant Phil Spangenberger (center).

John Wayne's daughters Melinda and Toni, son Michael, and the rest of the Wayne family were at the Frontier Museum for its gala opening event. "There was a lot of the 'Duke' in that museum," says Bianchi.

we wanted to recreate, from Geronimo, Annie Oakley and Buffalo Bill, to famous outlaws, lawmen, and film stars."

To get the correct height, weight, and stature of famous Western lawmen and outlaws, Bianchi went back through early Pinkerton Detective Agency records. "It was surprising what we were able to find, right down to eye color, so many of the figures we created were correct in every way." John went to Henry Alvarez, the premier wax figure maker in America for the heads, and purchased real glass eyes from the best maker in Germany. "It makes all the difference in the world between plastic eyes and real glass eyes," explains Bianchi. "When you put real glass eyes in a figure and you walk past it, the eyes almost follow you because of the liquid look they have. We used a special wax for the heads that created the translucency you have in human skin, and every hair, from heads to beards, mustaches, even hair on the

arms and hands, was individually applied using the hot needle technique, one strand at a time. When you look at most figures in a museum they have a wig on. Every one of our figures had real hair. It averaged $1,000 more per mannequin to do things this way, but the finished results were impeccable. It took Henry Alvarez 60 months to do all of the figures, delivering one a month for five years. I think the realism of the mannequins contributed to the emotional response people had going through the Museum and the respect they showed for each of the exhibits." Of course, there was a closed circuit monitoring system and uniformed guards walking through the Museum to keep a watchful eye, but as John recalls, people were just awestruck by what they saw and heard as they followed the carpeted footpaths from one area to another and walked through the buildings.

"We had a number of great parties in our 1880s saloon," recalls Bianchi. "Everything worked, the bar was authentic, we even shot an ad in the saloon and had a number of charitable and fund raising events there. Any of the buildings that you could walk into were full size. Everything worked and was authentic to the era, even the old cash register we had in the gun shop."

Although the grand opening had been spectacular with a huge turnout, newspaper and TV coverage, the trip to Temecula remained along a two-lane highway. The locals came

Michael Wayne signing one of his father's movie lobby cards from *McClintock* in front of the John Wayne bronze in the museum lobby.

Patrick Wayne signing the *McClintock* movie poster.

often, so did visitors and guests of Bianchi International, along with diehard Western fans, but Temecula wasn't a destination. Without the high volume of traffic that Interstate 15 would have carried, had the section of highway through Temecula been completed in time, John realized there was no way to cover the operating costs of a 25,000 square foot building and a full-time staff. "We carried it for four years, which was draining the operating funds of the manufacturing company. Finally we had to make the excruciating, painful decision to transition the Museum to a major financial entity that could support an operation like this. We knew that Gene Autry had taken an interest in it when he had visited. He told me that there were two things he still wanted to do in his lifetime, one was for his baseball team, the L.A. Angels, to win a pennant, and the other was to build a Gene Autry Museum. So we began to talk about all that was involved in building a museum, putting the collection together, and costs of the administrative staff. It had taken us years of prep work, studying, putting together a research library, and so on. We came to the conclusion that the Autry Foundation would acquire the contents of our Museum and relocate it to a high population center in Los Angeles."

It was a great emotional loss for John, but to do otherwise might well have brought his company to its knees after operating the Frontier Museum for four years in the red. "We arrived at a price and the financial terms were that a portion of the sale's proceeds would be donated to the Autry Museum. I naively expected there to be a John Bianchi wing in view of

the $2.7 million contribution we had made, but it became obvious after the close of the deal that there wasn't going to be one. The transition did not go well and there was no explanation. So much of what we had built was never used and it was and remains very disappointing to me. When the Autry took over, there was no comparison to the atmosphere we had created at the Frontier Museum. It became a very sterile environment, very different from what we had done."

Many of the items acquired were put into storage, others preserved in the Autry Museum's "white glove room" where clothing, guns, and other artifacts are cataloged and cared for. Others are still on display to this day, a silent but tangible homage to the man who put it all together.

When John Bianchi's Frontier Museum opened in 1982, it represented the largest privately-owned collection of Western memorabilia in the world. It was the realization of a dream. A dream a young boy once had as he marveled at William Parker Lyon's Pony Express Museum in the 1940s. It's hard to put a dollar value on dreams, but in today's dollars, Bianchi says, "the original contents of the Frontier Museum would be somewhere between $25 and $30 million." The Autry Museum is a magnificent repository of that dream. But in the end, as noted author R. L. Wilson details, it was now Gene Autry's collection and John Bianchi's contributions were never brought to light.

The original Ferrera artwork commissioned by John Bianchi for the first Frontier Museum poster.

The first poster had everything from hours of operation to directions. Like everything else John Bianchi did, there was no stone left unturned.

# THE GUNFIGHTERS

SEE LAWMEN · OUTLAWS · COWBOYS · INDIANS · THE OLD WEST

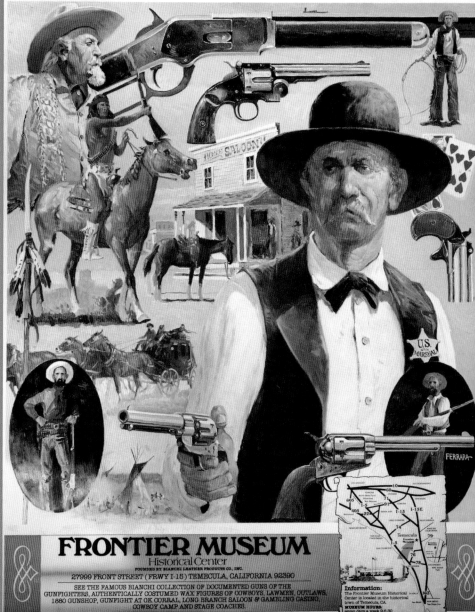

## FRONTIER MUSEUM
### Historical Center
FOUNDED BY BIANCHI LEATHER PRODUCTS CO., INC.

27999 FRONT STREET (FRWY I-15) TEMECULA, CALIFORNIA 92390

SEE THE FAMOUS BIANCHI COLLECTION OF DOCUMENTED GUNS OF THE GUNFIGHTERS, AUTHENTICALLY COSTUMED WAX FIGURES OF COWBOYS, LAWMEN, OUTLAWS, 1880 GUNSHOP, GUNFIGHT AT OK CORRAL, LONG BRANCH SALOON & GAMBLING CASINO, COWBOY CAMP AND STAGE COACHES.

**Information:** The Frontier Museum Historical Center is located in the historical town of Temecula, CA. MUSEUM HOURS: seven days a week 9-5:30

The John Wayne exhibit was one of the largest in the Frontier Museum with an assortment of costumes and holsters worn by John Wayne in so many of his movies, including *Red River*, *The Shootist*, and *True Grit*. The Cavalry tunic was actually worn by Patrick Wayne in *The Searchers*. The most famous gun belt in the display was the original two-tone belt and holster worn in *Hondo*. This became the Duke's trademark rig and there were several versions worn in later Wayne Westerns. It is said that the original was given to Wayne by his friend, famed trick rider, Western stuntman, and director Yakima Cunutt. Bianchi was also presented with the eye patch that Wayne wore as Rooster Cogburn in *True Grit*.

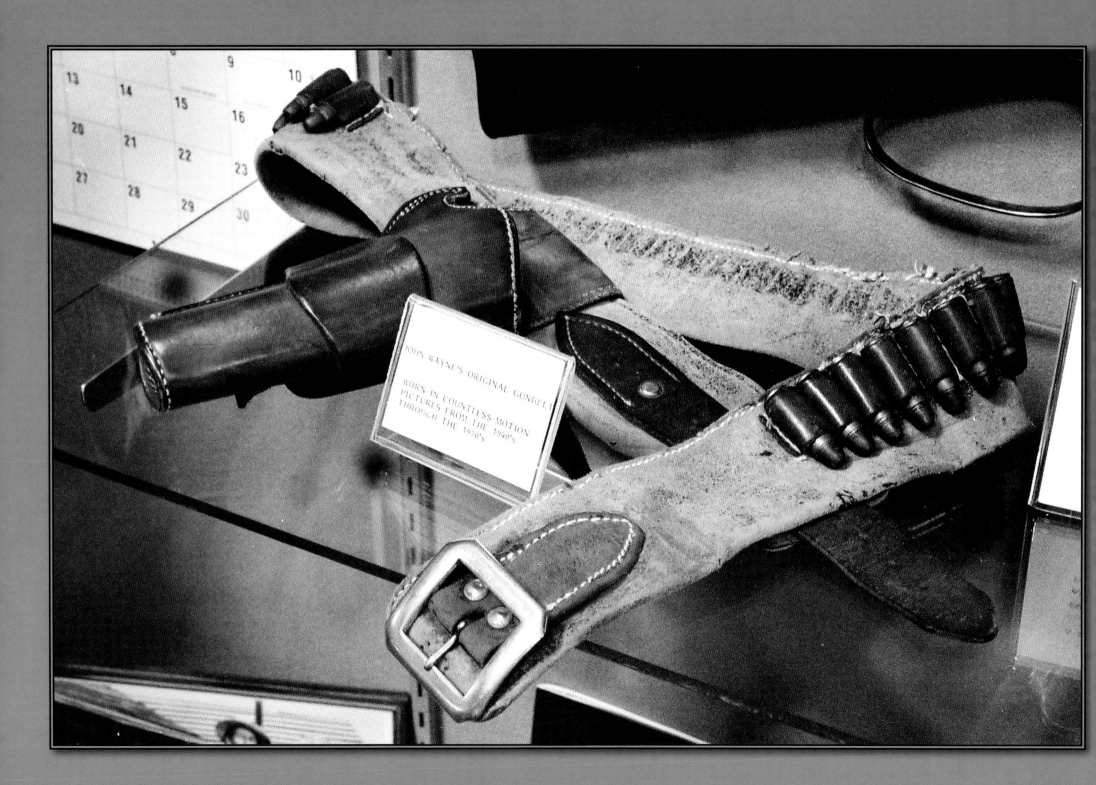

JOHN WAYNE'S ORIGINAL GUNBELT

WORN IN COUNTLESS MOTION
PICTURES FROM THE 1940's
THROUGH THE 1970's

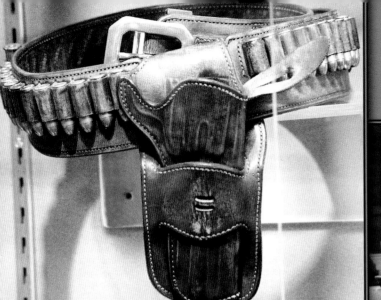

This was a custom made holster that John Bianchi did for John Wayne. Note the extensive wet fitting that Bianchi did to make the holster to the exact contours of the gun.

There were two stagecoaches, both restored originals and two scaled miniatures handcrafted by Jim Means, of the Wells, Fargo & Co. stage, both of which are displayed in Bianchi's home today. "Means was one of the best model makers in the world. He also did copies for Wells Fargo Bank." The stagecoaches were central figures in the Museum; the Wells, Fargo & Co. with passengers disembarking.

The gun shop was a walk-through building from one street to the other. It was designed to duplicate an 1880s gun shop and was fully stocked with rifles, shotguns, and pistols with all of the original 1880s prices on the guns.

The Main Street facades were built against the Museum's outside wall. The opposite side had complete buildings that were walk-through exhibits to take visitors from one street to another.

The harness shop was a walk-through exhibit that went from one street in the Frontier Museum to the other. The sign on the harness shop came from the *Buffalo Bill and the Indians* movie set. The shop itself had Bianchi's original leather working bench and tools in it and his original Landis No. 1 saddle stitcher that he had used to make his first production holsters in the early 1960s.

If you look inside the U.S. Marshal's office, that's Pat Garrett and Billy the Kid standing in the background. Bianchi left no detail out, right down to an original rolltop desk, ceiling fixtures, the gun rack, and wanted posters tacked on the wall. In the background is a lighted cabinet with hundreds of lawmen badges. The Marshal's office was another walk-through exhibit. "I think I paid $5,000 for that restored antique rolltop desk back in the 1970s," recalls Bianchi. "It was a premier piece of furniture." The exhibit also had the file office on another wall.

The saloon was a full size walk-in exhibit. At the card table are three gamblers with Wild Bill Hickok (notice the 1851 Navy revolvers in his waist sash) standing next to Calamity Jane. The shotgun guard at the top of the stairs was actually a mannequin of Frank Boyer, the museum curator. "You could walk all around the saloon but not upstairs, that's why we had Frank there!" laughs Bianchi. Take a close look at the dealer in front of the roulette wheel, it's a mannequin of John Bianchi!

Bianchi managed to get a very nice Gatling gun, but it did not have a cart. He acquired an un-restored cart that was literally in pieces. "One of the workers in the leather shop was also a wood worker and he took it upon himself to completely restore the cart to original U.S. Government specs," says Bianchi, "right down to the type and width wood used. The shop staff also made reproductions of the Gatling gun magazines to fill the slots in the cart. Everyone in the company went out of their way to get things done."

The Buffalo Bill display in the Museum was part of the actual set from the Paul Newman film. "After the filming was done, they gave me the Buffalo Bill backdrop and a lot of other stuff: banners, the billboards, even the copy of the original saddle we had in the Museum," says Bianchi, "so pretty much everything we had for the big Buffalo Bill exhibit, except for the mannequins, came right from the Paul Newman film." The Buffalo Bill mannequin is resting his hand on the saddle used in the film. On the other side is Annie Oakley. The Indians at far right are wearing authentic costumes that Bianchi paid over $10,000 for in the late 1970s. "The significance of the costumes," explains Bianchi, "is the elaborate bead work which was never before achieved on that scale for an exhibit. It probably couldn't be duplicated today."

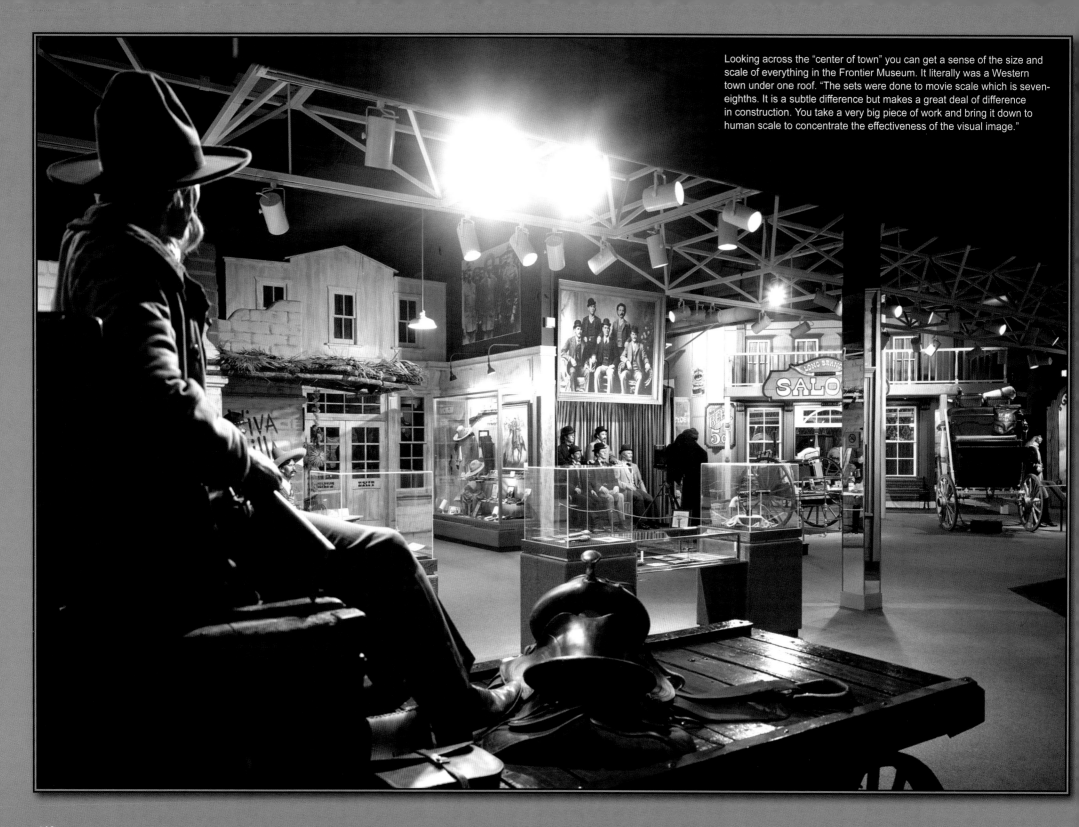

Looking across the "center of town" you can get a sense of the size and scale of everything in the Frontier Museum. It literally was a Western town under one roof. "The sets were done to movie scale which is seven-eighths. It is a subtle difference but makes a great deal of difference in construction. You take a very big piece of work and bring it down to human scale to concentrate the effectiveness of the visual image."

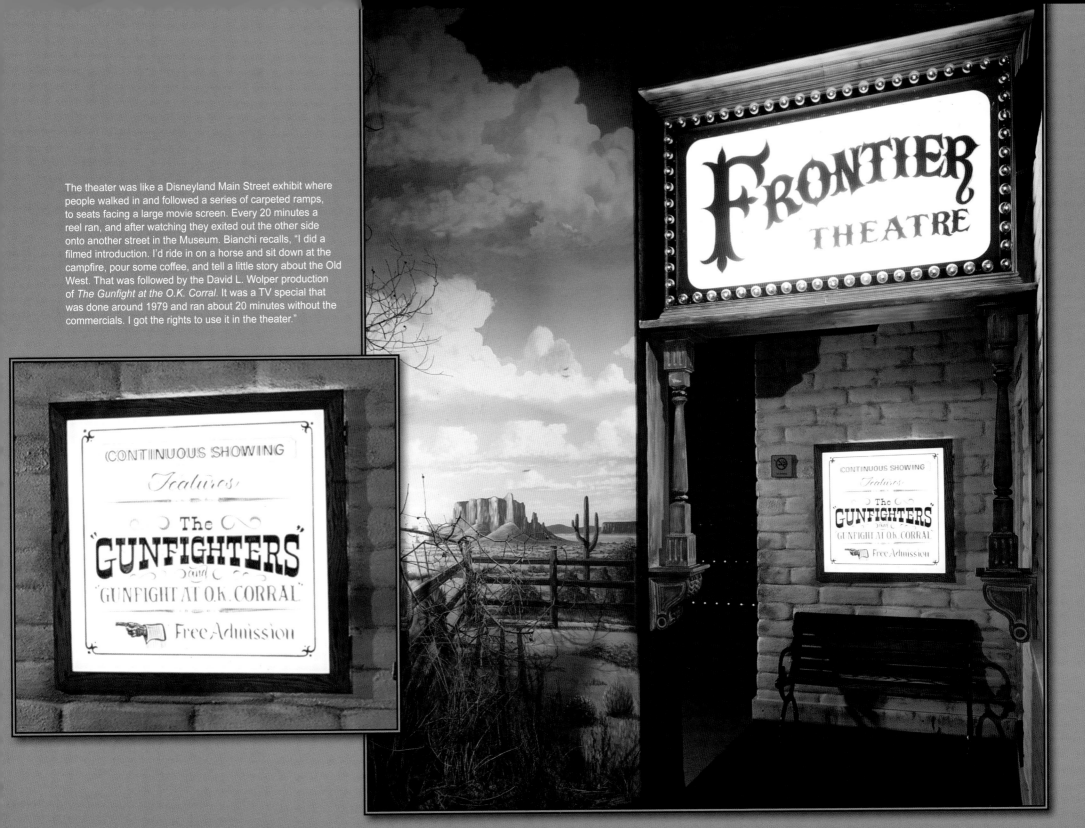

The theater was like a Disneyland Main Street exhibit where people walked in and followed a series of carpeted ramps, to seats facing a large movie screen. Every 20 minutes a reel ran, and after watching they exited out the other side onto another street in the Museum. Bianchi recalls, "I did a filmed introduction. I'd ride in on a horse and sit down at the campfire, pour some coffee, and tell a little story about the Old West. That was followed by the David L. Wolper production of *The Gunfight at the O.K. Corral.* It was a TV special that was done around 1979 and ran about 20 minutes without the commercials. I got the rights to use it in the theater."

CONTINUOUS SHOWING
*Features*
The
"GUNFIGHTERS"
*and*
"GUNFIGHT AT O.K. CORRAL"
☞ Free Admission

CONTINUOUS SHOWING
*Features*
The
GUNFIGHTERS
GUNFIGHT AT O.K. CORRAL
Free Admission

In the setup of the shootout at the O.K. Corral, Bianchi had an artist's rendition on the side wall of Fly's Photo gallery that accurately showed the positions of the Earps, Doc Holliday, the Clantons, and McLaurys. The illustration can be seen in the photo of the Clantons and McLaurys. The Frontier Museum staging was such that you could see the entire setting from different angles.

THE GUNFIGHT
(NEAR THE OK CORRAL)

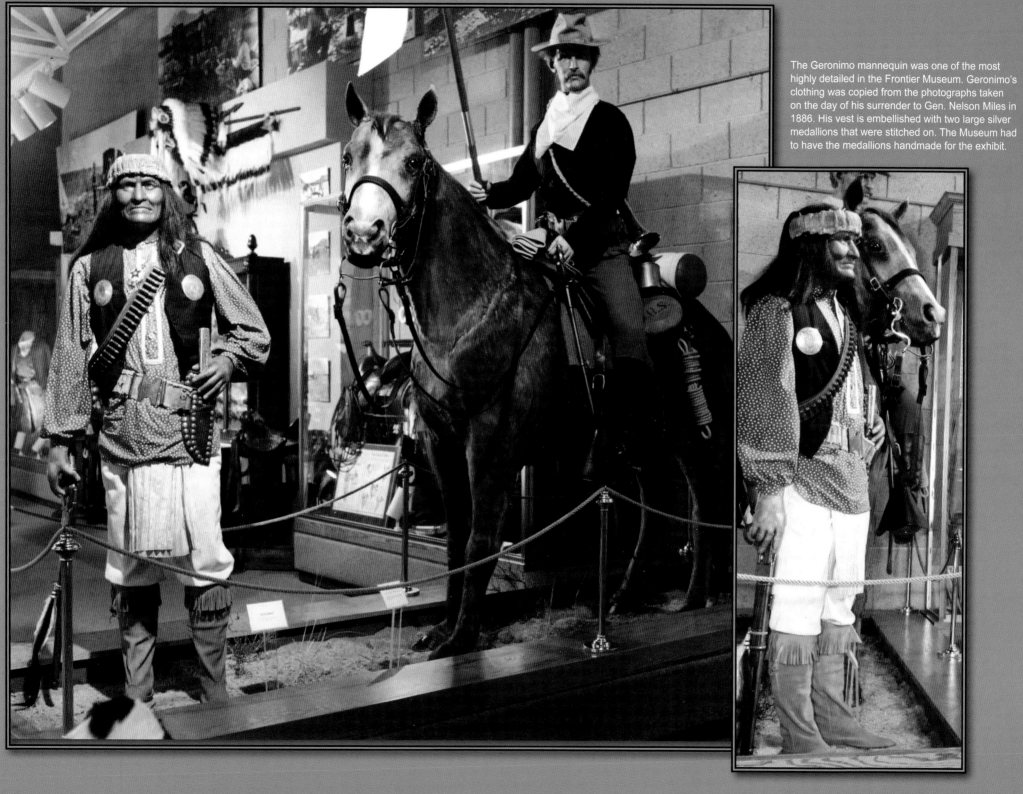

The Geronimo mannequin was one of the most highly detailed in the Frontier Museum. Geronimo's clothing was copied from the photographs taken on the day of his surrender to Gen. Nelson Miles in 1886. His vest is embellished with two large silver medallions that were stitched on. The Museum had to have the medallions handmade for the exhibit.

John wore the Pancho Villa costume for the "Los Bandidos" Histograph in 1977, and it became part of the Museum exhibit of Villa (standing) and one of his men. "We were able to make everything seem so natural, like the way Villa's fingers are holding the glass and how his *compañero's* hand wraps around the tequila bottle. It was the little details that made every exhibit seem so realistic," says Bianchi.

Every character in the Museum was built to look totally lifelike. Every piece of the wardrobes was handmade, as was all of the leather. The attention to details in posture and expressions was essential to total realism.

Custer with the Butterfield Express coach was one of the most elaborate mannequins in the museum when it came to costuming detail. "The Custer shirt was custom made from the original using the same type of Melton wool from England. We found the mill and got the duplicate fabric for the pants and shirt," says Bianchi.

The Bianchi Gun Cabinet contained examples of various Colt SAA models. It was one of the most complete sets of original guns at the time. "After it was transferred to the Autry, the Museum auctioned off the gun cabinet," laments Bianchi.

The three gunmen in front of this backdrop are the James Boys, Jesse and Frank, headliners in the Outlaws exhibit. All of the guns used with the mannequins were real. They were wired into the holsters so they couldn't be pulled out.

This casual street scene conveys the times it was designed to depict through the clothing, wagon, and physical characteristics of the two individuals. "It was like looking at an old daguerreotype in living color."

This is the chuck wagon that was used in "The Cowboys" Histograph. The chuck wagon was another centerpiece display in the Museum depicting Western life on the prairie. It was positioned next to the cattle drover's camp. "You could step right up to the encampment and hear one of the cowboys playing a harmonica. There was a coyote howling in the background. The sound effects really pulled you into the picture," recalls Bianchi. "Each of the open exhibits had its own soundtrack."

The Texas Ranger display depicts the end of the Old West as the Ranger has given over to driving a Ford instead of riding his horse in pursuit of outlaws. "In the 1920s the Rangers would haul their horse in a trailer until they reached the end of drivable roads and then continue their pursuit on horseback," explains Bianchi.

Since the Old West town of Temecula was home to the Frontier Museum, John Bianchi dedicated an entire exhibit to the town's history. It had been home to the 100,000 acre Vail Cattle Ranch. Temecula was established in the 1850s and was a stop for the Butterfield-Overland Stage Line. The old depot still existed at the time the Museum was opened and was used for the Histograph "Last of the Lawmen."

This incredible work of art done on a mirror was loaned to the Frontier Museum by Michael Wayne. The corridor led past the executive offices to the research library and conference room at the end of the hall.

The Bianchi Frontier Museum had an elaborate conference room and research library.

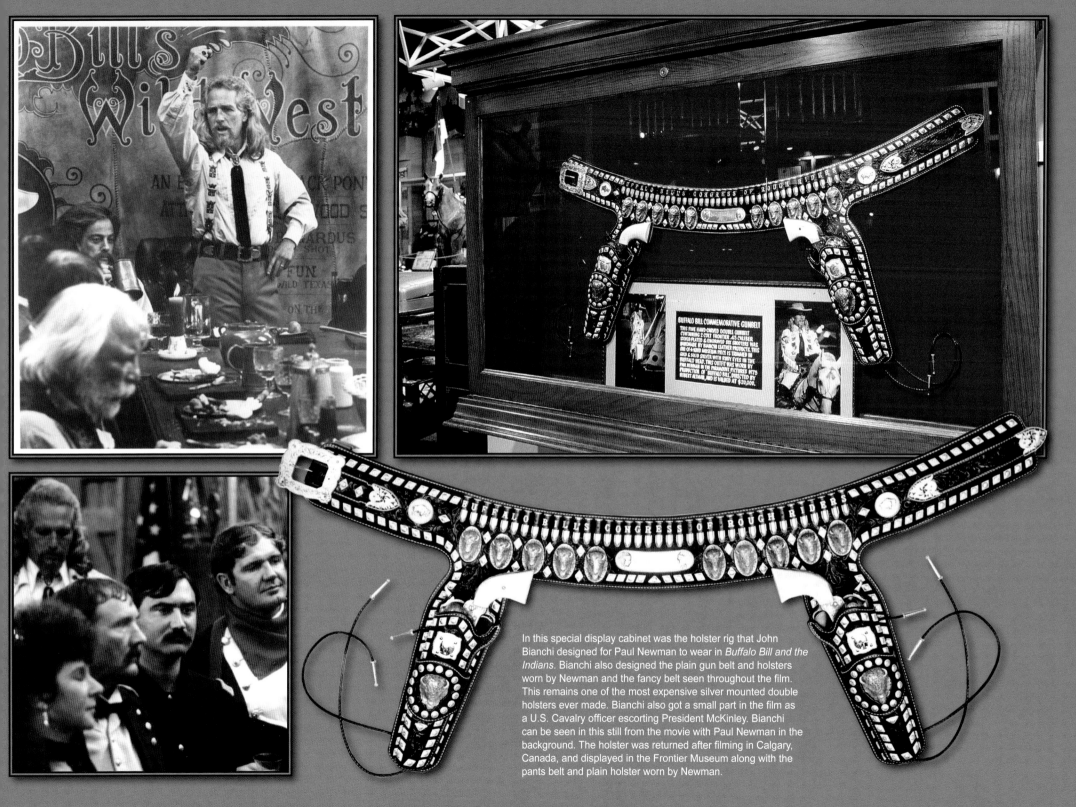

In this special display cabinet was the holster rig that John Bianchi designed for Paul Newman to wear in *Buffalo Bill and the Indians.* Bianchi also designed the plain gun belt and holsters worn by Newman and the fancy belt seen throughout the film. This remains one of the most expensive silver mounted double holsters ever made. Bianchi also got a small part in the film as a U.S. Cavalry officer escorting President McKinley. Bianchi can be seen in this still from the movie with Paul Newman in the background. The holster was returned after filming in Calgary, Canada, and displayed in the Frontier Museum along with the pants belt and plain holster worn by Newman.

The Movie Cowboys display contained more significant Western film memorabilia than anyone realized at the time. John had been collecting pieces for years, and when it all came together, the scope of the exhibit, with original clothing worn by Tom Mix, Buck Jones, Joel McCray, Gary Cooper, Jack Holt, Wallace Beery, Robert Redford, and Hugh O'Brian, just to mention a few, is priceless today.

Among the famous Old West film memorabilia was one of the Stetsons worn by Tom Mix in his 1920's films.

In the top of this display case of Reel Cowboys was the plain gun belt worn by Paul Newman in *Buffalo Bill and the Indians*; below it, the decorative belt worn by Newman. Both were designed by John Bianchi for the film. Below, left, Joel McCrea's spurs; at right, Gary Cooper's spurs from *High Noon*.

Buck Jones' wooly chaps and the coat worn by Robert Redford in *Butch Cassidy and the Sundance Kid*.

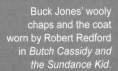

Three of the most historic pieces in the Frontier Museum were the fringe jacket worn by Buffalo Bill Cody in his Wild West Shows, one of Cody's hats, and a 12-ga. double barreled shotgun with the inscription *For The Honorable William F. Cody* engraved on the barrel rib.

# THE LAWMEN

In the Lawmen display case sitting on the left shelf was Bill Tilghman's engraved Colt Single Action revolver, presented to the famous U.S. Marshal by the grateful townspeople of Perry, Oklahoma, in 1893. Tilghman was one of the "Three Guardsmen of Oklahoma" who cleaned up the territory in the late 1890s and early 20th century. Heck Thomas and Chris Madsen were the other two heroic Deputy U.S. Marshals who rode with Tilghman.

THE HISTORY OF GUNLEATHER

The History of Gunleather display was a visual treatise on the evolution of holsters from the pre-Civil War era up to the early 1930s and included some of the rarest and most unusual holsters from the Old West. Many of these holsters formed the body of work presented in John Bianchi's seminal work on the history of holsters titled *Bluesteel & Gunleather*.

Among the holsters in the Museum displays was an original gun rig with a rare spark striker hanging from the gunbelt on a leather thong. It was used to start a campfire. The cut down 1860 Army belly gun (at far right) came to Bianchi with this equally abbreviated holster (below) with the throat cut down to expose the triggerguard for easier access to the gun.

Two significant holsters in the Gunleather exhibit were an early half flap 1860 Army holster and a rare Dragoon pommel holster.

"The most interesting of all the designs in the shoulder and pocket holster display was the pocket holster with the spring device. When you put the holster in your front or back pocket the spring pushed out to lock the holster in, so when you drew the gun the holster stayed tight in your pocket. At that time in the Old West, every gentleman carried a gun, if not in a holster then in a pocket. That was one of my favorites," says Bianchi. "Men went armed most of the time well into the early 20th century."

One of history's more unusual carry systems was the "Bridgeport Rig," a device designed to be attached to a cartridge belt by which a revolver could be suspended openly from the Bridgeport clip, either for fast draw or swiveling into action while still mounted to the gun belt. The Bridgeport used a forked clip into which the head of a large, mushroom-shaped screw (replacing the hammer screw) extended beyond the frame and slipped between the forks and into a recess in the mounting device. Originally intended to be used by the U.S. Cavalry, the design patented by Louis S. Flatau in 1882 was rejected by the military but found limited popularity in the civilian market among lawmen and Wild West showmen. At far left is a Cavalry saddle scabbard for the Springfield Trapdoor Carbine carried by troops during the Indian Wars.

"The elaborate studded holster at right was one of the very first that I collected, back when I was in my early twenties. It came with the 7-1/2 inch Colt," recalls Bianchi. "Cowboys back in the 1870s went for some pretty flashy stuff. That holster is unlined, one thickness, and the backings for the conchos were exposed on the inside of the holster." The holster at left is a later double loop design with hand stamping and border work, with an S&W .44 double action revolver. At far left is another unlined double loop holster and cartridge belt.

Among the various holsters in this display was an original money cartridge belt with a studded double loop holster. "That's an early belt," says Bianchi as he looks back on his old collection. "That belt would be worth thousands today!" The display was to show the diversity of holster designs in the 1870s as well as guns. The pair on the back wall are Richards Mason conversions of Colt 1860 Army revolvers; there is a pair of Colt 1878 double actions, a Single Action Army, and a Merwin Hulbert Bird's Head Pocket Army in a Mexican embroidered holster. "The embroidery was known as *piteada* and was done with woven fibers from the agave cactus. A lot of these old holsters still had the original guns with the holsters when acquired," recalls Bianchi.

GUN LEATHER
1865-1875

A variety of holster designs from the first decade following the Civil War. Many cap-and-ball revolvers were converted to fire metallic cartridges in the early 1870s and holster designs were modified to accommodate both the guns and belts with cartridge loops. Also note the unusual pocket holster with six cartridge loops.

The Guns of the Gunfighters display held 18 documented guns attesting to the provenance of having belonged to the famous and infamous personalities of the Old West, from Frank James to Judge Roy Bean and Pancho Villa, to guns carried by Pat Garrett, Col. Charles Askins, Bill Jordan, and Heck Thomas. This was in addition to the Reel Cowboys display, which held famous movie guns dating back to the earliest Westerns.

OUTLAW
**Frank James'**
Remington .44/40 Revolver
Belt and Holster
S/N 5116
CIRCA 1875

OUTLAW
**Frank James**
Colt Single-Action Bisley 32-20 Revolver
Carried By Frank James After Release From Prison When He Joined The Cole Younger Wild West Show Touring The Midwest From 1903 to 1909.
S/N 304918
Frank James Died A Natural Death In 1915

The Frank James gun came to John as a result of the *L.A. Times* article. "My secretary Elsie got a call and she knew what questions to ask, and she comes running in. 'Boss, you've got to take this call!' The man on the phone said he has one of Frank James' Remington revolvers. He brings it in with the gun in a cardboard box, and in a towel is a Remington in an old Slim Jim holster with the cartridges still in the belt loops. He had all the documentation and it was one of Frank's guns that he gave to a doctor that treated him after James agreed to surrender to the Governor of Missouri. Frank was sick and he wanted to be treated before he turned himself in. The doctor came to James and treated him privately until he recovered. He had no money so he gave the doctor his left-hand holster and gun. Many years later, the doctor's wife went to a Wild West Show where Frank James was appearing. After the show she got him to examine the gun and holster and write a note stipulating that it was his. He wrote it on the back of a cardboard cigarette box and she put it in the box with the gun. It went through three generations and the man who brought the gun to Bianchi was the grandson of the doctor."

This is a Colt Double Action .38 caliber revolver with swing out cylinder c.1899, carried by Oklahoma lawman and Deputy U.S. Marshal Heck Thomas in his later years.

Among the guns Bianchi acquired for the Museum was one of John Wesley Hardin's 1877 Colt Double Action revolvers and an 1873 Peacemaker. "I bought the John Wesley Hardin guns and memorabilia from Bobby McNellis of El Paso Saddlery," recalls Bianchi. "Bobby started locking on to that kind of stuff very early on before anybody had an interest."

John acquired the Judge Roy Bean Colt Single Action in the late 1970s. "When it was presented to me there was only a little bit of documentation. But in the back of my mind I kept thinking, 'I've seen this gun before.' Then I remembered. It was on the cover of *American Rifleman*. So I asked Elsie to check and see when. Within several days she had a copy of the magazine from July 1953, and the whole story of the gun was written up inside." The Roy Bean Colt was handsomely engraved in a combination of scrollwork and cattle brands, and had a shaved down front sight and cut barrel. This may be one of the first uses of cattle brand engravings. Legend has it that the Colt was a gift to the Judge purportedly from actress Lillie Langtry. There is no supporting evidence that Langtry ever met Roy Bean, but she did visit the saloon sometime after his death.

JUDGE
Roy Bean's
Colt Single-Action .45 Revolver
S/N 8054
Ornately Engraved With Early Texas Cattle Brands
Presented to the Judge By British Actress
Lili Langtree.
CIRCA 1874

Col. Charles Askins' .38 Colt Double Action revolver, c.1936, with a FitzGerald-style modified open triggerguard. "Beginning in the early 1960s we communicated often. He wouldn't talk on the telephone; he liked to write letters, and I have a file full of them. He would comment on holster designs and other Bianchi leather products, and he loved the museum," says Bianchi. "He was a very colorful character. We hunted and drank together. He was the elder statesman in that period. He carried that gun in WWII. There is a little known but great compliment granted by old time lawmen and border patrolmen, bestowed upon very few, but it speaks volumes… 'He's a good man to ride the river with'. I have been honored to receive that great vote of confidence from two legendary lawmen that I held in high esteem all my adult life. They're gone now, but their accolade remains. One was Col. Charlie Askins. The other was Texas Ranger Captain Clint Peoples, with whom I served with on the U.S. Marshals Bicentennial commission. Two fine gentlemen, but very tough cookies."

NATIONAL RIFLE ASSOCIATION OF AMERICA
INCORPORATED 1871

COL. CHARLES ASKINS
SENIOR FIELD EDITOR
NRA PUBLICATIONS

903 Melissa at Blanco Road
San Antonio, Texas 78213
29 January 1982

COL. CHARLES ASKINS
COLT DA .38 SPECIAL W/MODIFIED TRIGGER GUARD
Former lawman, U.S. Border Patrol Officer, Army Paratrooper, Author, International Big Game Hunter, Firearms Expert, and winner of many national and international shooting awards. He was a veteran of numerous gunfights in the 1930's and 1940's while with the U.S. Border Patrol.

S/N 339755

My Dear John:

Boy! This has got to be the finest vest in the West! I am a sucker for a vest anyway and this one is a pure delight. Like everytning that bears the name Bianchi it is highest quality and goodness. I am delighted with it, Old Stud.

Muchisimos gracias!

I heard at the SHOT Show that Elmer had suffered a stroke. Apparently one not too severe but then it don't take much of a stroke to put a feller in a bad way. He had developed diabetes and he had a severe heart attack in 1966. The last letter I had from him he said he would be 83 in March. He may not make it.

If it appears I can help with the formal opening of the Bianchi Museum just send me word and I'll come out. Recollecting the NRA Meeting this year is during the first week in April. I could not make that but any other time in April I could sure be with you.

I am pleased indeed with this gorgeous leathern vest, Old Hoss.

Many many thanks

Cordially as always

Askins

Emmet Dalton's Colt Single Action was an engraved model that the reformed outlaw used later in life as a Wild West Show performer. Dalton became a realtor in Hollywood, California after giving up the show circuit. It's uncertain whether Dalton used this gun to close any real estate deals!

**EMMET DALTON**
COLT S.A. .45 CALIBER ENGRAVED

**OUTLAW**

An original member of the Dalton Gang and veteran of many train robberies. The youngest of the 'Coffeyville Bank Robbery', Emmet Dalton served 15 years in prison for his crimes. After his release he became a wild west showman and later a real estate agent and lived in Hollywood, Calif. until his death in 1937.

S/N 147305

**SHERIFF**
**PAT GARRETT**
HOPKINS & ALLEN MODEL XL .32 REVOLVER
SERIAL NUMBER 3164

Engraved on barrel - "Patrick Floyd Garrett"

This gun was among Pat Garrett's possessions at the time of his murder in 1908. Affidavit related to this gun is signed by Pat Garrett's son, Jarvis Garrett of New Mexico. Pat Garrett was the sheriff

John acquired several significant guns from El Paso, Texas, collector Bobby McNellis (of El Paso Saddlery) including Pat Garrett's Hopkins & Allen Model XL .32 caliber pocket revolver.

John Bianchi knew Bill Jordan for many years and when he opened the Museum, Jordan gave him his custom modified .38 S&W used for trick shooting.

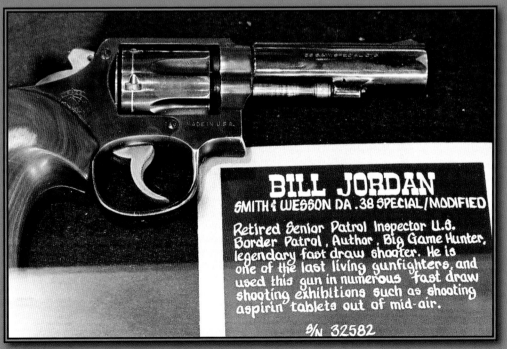

**BILL JORDAN**
SMITH & WESSON DA .38 SPECIAL/MODIFIED

Retired Senior Patrol Inspector U.S. Border Patrol, Author, Big Game Hunter, legendary fast draw shooter. He is one of the last living gunfighters, and used this gun in numerous fast draw shooting exhibitions such as shooting aspirin tablets out of mid-air.

S/N 32582

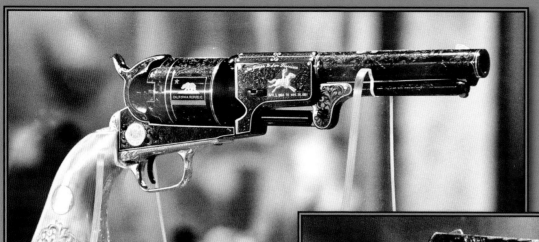

This second generation, Colt 3rd Model Dragoon was fully engraved with frontier history of California by world renowned firearms engraver Howard Dove in the late 1970s and presented to John Bianchi by Colt's for display in the Frontier Museum. When the museum was later transferred to the Autry, the Bianchi Colt was placed on display along with a collection of highly engraved second generation Colt Blackpowder models engraved by Dove, Alvin A. White, and other American Master Engravers. They are still on display to this day at the Autry and the Bianchi Colt stands alone as a tribute not only to John Bianchi, but the talent of late engraver Howard Dove.

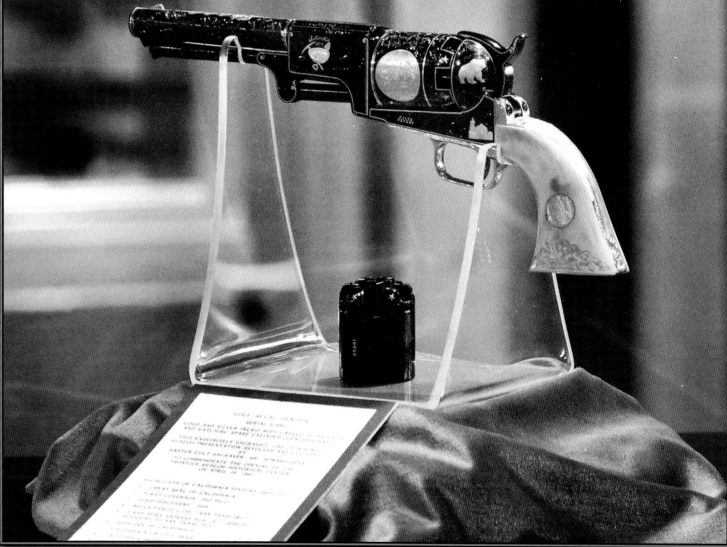

Ornate spurs made in Chile and worn during the Mexican Revolution, c.1914. These were the second most elaborate pair of spurs in the collection, second only to those worn by Death Valley Scotty.

"The most magnificent pair of spurs I ever owned were Death Valley Scotty's," says Bianchi. "Scotty was very adept at spending other people's money and built Scotty's Castle in Death Valley, California, financed by a Chicago industrialist." Much history is written about this 1920s historical figure.

Here are two examples of the incredible detail that went into the Frontier Museum mannequins. "Every strand of hair was individually inserted into the mannequins using a hot needle procedure. We used real glass medical replacement eyes made in Germany to give each of the figures a more lifelike appearance," explains Bianchi.

Western personality and showman Joe Bowman appeared at the Frontier Museum, representing the state of Texas, and presented John Bianchi with a Texas State flag from the Governor. Bowman was one of the world's greatest trick shooters and gun handlers. "He was a great friend for many years, a straight shooter and gentleman," says Bianchi. "We last visited in May of 2009, prior to his untimely passing after the '09 End of Trail Single Action Shooting Society event in New Mexico."

In 1983, Lawrence Welk filmed one of his shows titled "Our Western Heritage" at the Frontier Museum. That's Welk in an Indian headdress beating a tom-tom, and with John Bianchi after the filming. "Lawrence Welk had a housing development about 20 miles away," explains Bianchi, "so he had come to the Museum and was fascinated by it."

# The Key Role of John Bianchi and His Frontier Museum in the Formation of The Gene Autry Western Heritage Museum

### By R.L. Wilson

This is the inventory book and appraisal of the Frontier Museum, which was prepared for the transition to the Autry Museum. "This was in 1985 to inventory the entire contents of the Museum. There were 3,000 artifacts with a total of 10,000 components. In other words, if there was a collection of badges, each one had to be accounted for, and I had hundreds of original badges. Everything had to be separately inventoried and cataloged," explains Bianchi. Also shown are the actual documents that were signed by Gene Autry, acknowledging the donation contribution John made to the Autry Museum.

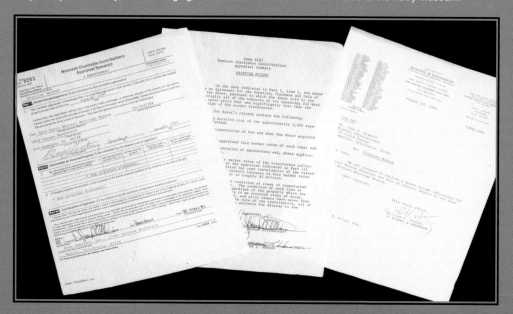

**H**aving manufactured millions of holsters for Colt firearms over the years, it is fitting that John Bianchi and his Frontier Museum would play a key role in the future of three major collections: the private gun museum of Colt Industries, the private arms collection of Colt Industries Chairman, George A. Strichman, and the soon-to-be-immense holdings of the Gene Autry Museum of Western Heritage. Because of the significance of all of these entities, the subject is dealt with in some detail.

In collaboration with George A. Strichman, late Chairman of the Board of Colt Industries, I had been privileged to organize the Colt Industries Museum Collection. This complex, ten-year long project began with the recommendation to Strichman of my services, by Colt President Paul A. Benke, in 1972. Only seven years previously I had resigned my position at Colt's, as Assistant Manager, Public Relations and Advertising, to become a freelance author and antiquarian. *The Book of Colt Firearms*, begun in 1967, had been published in its 616-page First Edition, in 1971. I had assisted the Colt company on many projects as a freelance since 1966, and Paul knew that I had been instrumental in building the collection of the book's publisher, R.Q. Sutherland. Benke had been particularly impressed with our book, and the Colt-Hartley & Graham Display Board, which I had been able to acquire from the Remington Arms Co., for the Sutherland Collection.

Not only did Paul Benke's recommendation result in formation of the Colt Industries Museum, but the project also led to George Strichman's own 170-piece Colt collection. The Colt Industries group was superbly balanced in firearms and memorabilia from 1836 to c. 1980, while George's was primarily post-1961. Each collection complemented the other, with George emphasizing in his best pieces the art of the gun engraver – featuring the genius of Alvin A. White, Leonard Francolini, and other artisan engravers. One of the special attractions of the Colt Industries Museum was a series of revolvers engraved and gold inlaid for Presidents of the United States, a superb archive of Colt patent papers and related documents, a carefully selected library (including an original copy of the first Colt book, *Armsmear*, published by Mrs. Colt, in 1866), and miscellaneous key objects of memorabilia. Among the latter treasures were Samuel Colt's cigar stand in sterling silver, the silver bell that he rang for his nurse (while on his deathbed in the Armsmear mansion), and the original ledger book of the Colt's Patent Fire Arms Mfg. Co. Board of Directors.

Thanks indirectly to John Bianchi, and to the retirement, and eventually the unfortunate passing of George Strichman, both arms groups became featured exhibits at the Gene Autry Museum of Western Heritage. After the Autrys, assisted by Joanne and Monte

Hale, made the momentous decision to proceed with their plans for a museum, it was evident that Gene's own collection, as fascinating as it was, centered largely on his own career – and as he finally came to realize – was not as large as Gene himself had remembered it to be. The fledgling Autry Museum was in definite need of digging into the past, the Old West, to add significantly to the appeal to the public, and to scholars and collectors in that genre.

## Gene Autry's Dream of His Own Museum of the West

Internationally known as the "Singing Cowboy," Gene Autry's meteoric career was launched when he was discovered by Will Rogers in a small town in Texas, strumming a guitar while he worked as a telegraph operator for Western Union. Rogers advised Autry to head to New York. Quickly the astute youngster re-directed his energies to Hollywood, and in 1929 the Autry legend was on its way. Soon he was making as much as $10,000 a week, and was starring in grade B Western films, regaled in fancy cowboy outfits, and equipped with silver-mounted gun rigs, fine Single Action Colts, and saddles by artists like Ed Bohlin.

Having accumulated an extraordinary Wild West collection in the process of developing his career, the concept of a museum of these artifacts was guaranteed by an endowment established by Ima, Gene's wife of several decades, in her will. By the time this idea was re-kindled, in 1980, that sum totaled approximately $75 million. Gene's own collection was intended to be the basis for the museum. But the seed funding and the seed collection needed to be organized and this required some careful planning. This exciting and challenging endeavor would be the joint effort of Gene and his new wife, Jackie, and Gene's best friend Monte Hale, and his wife Joanne.[1]

## Bianchi Museum a Giant Leap Forward for Autry Project

The Autrys and the Hales had decided early in the evolution of their museum plans that John Bianchi's Frontier Museum collection would provide a giant leap forward. Having been privy to working with this well-financed quartet from within two weeks of their decision to forge ahead, and having specialized expertise on the objects displayed in Temecula, I was asked to accompany the ladies on their trip to view the museum. It was clear to me that Jackie and Joanne had been given the authority to make a deal, on the spot. Gene was eager to move, and he had the wherewithal to do it. Not only would he draw on the fund established by Ima's estate, but he would also draw on his own considerable fortune. Well known for his wealth and generous spirit, *Forbes'* magazine's annual "Forbes 400" regularly included Gene Autry as among the leading 400 American multi-millionaires.

Watching Jackie and Joanne in action was something to see. They had been absorbing every bit of knowledge they could about how to put together a world-class institution. I had urged them to look into affiliation with the American Association of Museums, a group that I first learned of while interning at the Corcoran Gallery of Art, Washington, D.C., in the summer of 1960. At that time, the director of the AAM, Lamont duPont

Copeland, would come into the Corcoran, and was friendly with the institution's director, Dr. Hermann Warner Williams, Jr. A keen antiquarian and arms collector, Williams knew virtually everyone at the top in the art and museum world, and was an early mentor in my own career. That summer I was privileged to be assigned to help organize what became the Centennial exhibition of the Corcoran and the Museum of Fine Arts, Boston: *The Civil War: The Artists' Record*.

Affiliation with the American Association of Museums, which accredits institutions, and then assists them in a myriad of ways – and lists them in the now 1,800 page *Official Directory* – would be a crucial step in the Autry Museum's future. In order to obtain that accreditation, it was also crucial to have a world-class collection. The first giant step would be the purchase of John Bianchi's Frontier Museum.

While in California on an Autry Museum-related trip, I was informed that Jackie and Joanne were planning a trip to Temecula to negotiate with John Bianchi on the purchase of his Frontier Museum. I was asked to accompany them, and to do a careful examination of the collection, and provide extra assurance that acquiring John Bianchi's prized creation was a correct decision.

I had known John for years, having met him as early as 1966 at the NRA Show, and seen him from time to time at antique arms shows, including the fabled Great Western, held in Pomona, at the California State Fairgrounds. He was also a regular at Harry Mann's Las Vegas Arms Shows, which were later owned and managed by Wallace Beinfeld (from the early 1970s).

John had become the Samuel Colt of the holster industry. Not only had he mastered the art of design and manufacture, but he understood materials, had a keen business sense, was gifted in advertising and public relations, and had his own experience as a peace officer, and as a shooter, and indeed, a historian and student of firearms and of that most vital of accessories – especially in the Old West – the holster.

Bianchi's advertising, and his use of beautifully produced posters and "Histographs," proved to be key tools in the rapid rise of his reputation, his company, and their impressive product line. Vital to Bianchi's meteoric success were his promotions at the NSGA (National Sporting Goods Association) trade show, begun in 1967. Eventually the NSGA was succeeded by the SHOT (Shooting and Hunting Outdoor Trade Show), organized in 1971 by the NSSF (National Shooting Sports Foundation). Bianchi (and his company) was the first participant to come on board – at what quickly became the most important single trade show in the history of the shooting sports.

Bianchi perceived quickly the importance of advertising and public relations – communications (as it is called today). As was the case with Bill Ruger, and had been the case with the original marketing genius – Samuel Colt – Bianchi was able to meld his knowledge of and his passion for his product line, and capitalize on the significant role of leather goods in American history, particularly in the Old West.

"Bianchi Leather" became as famed a product line as "Colt Revolvers." And, instinctively (as had been the case with Colonel Colt), Bianchi early began collecting holsters and frontier leather along with the firearms they served. His creation of the Bianchi Frontier Museum, begun in 1970, and completed in 1981, was history repeating itself, Colt's concept for a museum dated from early in his success in the late 1840s and early 1850s. The museum collection Sam Colt created became two: that from his home, Armsmear, was willed by his widow to the Wadsworth Atheneum Museum of Art (in fact, part of that collection was due to her own input). The collection at the factory became the Colt Collection of Firearms, at the Connecticut State Library, exhibited within the Raymond Baldwin Museum of Connecticut History.

The Bianchi Frontier Museum had its own transition, into one of the world's premier institutions devoted to the collection, display, and study of the culture and history of the great American West. The Autry Museum of Western Heritage, opened in 1985, and John served on the Board of Directors from the founding year to 1988. The evolution of this transition is fascinating history in itself, and stands as a classic example of the old cliché, "Timing is everything."

I had been fortunate to visit the Bianchi Frontier Museum, where I also received a guided tour of the huge and modern factory, as well as being hosted by John and Donna at their spacious home, overlooking Temecula - with an extensive grove of avocado trees. I was delighted a short time later, returning home to Hadlyme, Connecticut, to find a box of fresh avocadoes on my doorstep.

Having already toured the collection, I was fully prepared to accompany Jackie and Joanne on their drive to Temecula. While they discussed business matters with John, reviewing various records and negotiating an agreeable price, I was assigned to examine the collection, give my impression of the usefulness of the holdings for the Autry's own museum plans, and estimate an overall value. The question of originality of the firearms and artifacts was yet another task. Agreeing that the collection was an ideal opportunity for the Autry Museum project, and presenting details of my findings, the ladies proceeded to close the deal with John.

What a thrill it was to me while returning to Los Angeles in Jackie's beautiful white Mercedes, to hear the car phone ring. I was sitting in the right front seat, Jackie at the wheel. It was Gene calling. His first question was whether or not the ladies had made a deal. His second question was "Did you get the Colt Single Actions." That was how important those 2nd Generation Colts were to Gene himself.[2]

The Colt Industries Museum was located on the fourth floor of Colt Industries' corporate headquarters, at 430 Park Avenue, New York. The Colt Industries Museum Collection was the biggest N.Y. Police Department firearms premises permit in the city. Strichman and other executives showed that collection to visiting dignitaries. When the display, designed by architect Bonnell Irvine, assisted by myself, was first unveiled, the first to view it were members of the Colt Industries Board of Directors. I particularly remember George Strichman's pride in showing the displays to retired General Matthew

John Bianchi (far left) at the official opening of the Autry Museum, which became the depository for the entire Frontier Museum collection in 1985. Pictured left to right are the first board members, Bianchi, Clyde Tritt, Jackie Autry, Joann Hale, Gene Autry, Stan Schneider, and Monty Hale.

B. Ridgeway, a heroic figure from World War II and the Korean War – and the most high profile board member.

What eventually led to the purchase of these collections by the Autry Museum was when Gene Autry's private pilot had called me in 1980, with the request of Gene to visit him in Los Angeles. The intent was for an appraisal of Gene's personal arms collection. A miscellany of guns totaling about 100 firearms, these were primarily Colt Single Action Armys, and a smattering of Winchesters and other makes. It was clear that Gene's guns had enormous potential for the planned museum, though they represented only a beginning. Since several of these had been used in making his 50 or more B Western movies they had a known history, and could be seen on film, firing blanks, making that peculiar "pow" sound common to all of those Saturday matinee productions.

I have always felt an affinity for museums, and the opportunity they often present for a better understanding by the public and media of the special, indeed unique, positive role of firearms in history, art, and culture. Over the decades it has been exciting to be involved in placing great pieces into important public collections. In the instance of the Autry Museum of Western Heritage, that rapidly developing organization came into reality with perfect timing. The Colt Industries Museum Collection would soon be available for purchase, since the corporate executives decided to sell off the Colt

Firearms Division, following George Strichman's retirement, in 1984.

At that point I had already been working with the Autrys and the Hales in creating their museum, to be based in Los Angeles. With the retirement of George Strichman, the new management was no longer interested in maintaining a gun collection on site in the Park Avenue offices. I advised them that the best means of selling the collection was to a single purchaser – and that the most likely candidate was the Autry Museum.

## Autrys Acquire the Colt Industries and Strichman Collections

I was authorized to invite Joanne Hale and then Chief Curator James Nottage to New York for viewing the still-intact display. Assisted by Pete Williamson, Colt Industries Director of Public Relations, the highly secured entrance to the Gun Room was unlocked. And in we entered – to a site few in New York had ever seen, and virtually no collector – other than my friend and later patron, Robert M. Lee (founder and president of Hunting World, Inc.) – had viewed.

It was obvious from the minute Joanne Hale and James Nottage viewed the collection that the Autry Museum would soon own it. Within a few weeks the deal had been made, and the collection was packed and shipped to the Museum's temporary storage facility in Los Angeles. Although Strichman was upset that the collection had been sold, he was delighted to learn that it would be the Autry Museum that would maintain the collection that he had authorized and that we had enjoyed immensely putting together. It was also a source of great satisfaction to me, knowing that our hard work over ten years had resulted in the finest collection of Colt firearms from New York City to the West Coast.

Quickly following George Strichman's death from cancer in April 1989, I encouraged the Autry Museum to acquire his own Colt collection as well. With the Colt Industries and Strichman acquisitions, the Autry instantly became one of the foremost institutions exhibiting Colt firearms anywhere in the world.

True to my feelings about commerce, I told the Museum that rather than pay me a commission, I would be proud to have my name up on the credits in their expansive entrance, where the main donors were honored, among them Gene and Jackie Autry, Frank Sinatra, Bob Hope, Wells Fargo Bank – and now me! But there is another name fully deserving placement on that coveted display of credits, John Bianchi.

## The Autry Museum Gala Colts, Built from the Bianchi Museum Collection

Never in the history of American arms engraving has a series been created to equal or surpass the Autry Museum Gala Colt Single Action Army revolvers. These were conceived to coincide with the annual fund-raising Gala fundraising evenings, a highlight of the Autry Museum year. Each revolver was from the Autry Museum's own collection of Second Generation (post-World War II) Single Actions, which had been a key portion of the purchase of John Bianchi's Frontier Museum collection.

The Gala Colt Single Action Army series began in 1991 and continued through the last of the millennium, that of 2000 – the Colt presentation revolver no. 356262. None of this would have happened if John Bianchi had not shared the same love of the Colt Single Action that was instilled in Gene Autry. That block of over one hundred of these treasured Colts was as treasured by Gene, as it was by John.

For years I had assumed the Single Actions had been acquired by the Autrys in the purchase of the Bianchi Frontier Museum. Only recently did I learn from John himself that he had presented that collection to the Autrys, as part of a $2.75 million dollar donation, coinciding with his sale of the Frontier Museum.

John Bianchi's recollection of these revolvers brings back other memories as well. "When Gene Autry and Monte Hale and their wives visited my museum, they were absolutely fascinated with the collection and the manner in which it was exhibited, and could not have been more complimentary. During that second visit, Gene said 'This collection is overwhelming. How long did it take you to put it all together?' When I told him it took me a lifetime, his response was indicative of his quick cowboy wit, 'I don't have that much time.' Gene told me that he had quite a collection gathered during his career that he had in storage, which he truly believed. When he invited me to his home in Studio City, and to Melody Ranch, we made the disappointing discovery that much of what he thought he had saved over the years had been lost, stolen, misplaced, or damaged by fire and water. The only thing we could find of value at Melody Ranch was a couple of old saddles and a highly embellished 1953 Buick Woodie convertible elaborately decorated with Western décor, probably by 'Nudie's of Hollywood' – makers of costumes for Gene, Roy Rogers, and other stars of the 1930s, '40s and '50s. Nearly everything else of importance from Gene's collection was gone.

"The most important remaining treasure, which fortunately was stored elsewhere, was a heavily gold- and silver-mounted Bohlin saddle, with all the trappings, Ed Bohlin had made this magnificent item for himself in the 1930s. I remember that saddle well: as a young man, just beginning in the holster business. The then quite elderly Ed Bohlin had offered that saddle to me. His price was, in retrospect, cheap: $50,000. Today that work of decorative art, which was lent to The Metropolitan Museum of Art for a major exhibition on 'The Horse,' is one of the prized exhibits at the Autry, and worth a fortune.

"At one point, the conversation turned to baseball. Gene asked me what my favorite baseball team was. I thoughtlessly replied, 'I'm not much of a ball fan.' Gene had a perplexed look on his face, not understanding that a red-blooded American did not like baseball. However, he insisted that my wife and I be his guest in the Owner's Box at the Angels' Stadium in Anaheim. We went, although I had a very hard time sitting still for 3-1/2 hours!"

Unfortunately for John, when the transition took place from the Bianchi Frontier Museum to the Autry, things began to turn sour. "It was obvious to me that the collection was [being] postured as Gene's lifelong accumulation of artifacts and every effort was made to diminish my role in the project."

Despite Bianchi's $2.7 million dollar donation to the Autry Museum and the gift of over a hundred, new in-the-box Colt Single Action revolvers, the contributions were never recognized or appreciated, and no thank you to John for the gift ever resulted. "By this time Gene was pretty much out of the picture, leaving the administration and transfer to his wife Jackie and her friend, Joanne Hale. Their lack of appreciation and sensitivity was at times offensive, without provocation or reason," recalls Bianchi.

I have had a long and friendly relationship with Jackie Autry and Joanne Hale, and consider them dear friends. Sadly, I remember distinctly at the first annual Gala fund raiser of the Museum, in October of 1986, Bianchi was standing at an entranceway to the huge ballroom, obviously quite upset. The table he and his party had been assigned was

The Autry National Center of the West as it appears today. The Autry houses many of the original guns, holsters, clothing, and mannequins from John Bianchi's Frontier Museum. Without the Bianchi collection, the Autry would not have many of its most prominent pieces. (Photo by Clark Fogg)

as far away from the stage as possible (in "Siberia"), and the recognition and respect he had anticipated was clearly not a part of the evening's festivities. He and his party left, and he has yet to return to the Museum for even a cursory visit.

The only visible recognitions to John Bianchi are on the display of credits in the Museum lobby, and a bronze founder's plaque, at the entrance to what is now known as the Autry National Center of the West. ✍

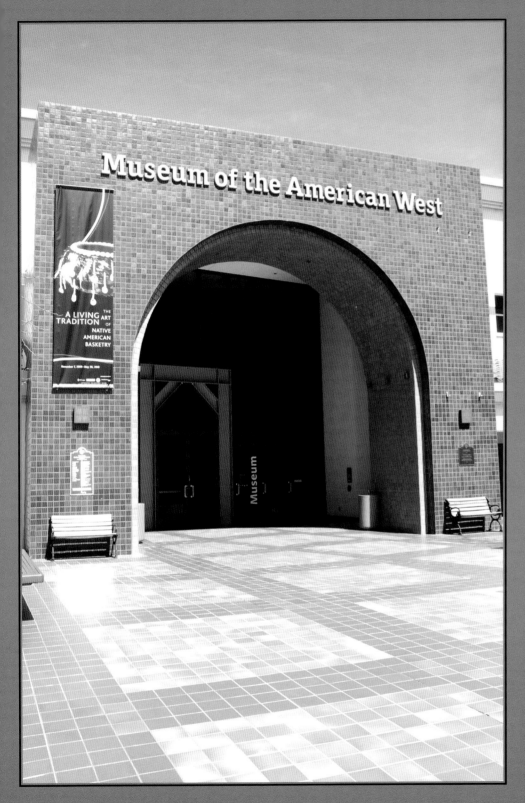

Gene Autry
Western Heritage Museum
NOVEMBER 22, 1988
FUNDED BY THE AUTRY FOUNDATION

BOARD OF DIRECTORS

GENE AUTRY
CHAIRMAN

JACKIE AUTRY
PRESIDENT

JOANNE D. HALE
VICE PRESIDENT/
SECRETARY AND
EXECUTIVE DIRECTOR

STANLEY B. SCHNEIDER
VICE PRESIDENT AND
TREASURER

MONTE HALE
VICE PRESIDENT

COUNCILMAN
JOHN FERRARO

CLYDE TRITT

JOHNNY GRANT

REVEREND LARRY STAMPER

JOHN BIANCHI

THE HONORABLE TOM BRADLEY
MAYOR, CITY OF LOS ANGELES

THE HONORABLE JOHN FERRARO
PRESIDENT, LOS ANGELES CITY
COUNCIL, 4TH DISTRICT

THE HONORABLE PAT RUSSELL
PAST PRESIDENT, LOS ANGELES
CITY COUNCIL

THE HONORABLE JOEL WACHS
LOS ANGELES CITY COUNCIL
2ND DISTRICT

THE HONORABLE DAVID CUNNINGHAM
LOS ANGELES CITY COUNCIL
10TH DISTRICT

JAMES E. HADAWAY
GENERAL MANAGER, DEPARTMENT
OF RECREATION AND PARKS

WIDOM WEIN COHEN
ARCHITECTS

KIEWIT CONSTRUCTION COMPANY
CONTRACTOR

ENGINEERING TECHNOLOGY INC.
PHILIP KRAKOVER, CEO

WALT DISNEY IMAGINEERING
EXHIBIT DESIGN

EMMET L. WEMPLE AND ASSOCIATES
LANDSCAPE ARCHITECT

"IT HAS ALWAYS BEEN MY VISION TO BUILD A MUSEUM WHICH
WOULD EXHIBIT AND INTERPRET THE HERITAGE OF THE WEST,
AND SHOW HOW IT HAS INFLUENCED AMERICA AND THE WORLD."

The plaque honoring those who contributed to the establishment of the Autry includes John Bianchi, who also served on the original Board of Directors. (Photo by Clark Fogg)

1. A salute to the extraordinary role played by Jackie and Joanne appears in the R.L. Wilson's *Silk and Steel Women at Arms*, pages 253-54, "The Autry Museum of Western Heritage – the Dynamic Duo of Jackie Autry and Joanne Hale."

2 This also brings to mind the efforts of Robert E. Petersen, famed publisher, real estate magnate, and entrepreneur – who wished to open a firearms museum in Los Angeles, near the site of the Petersen Automobile Museum. The powers that be refused to allow a "gun museum" in their beloved city. But, in effect, the Autrys were able to do it – because they proposed a museum of the West. In retrospect, the most compelling collection in the Autry museum is that of firearms.

**CHAPTER**

# The NRA Bianchi Cup

## The World's Shooting Competition

*John Bianchi – An American Legend*

"I'd been a pistol shooter all my life, and as I shot with friends at different ranges around the country I was slightly distressed by the image of pistol shooters, where they shot and how they conducted themselves on the range. Although there were some fine outdoor ranges in a number of cities across the country, in many areas, the best range facility was usually the garbage dump, a rock quarry, or someplace close to that. At most, there was no code of conduct for safety or protocol for pistol shooting like I had grown up with. Many shooters who went out on a Saturday morning looked like they'd just come back from a week in the wilderness. Of course, this is long before the Western culture came into popularity through SASS (Single Action Shooting Society) and other organizations and people started dressing up in costumes. Overall, the public image of weekend pistol shooters in the 1960s was pretty disparaging and this disturbed me because I was supplying products to the shooting hobby."

Outside of Olympic competition, there weren't any formal shooting organizations until the 1970s when the IPSC (International Practical Shooting Confederation) was formed. In 1984, the USPSA (United States Practical Shooting Association) was organized as the U.S. Region of IPSC. However, five years before the USPSA was established, John Bianchi had a vision of his own for a formalized pistol competition.

"At the time, there weren't any factory shooting teams, and I thought this was a wonderful opportunity to get behind an organization and change the culture of pistol shooting in the eyes of the general public. We were (and still are) constantly fighting anti-gunners who choose the worst image to depict gun owners in the newspaper and on television, so I wanted to elevate the sport of pistol shooting to Olympic standards; clean cut, highly disciplined professionals, so nobody could ever take a potshot and say, 'Look at these redneck guys with guns, shooting tin cans at the garbage dump.' I started calling around to the other company presidents and said, 'Here's what I'm thinking. I'd like to launch something that will benefit the entire industry. Will you get behind the program?' Colt, Smith & Wesson were the first; a couple of years later Ruger got on board, along with all the accessory companies and ammunition makers. But at the beginning, in the planning stages," explains Bianchi, "when I had talked to these other company presidents, I told them I wanted to establish a new image. I said, 'I'm going to tell them what they can and cannot wear, what they can and cannot do, where they have to be and when they have to be, and I went on down the list.' I said 'We're going to have an award banquet, and it's going to be a formal event. The winners and anyone who wants to claim a prize is going to have to be there or they're not going to get it. They have to be there to applaud for the second, third, and fourth place winners and all the other people.' The question everyone asked was, 'Do you think you can enforce all those standards?' I said 'Yes, every one of them.' And I did.

"It was not unusual to have a very large crowd. We had over 300 people at the first banquet. We went a step further. When the invitations went out they included spouses. Spouses were never involved before," exclaims John in a booming voice. He was using the same philosophy that had made Bianchi International a success. "Family members were now involved. Every night we had a social event: a cocktail reception, a dinner, a Bar-B-Q, and the women loved it. Each of the companies would sponsor an event and that night

John Bianchi established the NRA Bianchi Cup competition in 1979. Now, 31 years later, it is the most respected shooting event in the world. (Photo of John Bianchi by Dennis Adler)

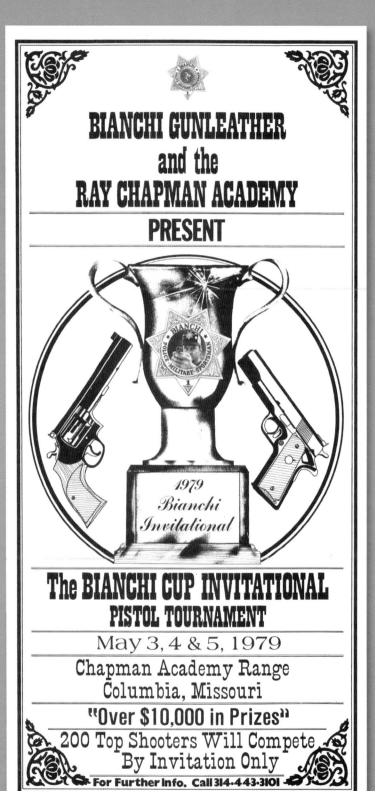

The original promotional flyer for the first invitational NRA Bianchi Cup held in May 1979. (Photo courtesy National Rifle Association)

Original NRA Bianchi Cup medals, Gold, Silver, and Bronze, now reside in this framed display in John Bianchi's office. Like everything else regarding the NRA Bianchi Cup, John was personally involved in the design of the medals. (Photo by Dennis Adler)

their banner was up. It became an annually anticipated event.

"The National Rifle Association, however, sat back and said, 'We don't know how it's going to shape up before we get involved. We have the NRA image to be concerned about,' and I said 'That's fine.' The NRA sent representatives to the first shoot, second shoot, and the third shoot. They were overwhelmed by the professionalism and the standards we set. In 1984, we came together and decided to make it the NRA Bianchi Cup. We were already national and international. We had shooters coming from Japan, Germany, Australia, Belgium, Switzerland, and France. The NRA liked the idea and they got behind it, and once we started putting factory teams together everyone realized the remarkable potential."

When John launched the first Cup, he instituted a mandatory entry fee. "I think the first year was $75. When the participants arrived to sign in they received a care package, the contents of which far exceeded the $75 entry fee by a wide margin. Every year a different company supplies the 'shooter's bag,' which is a functional, zipper nylon travel bag. In it are things like shooting ear muffs, shooting gloves, and all kinds of promotional items that the companies want the shooters to be seen wearing. Every participant gets a couple of hundred dollars worth of stuff."

The NRA Bianchi Cup was directly responsible for the creation of factory-sponsored shooting teams. Before that, shooters had been individuals, some from organized shooting clubs, "But none of the manufacturers had an organized, factory funded team using their guns and accessories," explains John.

When the NRA Bianchi Cup was first organized in 1979, the event took place at Ray Chapman's Green Valley Rifle and Pistol Club shooting range in Columbia, Missouri. Chapman was a shooting buddy of Bianchi's and also the 1975 IPSC World Champion. "There was a great deal of political controversy between two of the big shooting clubs, and that was a big obstacle to overcome because Chapman's club was one of them. I figured out how to break the ice by having Chapman host a reception for the other club at the hotel the night before the first match. He said, 'What!' I said 'You're going to host a cocktail party and the two clubs are going to come together. They're going to be delighted to be personally invited, and your group is going to interface with their group and that's it.' Boom, the controversy went away," says John with a wave of his hands, like completing a magic trick. The only person that John was never able to bring into the NRA Bianchi Cup fold was legendary shooter Jeff Cooper. "I knew him very well," says John, "but he would never accept an invitation to attend. He boycotted the NRA Bianchi Cup his entire life. But we brought together a lot of diverse contestants, competitors, and companies through the course of events."

The first company to sponsor shooters who used their brand of guns opened the door for team competition, "and soon there was an S&W team, a Colt team, a Glock team, and others," says John. "The one thing that I felt that I was honor bound to do was never take commercial advantage of the Cup as long as others were contributing to the event. We put up a lot of money to start it, but we never displayed Bianchi products at the Cup. Catalogs?

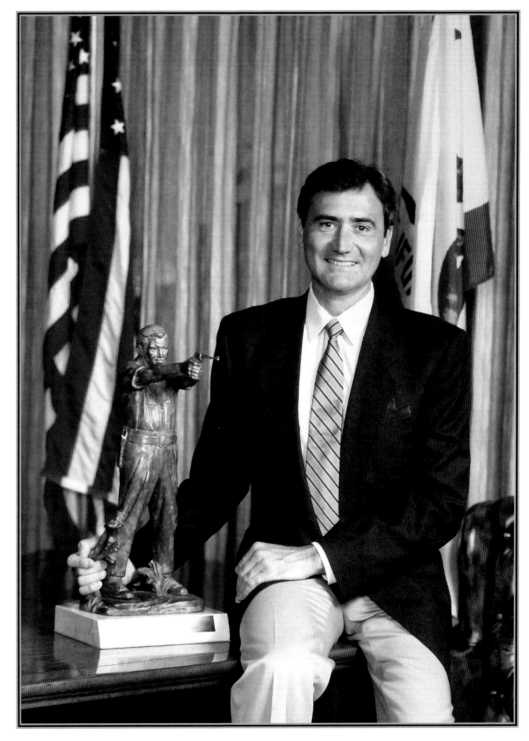

John Bianchi was the recipient of the 1986 Outstanding American Handgun Award Foundation trophy for career lifetime achievement.

**BIANCHI CUP**
INVITATIONAL PISTOL TOURNAMENT

CHAPMAN ACADEMY RANGE
COLUMBIA, MISSOURI

609 E. Broadway
Columbia, Missouri 65201
Phone: (314) 443-3101

# BIANCHI CUP INVITATIONAL PISTOL TOURNAMENT 19 79

An original 1979 NRA Bianchi Cup Invitational brochure. (Photos courtesy National Rifle Association)

# Bianchi Gunleather Cordially Invites You To Compete in the World's Finest and Most Prestigious Shooting Event...

**The first annual Bianchi Cup Invitational Pistol Tournament.**
We are inviting only a few hundred of the worlds' top handgunners, and your shooting records shows you to

be part of this elite group.

**Bianchi Gunleather has been contributing to the shooting sports for decades.**
Our products and programs have had significant effects on these sports and added professionalism to a growing field of interest. To add a new challenge for pistol competitors, we have collaborated with Ray Chapman and his Chapman Academy to put on a first-rate, first-quality match.

**The Bianchi Invitational has been designed by Ray Chapman.**
A top-flight shooter and competitor himself and head of the Chapman Academy of Practical Shooting. As Match

Director, Ray has designed a four-part match that provides an equal challenge to both revolver and automatic pistol. There is no reloading, running or climbing during timed matches. The minimum calibers are 9mm Parabellum and .38 Special, and handgun type is relatively unrestricted, so nearly all popular handguns will be competitive.

**Dates for the Invitational are May 3rd, 4th & 5th, 1979**
The tournament will be held at the Chapman Academy Range in Columbia, Missouri. This new range offers

excellent facilities. Columbia is centrally located in the United States, has excellent lodging facilities, and the weather during May is excellent.

**First prize is an impressive $1,500.**
Plus other outstanding prizes. Second prize is $750, and third prize is $500; both include other prizes. Prizes will be awarded for places up to tenth overall and for the individual matches. These prizes will include guns and accessories from nationally-

famous manufacturers.

**The headquarters hotel selected for the Bianchi Invitational is the Hilton Inn in Columbia.**

The entire hotel has been reserved for competitors and their spouses and returning the enclosed card 45 days prior to the Invitational will ensure your lodging. Rates are quite reasonable at $30 single, $37 double. We would be pleased to have your spouse attend too, as there will be plenty of social activity. This will include a cocktail party Friday night, the Awards Banquet on Saturday night, and other activities. Dress for the social hours will be jackets for gentlemen and matching

attire for the ladies. All prizes will be awarded only at the banquet, so winners must attend; everyone else will want to attend, also.

**Transportation will be made available to and**

**from Columbia airport and between the range and the Hilton Inn.**
Directions to the range will be available at the Hilton. Shooting starts at 9:00 A.M. each day, and will consist of one match fired in the morning and one match in the afternoon, on two consecutive days. Mark your preferences for dates and match sequences on the enclosed card, but please plan to be available all three days.

**The entry fee is only $50 per entrant, and includes the banquet and transportation.**
Many other benefits were already mentioned. Tickets for your guests at the Awards

Banquet are available at our cost of $10.00 per person. The Bianchi Cup Invitational Pistol Tournament is a first-class opportunity for the world's best shooters to compete and thoroughly enjoy themselves. We look forward to seeing you in Columbia on May 3rd, 4th and 5th, 1979.

For further information, call or write
BIANCHI CUP INVITATIONAL
609 East Broadway
Columbia, Missouri 65201
Phone (314) 443-3101

1979

Bianchi Cup

Invitational

Pistol Tournament

The Selection Committee of the
1979 Bianchi Invitational
Pistol Tournament
cordially extends an invitation to

*Mr. Ted Hunt*

to participate
on the third, fourth and fifth of May
nineteen hundred and seventy-nine
Chapman Academy Range
Columbia, Missouri
Awards Banquet to follow

R.s.v.p.

*Ray Chapman*
Ray Chapman
Match Director

*John E. Bianchi*
John E. Bianchi
President, Bianchi Gunleather

An original 1979 invitation to participate in the inaugural NRA
Bianchi Cup. (Photos courtesy National Rifle Association)

A collection of photos from the 1980 NRA Bianchi Cup competition shows the roots of this world class event. In the beginning, competitors used production handguns to compete. Some fine tuning of the actions was as far as it went in the early years. (Photos courtesy National Rifle Association)

Sure, you could have all the catalogs you wanted, and we invited all the other companies to bring their catalogs and display their products. But I never wanted there to be even the slightest hint of a conflict of interest, so I never allowed our products to be displayed. When I went to a manufacturer and asked for $25,000 they couldn't say, 'What, to help you promote your products? Why would I want to do that?' With Bianchi International's commercial exposure diminished, nobody could ever say 'No,' and it worked really well."

Over the years since the first Cup in 1979, the competition has changed, becoming very professional with factory-sponsored teams and competitors from all around the world. "My original concept was to focus on personal defense combat shooting with conventional guns and holsters," explains John. "As the years have passed it has become more and more sophisticated with specially built guns, and holsters designed especially for competition use that are just platforms to rest the gun in. Both the guns and holster platforms are totally impractical in the non-competitive shooting world, and this wasn't the way I wanted the NRA Bianchi Cup to go at the beginning. I began talking with Tommy Hughes, the current match director, and Larry Potterfield from Midway USA, Inc. in Columbia, Missouri, and we came to the conclusion that we had to get back to basics. We needed a program for youth shooters and for production guns." As a result, for the 30th anniversary of the NRA Bianchi Cup in 2009, a new "Production Division" and "Pro-Am" shooting category were introduced. Initiated as the Ray Chapman Nostalgia Event in May 2009, only "production firearms" were permitted, just like at the first NRA Bianchi Cup in 1979.

At the first NRA Bianchi Cup, all the competitors were from the United States. Now thirty years later, the NRA Bianchi Cup (National Action Pistol Championship) hosts shooters from more than fifteen countries including Austria, Australia, Canada, Germany, Italy, Japan, the Netherlands, New Zealand, Norway, the Philippines, the Republic of South Africa, Switzerland, and the United Kingdom. To quote the National Rifle Association, "Action Pistol has become one of the NRA's crown jewels, and is renowned as one of the world's most spectacular shooting events."

After three decades, John Bianchi looks back on the Cup as one of his greatest achievements, but, as with all things in his life, he still sees further potential. "We need to focus on the next generation of shooters. There is one coming up and we're helping develop it. The people who are running the match now have a renewed vision. We need to tailor it to appeal to a wider range of shooters, and we are doing that by getting back to basics with the production category. The cost of competing with production guns and holsters is much less and allows a greater diversity of competitors and skill levels. Today we have shooters who have competed in every match since the first, who are now in their sixties, and we have young competitors just entering the shooting sport. The international side of the competition is also so important. I remember a young woman from Japan, Yoko Shimomura, who won the ladies category in 1989. She had to travel from Tokyo to Guam in order to practice and shoot because she was not allowed to have a gun and shoot in Japan. A couple of times a month she and her husband would travel to Guam just for her to be able to practice! I think that made her victory all the more impressive." It also shows how important the NRA Bianchi Cup is on a global level, how many doors it has opened, and how one man's vision can make a difference. ✍

By 1999, the complexity and sophistication of competition firearms was becoming apparent and competitive shooting skills rising to new levels. (Photos courtesy National Rifle Association)

With the dawn of the 21st century, the 2000 NRA Bianchi Cup was now regarded as the crown jewel of the NRA, and manufacturer supported factory team competition was at an all-time high. Photos are from the Match V Speed Event. (Photos courtesy National Rifle Association)

Pictured at the 2008 NRA Bianchi Cup are (L to R) John Sigler (NRA President 2007-2009), S&W's Doug Koenig (11 time NRA Bianchi Cup Champion), event founder John Bianchi, and Scott Carnahan (V.P. Marketing Bianchi International and Safariland). (Photos courtesy National Rifle Association)

Caspian Arms Ltd.'s Bruce Piatt won the 2009 30th Anniversary Bianchi Cup competition. (Photo courtesy National Rifle Association)

Always a great meal at the NRA Bianchi Cup. Here at the 2008 Bar-B-Q are (L to R) Tom Hughes (NRA Pistol Manager), John Bianchi, and Midway USA founder Larry Potterfield. (Photo courtesy National Rifle Association)

# NRA BIANCHI CUP

## NATIONAL ACTION PISTOL CHAMPIONSHIP

*30th Anniversary 1979-2009*

### 18-23 MAY 2009

GREEN VALLEY RIFLE & PISTOL CLUB, COLUMBIA, MO

Sponsored By

Midway USA
midwayusa.com

NRA SPORTS

For More Information: National Rifle Association of America—Tom Hughes
11250 Waples Mill Road • Fairfax, VA 22030 • 800.672.3888 Ext 1478 • BIANCHICUP@NRAHQ.ORG

Bruce Piatt in the Speed Event on his way to the 2009 NRA Bianchi Cup Championship. (Photo courtesy National Rifle Association)

The 30th Anniversary NRA Bianchi Cup poster.

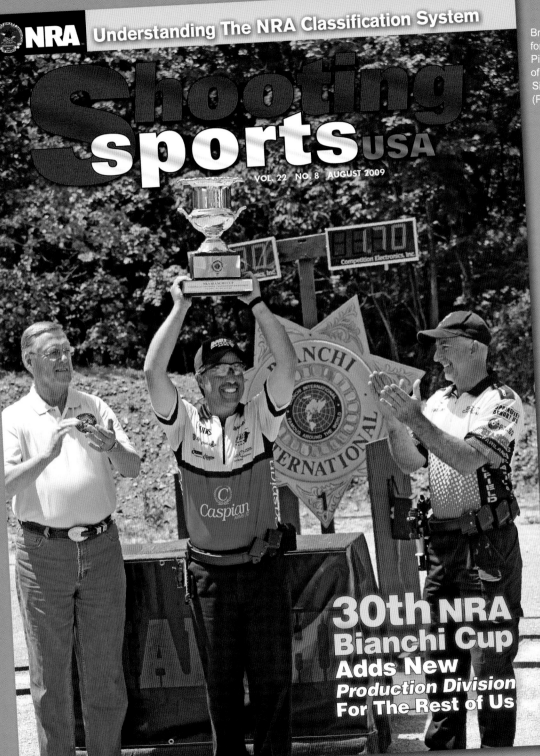

Bruce Piatt claims his championship trophy for the 30th Anniversary NRA Bianchi Cup. Piatt was featured on the August 2009 cover of *Shooting Sports USA* along with John Sigler (left, NRA President 2007-2009). (Photo courtesy National Rifle Association)

Bruce Piatt receives his trophy from Tom Hughes (NRA Pistol Manager). (Photo courtesy National Rifle Association)

The 2009 NRA Bianchi Cup Champions were (L to R) John Pride, Senior Champion and four-time NRA Bianchi Cup Champion; Rob Leatham, one-time NRA Bianchi Cup Champion and seven-time Metallic Division Champion; Jordan Dick, Junior Champion; Bruce Piatt, NRA Bianchi Cup Champion; Julie Golob, Women's Champion; and Dave Sevigny Production Division Champion. (Photo courtesy National Rifle Association)

Shown in the 2009 NRA Bianchi Cup Speed Event is the 30th Anniversary Production Division Champion, Glock's Dave Sevigny. (Photo courtesy National Rifle Association)

Competing in the 2009 NRA Bianchi Cup Speed Event, Julie Golob, Captain of Team Smith & Wesson, became the 2009 Women's Champion. (Photo courtesy National Rifle Association)

Team Glock's Jessie Abbate competing in the 2009 NRA Bianchi Cup Speed Event with a highly modified competition Glock. (Photo courtesy National Rifle Association)

Sig Sauer Team Captain Max Michel is pictured competing in the 2009 Speed Event. (Photo courtesy National Rifle Association)

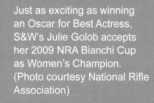

Just as exciting as winning an Oscar for Best Actress, S&W's Julie Golob accepts her 2009 NRA Bianchi Cup as Women's Champion. (Photo courtesy National Rifle Association)

Julie Golob, Team Smith & Wesson Captain, on her way to winning the 2009 Women's Championship at the 30th Anniversary NRA Bianchi Cup. (Photo courtesy National Rifle Association)

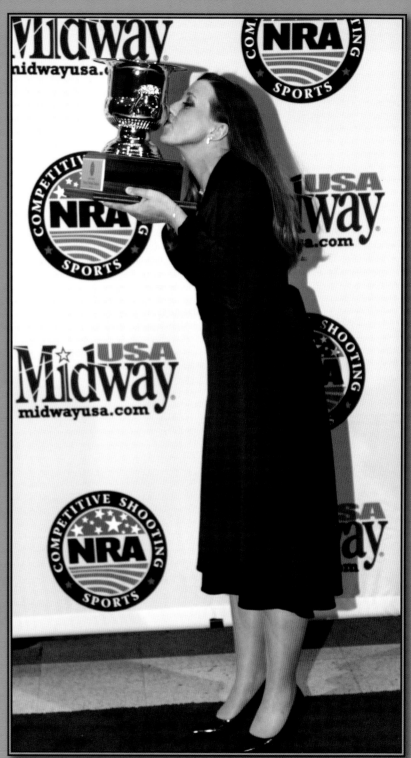

The inimitable master of the NRA Bianchi Cup and 11-time
Champion, Smith & Wesson's Doug Koenig in action at the 2009 30th
Anniversary competition. (Photos courtesy National Rifle Association)

Teams and teamwork, 2009 NRA Bianchi Cup competitors and the 2009 NRA Bianchi Cup volunteers who helped put it all together. (Photos courtesy National Rifle Association)

The men behind the cup and the winners, from (L to R) NRA Bianchi Cup founder John Bianchi, Scott Carnahan (V.P. Marketing Bianchi International & Safariland), Tom Hughes (NRA Pistol Manager), Doug Koenig (11-Time NRA Bianchi Cup Champion), and John Pride (2009 30th Anniversary Senior Champion and four-time NRA Bianchi Cup Champion).

# CHAPTER

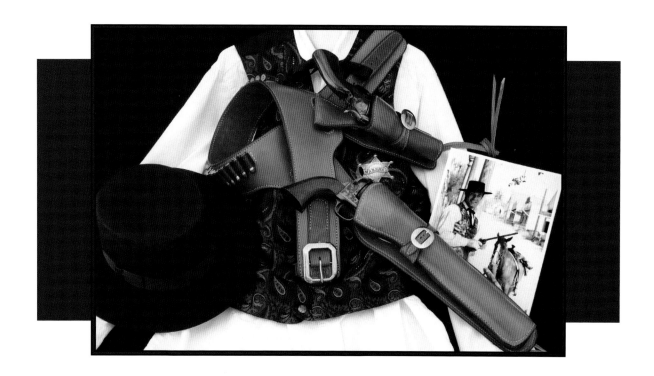

# Frontier Gunleather and the 21st Century Old West

### Still the Innovator

When John decided to get back into making Western gun belts and holsters in the early 1990s he hadn't planned on it becoming a second career. "At that point in my life I regarded Frontier Gunleather as a hobby craft, but the phone kept ringing, and still does to this day, every day, with orders."

John's first love has always been the Old West and Western gun leather, or as he has coined it, "gunleather," and he had an immediate following as soon as he started making Western holsters from his home in Palm Desert, California. "When I started over, and I really did start over because I had sold everything, I rounded up some old tools I had kept and an old saddle stitcher and started putting together Western style rigs one at a time from my garage. It was like going back half a century. After the first couple of rigs people figured I was back in business, and magazines wanted to write about it. I don't play golf, I don't hang out at the country club, and I was getting restless," says John with a laugh, "so I decided to open up a small shop in an industrial park, take out a few ads, and well, it happened again."

At about the same time, John was approached to design a new kind of high-tech shoulder holster. "I had done just about every kind of leather holster imaginable over the years. What I came up with was an injection molded holster with a spring loaded device to secure the gun. It was fully adjustable for a variety of different semi-autos. It was very concealable, very fast on the draw. I called it Gun-Quick. I licensed the design to my old partner, Neil Perkins at Safariland. I not only designed the rig, I designed the packaging, did the marketing, and even appeared in the ads. It was the first time I ever designed a holster that was marketed by a competitor! It was a big hit and I've collected royalties on it for seventeen years."

Just about every holster John designed has become a classic, from the original Speed Scabbard right up to his latest Western holsters and custom leather. Back in the early 1990s when he decided to get back into making the Western holsters, he priced them at twice what any competitive product might have been. "If a rig sold for $200, one by Frontier Gunleather would have been $395, and the customers felt it was worth it. I had decided I did not want to become an industrialist again; I'd been there, done that. And I wanted to keep output to a reasonable level and the quality at the highest level. I wanted the business to be small and manageable and I made it mail order only, no dealers. It was very much the same way of doing business as I had in 1958. Every holster and belt that we have put out of that little shop since 1993 has been handmade."

The bulk of Bianchi's Frontier Gunleather is based on 19th century designs and early 20th century Western Buscadero holsters made famous in the movies. "The operation has continued to grow and prosper for seventeen years, and it is still a small, highly specialized operation, with just a bit of custom floral carving and beadwork, farmed out to individual craftsmen. The inspiration for the designs comes from two things; my knowledge and fascination with the history of the American West and my passion for fine leather. When you combine the two you get the mix of designs we now offer. Our clientele want fine, handcrafted, custom rigs and that's all we do."

John Bianchi's famous silver mounted double rig worn in one of the latest catalogs and in his signature black backdrop poster. John made the gun belt in 1995 and it is one of the most elaborate silver mounted belt and holster designs he has done. The Colt Single Actions, (serial Nos. S12578A and S12579A) were fully engraved by Phil Quigley and fitted with ivory grips.

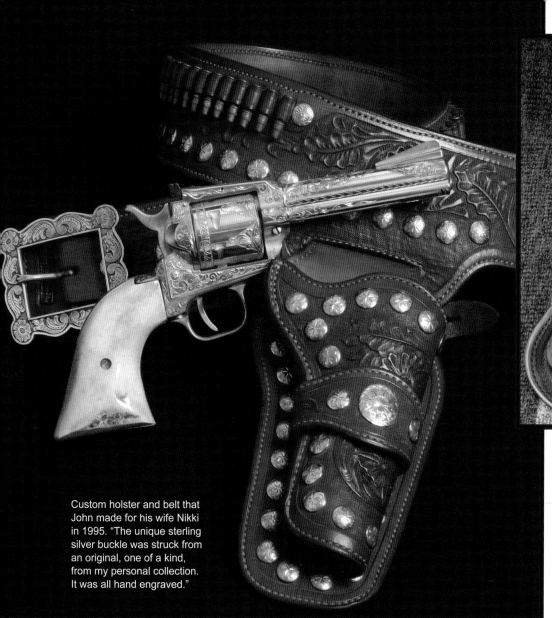

Custom holster and belt that John made for his wife Nikki in 1995. "The unique sterling silver buckle was struck from an original, one of a kind, from my personal collection. It was all hand engraved."

A first look at the latest double rig from Frontier Gunleather, featuring an exclusive antiqued finish.

The second half of the "we" is Matt Whitaker, Bianchi's shop manager. "Matt is a very gifted leather crafter, and a number of the holsters we offer today are his own designs or interpretations of historic frontier rigs like 'The Wichita.' Matt researched the design, perfected the pattern, and added an exceptional holster and belt to the Frontier Gunleather line."

Whitaker came to visit Bianchi right after he had set up shop and became an apprentice. "He gravitated to the craft very quickly and today he can do anything I can do, if not better. Matt also does his own work, he has his own stamp, his own little operation, and he runs my operation now, so that I can do a variety of other things."

The most popular rig requested today from Frontier Gunleather is a mixture of the 1870s, 1880s style holster for SASS shooters. John notes that, "We probably average one request a day for the Model 100, which is the trademark John Wayne rig, like we originally did at Bianchi International. In 1978 when we first made it for John Wayne, he wrote me a note, 'John, now that's to my liking! Duke.' That actual design dates back to the film *Hondo* made in 1953 with Wayne, Ward Bond, and Geraldine Page. Since I had the original from *Hondo* in the Frontier Museum, we were able to faithfully reproduce it in every detail. In 1981 we put together a special John Wayne commemorative Limited Edition Tribute gun belt sold by Bianchi International. It was the first time that a gun belt had ever been used for a tribute. Almost thirty years later, the John Wayne holster continues to be as popular as it was back then."

Another commemorative rig Bianchi added in 2009 is the Model 1953, a limited edition copy of the holster and gun belt worn by James Arness as Matt Dillon on *Gunsmoke*. Each rig is serial numbered and stamped with the James Arness signature block. The latest addition to the Frontier Gunleather line is the Fort Apache series of rough out leather holsters with rolled fringe and authentic Indian beadwork. "We designed these holsters and belts to resemble those worn by scouts during the period of the Indian Wars. They have matching knife sheaths and no two rigs are ever quite the same as each is handmade and hand beaded to museum quality," says Bianchi. "This series came about after we started getting requests from reenactors who wanted to wear something that reproduced some of the more colorful rigs worn during the 1870s. That included copies of the holsters worn by the U.S. Cavalry, such as our Model 1875 for the Schofield revolver, or Colt Single Action Army from the period of the Indian Wars, and outfits worn by the Indian scouts. In the period, the scouts were issued 7-1/2 inch nickel plated Colts. They were nickel plated because the scouts were less inclined to clean their guns as often and nickel was more durable. Many of them had their holsters, gun belts, and knife sheaths made on the reservation. Having handled so many originals over the years, I took the best of the diverse features of all the Indian-style rigs that I had seen and came up with one design. Matt and I decided that it had to have fringe and a suede-out finish. We put the first one together and it sold the same day. We get periodic orders for them because it is a very expensive and time consuming rig to produce. Everything has to be handmade and we have the beadwork actually done by American Indians in Albuquerque, New Mexico. There's a big Indian craft industry there, jewelry, beadwork, and so forth. For the belt and holster we use what is called cream cowhide. It is cowhide that has been tanned for moccasins. It's a five ounce, very mellow, very soft leather that is suede on one side, smooth on the other, and we use it suede side out."

The handwork, as John explains, is the most time consuming. "The fringe, for example, is cut one at a time with a razor blade and then it has to be soaked in hot water and each one rolled by hand. People say, 'Why fringe? How did that come to be?' We researched it and found that buckskin clothing worn by Indians, dating back to the 1700s, and even earlier, had fringe which wicked off water when the clothing got wet. Water will always gravitate to the lowest level and by creating the strings of buckskin fringe, the water would follow the strands and drip off, allowing the clothing to aerate and dry more quickly. This worked its way from Indian cultures to frontiersmen, fur trappers, and traders, and eventually became an accepted style of clothing. It faded out in the 1850s and 1860s but became popular again in the late 1870s and 1880s because of the Wild West shows and Buffalo Bill Cody."

In researching designs, John always finds something of particular interest, historically. "What we call beadwork today is different than what the American Indians had in the 18th and 19th centuries. It was originally quill work, multi-colored weavings in the leather done with porcupine quills. When the French and English fur traders started trading goods with the Indians in the late 1790s and early 1800s, the American tribes were introduced to steel bladed knives, which eliminated the need for stone cutting tools, steel tomahawk heads and arrowheads, copper kettles, bolts of fabric and felt, and many things which began to transform life on the plains. Among the various trade items were colored glass beads made in Hungary, hollow tubes of glass made in different styles and shapes."

Although the Frontier Gunleather catalogs, the latest for 2010, have more than forty-five different holsters and rifle scabbards available, along with belts, buckles, sheaths, and other accessories, Bianchi is always willing to make something special, i.e. a custom one-off, as there are usually one or two going through every month. In addition, Matt

John's personal collection of Colts Single Actions and rifles. Many of the Colts were presented to John by manufacturers and fans over the years. Among the guns are the engraved Single Actions used in his poster and catalog and the Single Action worn in many of the famous Bianchi Histographs from the 1970s and 1980s. His original .22 caliber Winchester Model 62 from his childhood (third from John's left) also occupies a special place in his office display cabinet.

John Bianchi in his home office in Rancho Mirage, California, surrounded by pictures and memorabilia from a lifetime of collecting and his career in law enforcement. (Photo by Taylor Sherill)

Whitaker has his own special designs that are also available, so there's no shortage of options in gunleather at Frontier.

## Wickenburg – Passing on the Tradition

In 2007, John Bianchi and Matt Whitaker began a holster maker's seminar in cooperation with *The Leather Crafters & Saddlers Journal* to instruct students on the art of holster making and leatherwork in historic Wickenburg, Arizona. The three-day classes are held each February, during the week long annual Southwest Leather Trade Show. There are also classes in boot making, saddle making and general leather craft along with Bianchi's popular holster making seminar.

"The first year we had about fifteen students and it became the most popular seminar that *The Leather Crafters & Saddlers Journal* had put on," says John. They decided to continue it because there were so many self proclaimed experts out there writing stories about how to make holsters that the *Journal's* staff wanted to establish a class that would lend credibility to leather crafting. "Our classes are very intensive and we have had many of the same people come back every year to further their training," explains Bianchi. John and Matt's classes attract people from all walks of life. "We have had doctors, hospital administrators, and senior military officers from the Pentagon, businessmen; we have had police officers and beginning holster makers looking to expand the scope of their work. Everyone who attends shares a common passion for the art and craft of holster making and our students' ages have varied from the mid-twenties to almost eighty," says Bianchi. Today, John and Matt's classes have from a dozen to eighteen students annually, "which is about as many as you can have in a class because it is a very hands-on course."

Most come to Wickenburg to learn leather craft as a hobby or a vocation. "We are often surprised at how well our students learn to craft gun belts, and once they learn the basic procedure, they can go on and make a wide variety of leather products. One common trait among all of our students is a deep seated desire to handcraft their own gun belt. They are gun enthusiasts who know that you can't go into a store and buy a handcrafted gun belt that is tailored to your exact needs. You either have to have one custom made or learn how to do it yourself. The students that attend the Wickenburg classes have the desire to make their own." John's "Secrets of Professional Holster Makers" classes have also turned hobbyists into professionals over the years, including the man John Bianchi calls his "…best student ever," Alan Soellner of Chisholm's Trail Leather.

Recalls Alan, "Several years ago I attended a large gun show in Birmingham, Alabama, when I passed a table full of gunleather that resembled gear made by John Bianchi. I have collected Bianchi leather since the 1960s. I also tried, without much success, to make cowboy leather since the 1970s. After striking up a conversation with the man behind the table I asked where he got all his leather. 'I craft my own leather,' was his reply. He said he had studied the examples of John Bianchi and his work comes out similar. His name was John O'Rourke and he operates O'Rourke Leather in Hartselle, Alabama, and makes mostly modern gunleather.

John and Nikki Bianchi on the patio of their Rancho Mirage home "Bella Vista" and a framed marriage invitation from April 1997. A noted Palm Springs interior designer, Nikki is also a member of the prestigious international gourmet society Les Dame's d' Escoffier and is active in many philanthropic and cultural activities. (Portrait photo by Taylor Sherill)

"After a lengthy conversation and my sad tale of trying to learn what I could about making cowboy leather correctly, O'Rourke said he would show me. It would take some time and much work, but if I wanted to learn, O'Rourke was willing to help. It was fortunate that I lived in the next town and was able to go over to his shop on weekends. So the following Saturday, off I went full of enthusiasm. Upon arrival he gave me a stack of twenty or so holsters and, after spending time showing how to get the edges just right, had me just edge the whole lot. That is all I did that day – edge. But, when I was done with that task, I did know how to edge. That is the way it went for what seemed to be forever. O'Rourke would continue to give me just one task until he saw proficiency.

"Finally, after months of learning, O'Rourke guided me in crafting a Western holster. To me it was the finest one in the world – I wish he still had it. The first holster ended up being sold to John Allen from *Blue Book of Gun Values* at the Orlando, Florida, SHOT Show. Allen still has it, uses it, and says it is not for sale. Finally, I found a set of DVDs that John Bianchi produced showing how to make gunleather. I studied them over and over. Slowly my work improved and I have been making gunleather ever since.

"In 2008 I found out that John Bianchi was going to offer a limited class to a few folks in Wickenburg, Arizona. I applied and was lucky enough to be one of the few students accepted for the class. By this time I was the owner of Chisholm's Trail Old West Leather and starting to reproduce authentic gunleather of the Old West.

"I flew to Tucson, Arizona, and spent the night with Mike Laurine, a friend and an Old West historian, before driving to Wickenburg. Matt Whitaker from Frontier Gunleather welcomed the 'leather craft' students to class. Not knowing what to expect, I was thinking that maybe John Bianchi had decided to take things a little easier after being in the business so long. Boy was I wrong. John almost bounced into the room, full of vim and vigor. He bonded with the class instantly, dressed in Western garb with a gorgeous hand tooled belt and sterling silver buckle set.

"Bianchi took the class through his history from making holsters in his garage up to the sale of his mega company then going back to a small building and making cowboy gunleather once again. Sharing stories with everyone about how he learned fast draw with wax bullets and how he dented his dad's truck when the bullets went though the target, just made the Bianchi experience more rewarding.

"The class then got down to business and each person chose a style of holster and belt to make. John went through how to make a pattern, sharpen blades, and 'case' the leather with water. Students edged, tooled, cut, stamped, and finally began to sew their leather projects. What a thrill to see the leather come together. I kept a journal and was constantly scribbling down what John called 'Trade Secrets.' When the leather was finished he taught everyone how to round and burnish all edges. We were even shown how to wet form holsters using nothing other than pieces of PVC pipe.

"During breaks in the action John would sprinkle in anecdotes of his associations with John Wayne and other famous Western actors. Too soon, the class was over. John

As you enter through an interior courtyard into the Bianchi's Tuscan-style "home on the range, Bella Vista," designed by Nikki Bianchi in 1998, you find a very welcoming, comfortable home that encompasses 6,300 square feet. There is an open beam ceiling great room, divided by a double sided sandstone fireplace into a family room and living room. The interior of the home, also designed by Nikki, is done in a traditional style with a combination of Western Americana…a few saddles here, an Indian breastplate and framed Plains Indian War shirt there. An elegant Western style leather sofa and Louis XIV side chairs, a large granite top cocktail table and Remington reproduction of "Wooly Chaps" accents the living room. An infinity pool and patio, off the great room, overlooks the northeastern Coachella Valley. (Photos by Taylor Sherill)

"The Shootist" bronze was done by artist Dave Manuel in 1984. The piece was a tribute to John Wayne and his last film. Bianchi was the master of ceremonies at the Los Angeles unveiling. The artist's proof of the Limited Edition series of thirty-five bronzes was presented to Bianchi by the Wayne family in appreciation of his long relationship with their father. The hat and vest on the wall were given to Bianchi by John Wayne. The painting is by Andy Degosta and was done in the early 1960s.

then took the time to allow a photograph with each class member holding their finished gunleather with him. He signed large color Bianchi posters of him in cowboy regalia. To my surprise he wrote across my poster "Master Holster Maker." What an honor to have been in John Bianchi's Master Leather Crafter class and receive this classic Histograph poster. Finally John said, 'I have a prize for whoever recorded the most Trade Secrets.' After asking a few folks he said, 'How many did you write down Al, you've been scribbling all week.' I responded, "One hundred and thirty-five single spaced notes typed on three pages.' John announced that I had won and presented me with a hard cover book about the life of George Montgomery, one of Bianchi's closest friends.

"I will always treasure this book and the time spent with John Bianchi. He taught me, inspired me, and became a friend. Whenever I have a problem or a perplexing question I call him. He never says I am bothering him, but he responds with prompt and good answers which work.

The author (left) in 2009 with John Bianchi (far right) and filmmaker Patrick Curtis. It was a celebration for Curtis, who was literally born into the film industry as Baby Beau Wilkes, in *Gone With The Wind*. The framed photo shows Curtis being held by Olivia DeHavilland (who played Melanie Wilkes) in a scene from the film. Curtis and DeHavilland have been friends for more than seventy years!

"Through the years I have found that many craftsmen are threatened by the work of peers. Not John, he wants to teach and help others learn. He wants the art of leather craft to go on. He is an American business example and living proof that you can start with nothing but an idea in your garage and make a million dollars. He is a true American treasure and someone I am proud to call a friend."

What's next for John Bianchi? He laughs at the question. "You know, voids beg to be filled. I'm enjoying what I'm doing, I'm enjoying the people I have known and worked with over the years. The industrial pressure of having to meet an enormous payroll, of having to forecast the needs of the market, and running a big manufacturing company are behind me. There is a growing interest in licensing my name and likeness for Western clothing and things like that, so I'm exploring that aspect while I still have some energy left," and John laughs again. "As for gunleather, we're doing what we enjoy right here in our little shop making custom, handcrafted Western holsters, and now we get six dollars for a catalog. People are saying, 'That crazy kid, he'll never get anyone to spend six dollars for a catalog!'" ✄

John's relationship with film and TV star Hugh O'Brian goes back more than twenty years. The two appeared together at a Western event about ten years ago. In 2009 they teamed up with Colt's to produce a Hugh O'Brian Wyatt Earp Limited Edition cased Buntline and Single Action pistol set with matching holsters copied from the rig worn by O'Brian on the television series. The guns and holster were unveiled by Bianchi and O'Brian at the 2010 SHOT Show (an annual international firearms manufacturers trade show) in Las Vegas, Nevada. (Holster display photo, by Dennis Adler)

For the 2009 SHOT Show, Bianchi International produced a one-of-a-kind double holster rig in conjunction with Colt's. Bianchi donated the gun belt and Colt's donated the guns. Tickets for the drawing were sold throughout 2008 and the drawing was held at the '09 show with the proceeds going to the NSSF (National Shooting Sports Foundation).

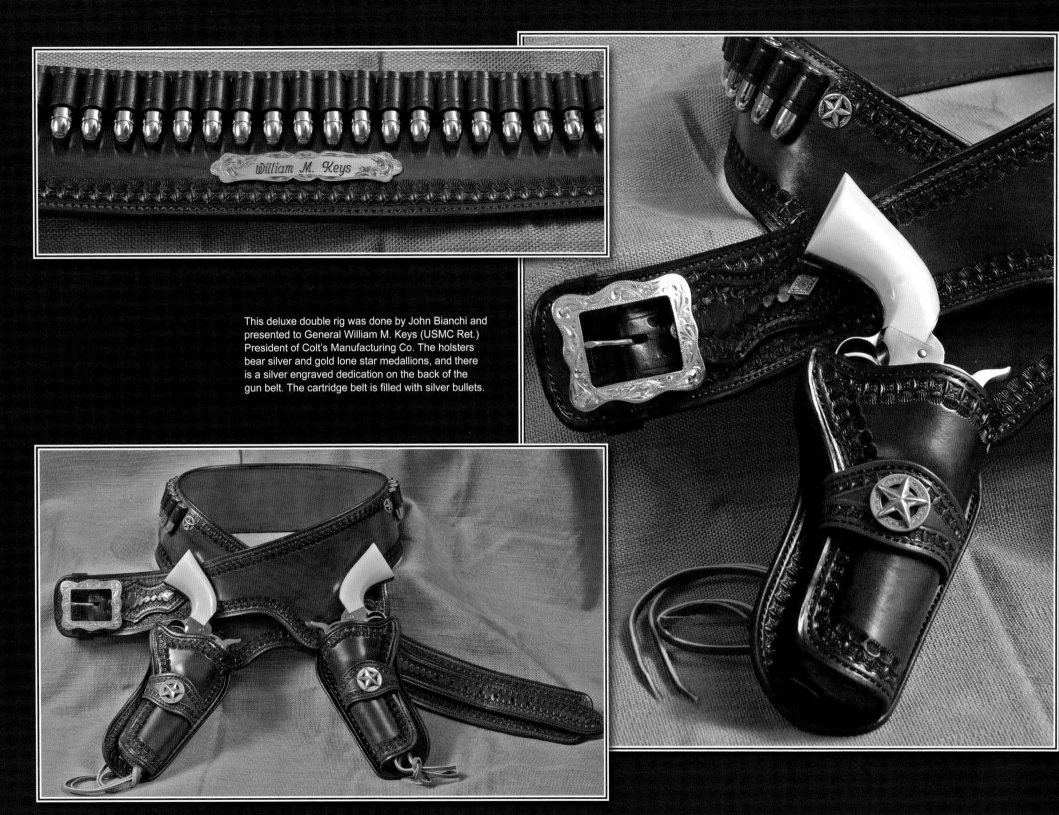

This deluxe double rig was done by John Bianchi and presented to General William M. Keys (USMC Ret.) President of Colt's Manufacturing Co. The holsters bear silver and gold lone star medallions, and there is a silver engraved dedication on the back of the gun belt. The cartridge belt is filled with silver bullets.

William M. Keys

"We designed these holsters and belts to resemble those worn by scouts during the period of the Indian Wars," says Bianchi. "In the period, scouts were issued 7-1/2 inch nickel plated Colts. They were nickel plated because the scouts were less inclined to clean their guns as often and nickel was more durable. Many of them had their holsters, gun belts, and knife sheaths made on the reservation. In duplicating this style, Matt and I decided that it had to have fringe and a suede-out finish. Everything has to be handmade and we have the beadwork done by American Indians in Albuquerque, New Mexico." The photo insert is of George Armstrong Custer with two of his Indian scouts, who are holding nickel plated 7-1/2 inch Colt Single Action revolvers. A similar style holster can be seen on the ground by the scout kneeling to Custer's right.

The author wearing Frontier Gunleather's new Fort Apache Indian Scout gun belt, holster, and knife sheath. The new rig is all handmade to order with hand rolled leather fringe, rough out elk hide, and adorned with handmade Indian beadwork.

Master craftsmen Matt Whitaker, general manager of Frontier Gunleather' shows the techniques used in making a holster pattern. This is where every custom holster begins.

Teaching how to use a saddle stitcher and stitching techniques.

At the annual Wickenburg holster maker's seminar held in cooperation with *The Leather Crafters & Saddlers Journal*, students are instructed in the art of holster making and leatherwork in historic Wickenburg, Arizona. The three-day classes are held each February during the weeklong annual Southwest Leather Trade Show. Here John is shown demonstrating the fine art of holster design to students from all over the country who pay a premium to learn from the master.

Matt Whitaker demonstrates stitching the lined holster. After this procedure, the excess leather from the liner is trimmed off with a special knife.

Cutting the leather pattern.

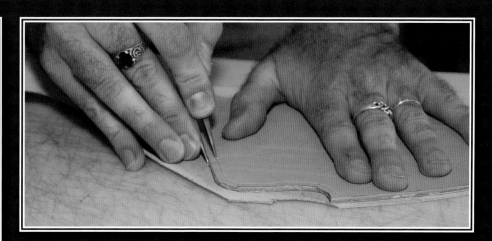

Using a scoring tool to impress the stitching line for the holster. This become the guide for initial stitching before the holster is folded and assembled.

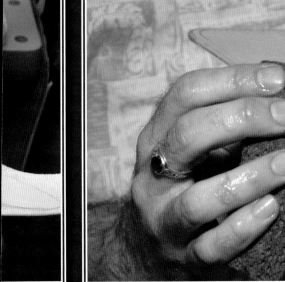

After the excess is trimmed off, the edges of the unassembled holster are dampened with a sponge to prepare the leather for burnishing the stitched edges.

Here Matt Whitaker burnishes the edges of the unassembled holster. This blends, smoothes, and polishes the edges of the leather. This step determines the quality of the finished product. Bianchi designed his own burnishing wheels.

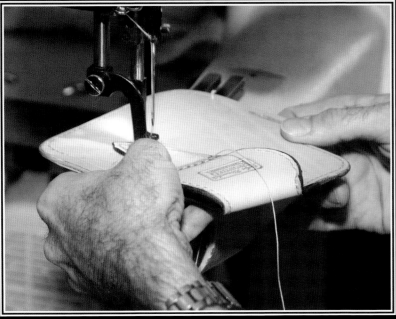

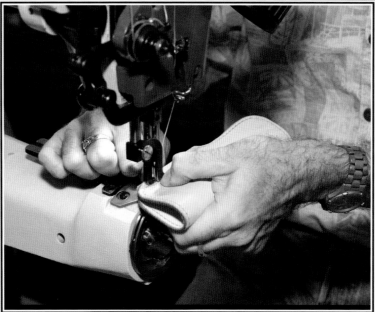

Beginning the holster's assembly requires precision stitching by attaching the leather to form the belt loop. Each step from this point on requires meticulous attention to using the stitcher. The proper thread selection, tension, needle style, and size determine the quality of the final stitch

The holster is folded and the outside edges stitched to form the holster pouch.

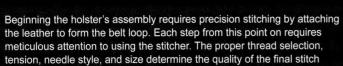

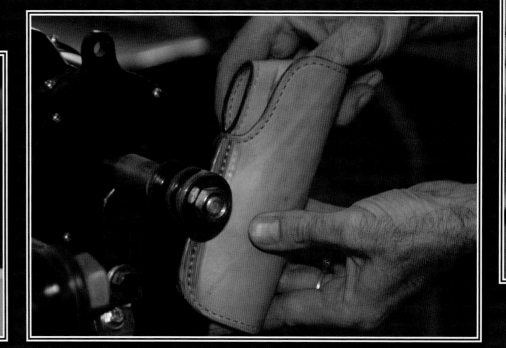

In the holster shaping process Matt Whitaker shows how to hand burnish the outside edges of the holster with a piece of polished elk horn. Elk horn is used because it is coarse enough in texture to blend and burnish the edges of the leather through a combination of pressure and heat produced by the friction of rubbing the elk horn against the leather. Sometimes hard rosewood or African ironwood is used for the burnishing process.

Another step with the burnishing wheel puts the final touches and polish on the holster's outer edges.

After the holster is stitched together it is quickly placed in a warm water bath that contains a little chemical water softening agent to better penetrate the leather and prepare it for form fitting over the gun shape (or gun mold). With an aluminum gun mold or the actual gun placed in the dampened holster, the leather is pressure shaped around the gun using hand and finger pressure on the contours of the firearm. This is necessary for the holster to take the shape of the gun. The holster is then allowed to dry overnight.

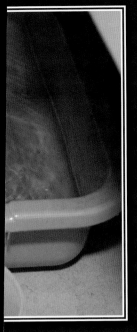

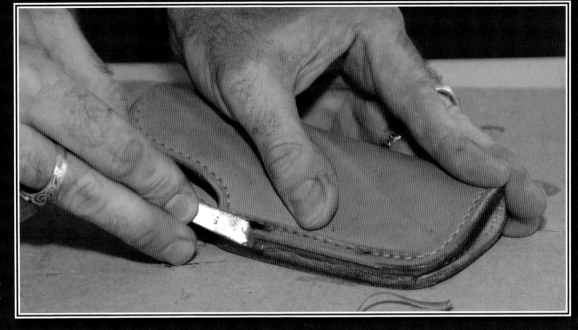

While the leather is still wet, Bianchi recommends doing edge trimming with the saddle maker's edge trimmer. This provides a smoother, more rounded edge for the finished product.

Leather dye is used to color and seal the edge of the leather. There are some old world saddle and holster makers who do not believe in using an edge dressing but prefer cotton canvas impregnated with bee's wax to rub against the edges of the leather as a final polish and seal.

The finished holster is quick-dipped in a warm oil bath to put a life-long preservative in the leather and produce the rich saddle tanned look. If the holster or belt is going to be a different color, such as black, it is dyed after the oil bath. "Depending on the complexity of the holster, explains Bianchi, dyeing may sometimes be done ahead of time."

Matt Whitaker hand applies a final leather dressing using a sheep's wool applicator. This seals the leather in the final production process.

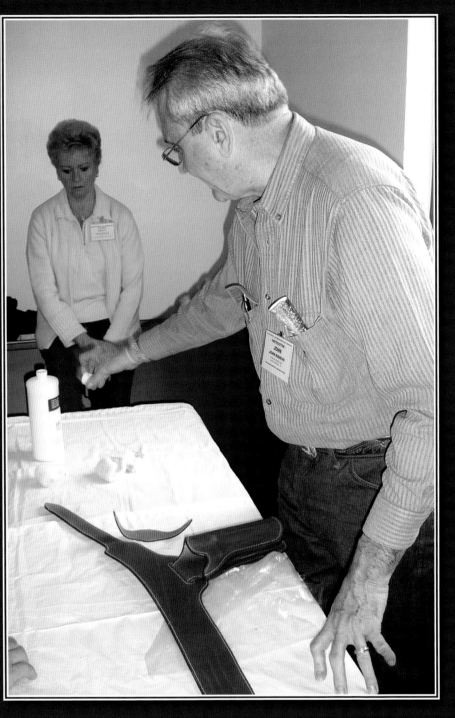

At the Wickenburg class, John Bianchi shows the hand finishing technique. "It is a 'technique' that must be done properly," explains Bianchi. (Photo by Alan Soellner)

Bianchi graduate Alan Soellner receives his diploma from John Bianchi after finishing the holster maker's seminar. Soellner went on to become one of the most successful custom Western holster makers in America.

John Bianchi and Alan Soellner at the 2008 Wickenburg class. Alan was presented with the Bianchi Master Craftsman Award as the best student in the class.

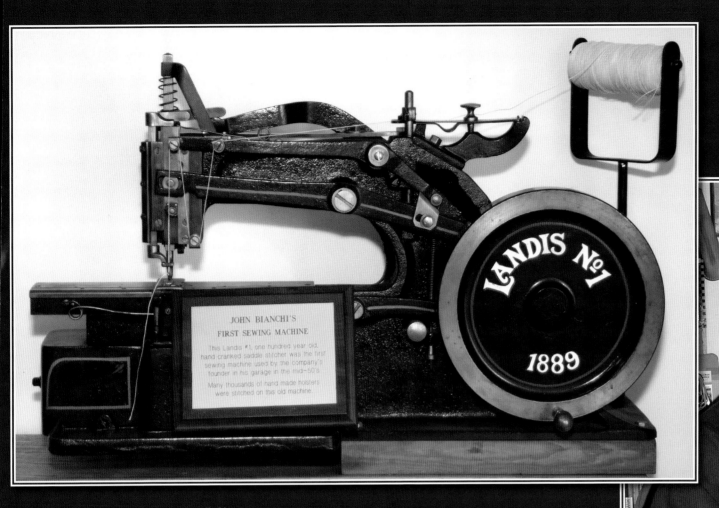

John Bianchi's first saddle stitcher, a Landis No. 1 is still on display in his Frontier Gunleather shop. "I have had the Landis since the 1950s".

**JOHN BIANCHI'S FIRST SEWING MACHINE**

This Landis #1, one hundred year old, hand cranked saddle stitcher, was the first sewing machine used by the company's founder in his garage in the mid-50's

Many thousands of hand made holsters were stitched on this old machine.

**LANDIS N°1**

**1889**

Working with John Bianchi was a second career for retired US Navy Captain James Travis Luz, who trained with Bianchi for five years before he retired as a Naval Aviator. As a Master Craftsman, he now operates his own custom leather shop in Durango, Colorado, where he handcrafts a wide variety of fine leather products. Bianchi says that "Jim's quick hand-eye coordination as a jet fighter pilot enabled him to apply these skills to a less stressful vocation as an artist and craftsman. He is one of the best I have known in fifty years," adds Bianchi.

John Bianchi's FRONTIER GUNLEATHER

John Bianchi's FRONTIER GUNLEATHER
STARQUEST INC.
Catalog $5.00

John Bianchi LIMITED EDITION FRONTIER GUNLEATHER 2005/2006

"When only the best will do."

# John Bianchi's

## — 50th Year —
# FRONTIER GUNLEATHER

## Limited Editions
## 2010

"The Standard By Which All Gunleather Is Judged" $6

---

# FRONTIER GUNLEATHER

Premier holster maker John Bianchi brings back the revival of the turn of the century styles and old west craftsmanship with the Frontier Gunleather brand. Twenty-six highly skilled hand operations, the use of seventeen precision hand tools and three machine operations are still used in the crafting of each and every custom-made holster and gunbelt. Many of these "Gunleather" rigs are actual replicas from the Frontier West, representing the best examples of the cowboy-gunfighter culture for today's cowboy shooters, collectors, and decorators alike.

Every John Bianchi rig is a handmade work of art, giving each outfit its own individual personality. From among the wide array of styles and selections offered, you choose your own combination of design, finish, and particular details to suit your preference. Your custom made holster will be wet molded to the actual model of the gun it will hold. Our beautiful, hand rubbed finishes are the true signature of a Frontier Gunleather gunbelt and holster. By limiting our annual production of rigs we can assure your custom made outfit will be of the utmost quality, bench made, one at a time, as in the days of the old west.

## Certificate of Authenticity

Each handcrafted gunbelt is individually serial numbered (with the exception of Model 100). Upon request, for a nominal cost your rig will be imortalized with a Certificate of Authenticity, embelished with a gold seal and suitable for framing. This certifies that each product is an original, custom made by John Bianchi and Frontier Gunleather.

## Gun Belt Sizing

### CRITICAL
### ORDERING INFORMATION

Accurate sizing is very important. Belts are **cut and sized** according to the information you provide.

Measure your **exact** waist and hip size.

**Do not** estimate your waist size or rely on your pant size.

WAIST MEASUREMENT

HIGH HIP MEASUREMENT

**ALWAYS USE A TAPE MEASURE TO INSURE ACCURACY.**

The proper position to wear western style gunbelts is immediately under the trouser belt line in a **HORIZONTAL** position as shown.

**IMPORTANT NOTE:** With the custom made nature of our products and suppliers, as well as our limited annual production, styles, trim and hardware may not always be as depicted. You can be sure that every rig that leaves our facility will have a unique personality and will be a one-of-a-kind work of art.

---

JOHN BIANCHI

## "New" Old West Antiqued appearance!

Frontier Gunleather is proud to announce our newest finish. We carefully age and antique your holster and gunbelt to give it that old world, aged look. This is the same special process we use for museums and movie studios. Get that instant antique look without waiting 100 years. Antique finish add $50 for your gunbelt.

www.frontiergunleather.com    1-877-877-470

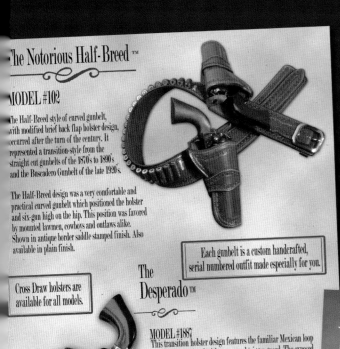

# The Notorious Half-Breed™

## MODEL #102

The Half-Breed style of curved gunbelt, with modified brief back flap holster design, occurred after the turn of the century. It represented a transition-style from the straight cut gunbelts of the 1870's to 1890's and the Buscadero Gunbelt of the late 1920's.

The Half-Breed design was a very comfortable and practical curved gunbelt which positioned the holster and six-gun high on the hip. This position was favored by mounted lawmen, cowboys and outlaws alike. Shown in antique border saddle stamped finish. Also available in plain finish.

Each gunbelt is a custom handcrafted, serial numbered outfit made especially for you.

Cross Draw holsters are available for all models.

## The Desperado™

### MODEL #1887

This transition holster design features the familiar Mexican loop style holster band with an exposed trigger guard. The exposed trigger guard allows faster access to the trigger. Favored by Gunfighters, Outlaws, and ... Desperados. Your choice of Santa Fe, Powder River, or Gunfighter Buckle on a straight or curved belt. Offered standard with hand rubbed antique chestnut oil stain and makers choice of border stamping.

Each gunbelt and holster is a handcrafted Limited Edition
All gunbelts and holsters are interchangeable to create a customized rig.

## The Original
# Model 100
### "Duke's Special"

## MODEL #100

This rig is a re-creation of the original versions John Bianchi made for the all-time greatest western film star. Seen in countless classic western films, the holster design is the Half-Breed style, and is mounted on a comfortable straight cut belt made from rough-out, mellow tanned cowhide. Offered in a rich, cream color and folded and saddle stitched. Many look alike, only one original. .22 Caliber not available.

*"John, now that's to my liking!"*
*Duke*

# Slick Jim

## Model 1870

Dating back to the 1850's, 60's & 70's, this holster style originated as the California or Slim Jim and was widely used by frontiersman throughout the west. Ours is an authentic frontier period design, fully leather lined, and features a fancy stamped border. Each one is custom handcrafted and made specifically to order for a variety of black powder, percussion and single-action revolvers. Specify straight draw or cross draw.

THE OLD WEST LINGERS IN THE HEARTS AND IMAGINATION OF EVERY AMERICAN. IT WAS A BRIEF AND COLORFUL ERA IN HISTORY BETWEEN THE END OF THE CIVIL WAR AND THE TURN OF THE CENTURY. IT WAS A TIME OF HIGH HOPE AND PROMISE. GREAT RISK AND HARDSHIP. IT BROUGHT OUT THE BEST AND THE WORST IN MEN. IT WAS THE TIME OF COWBOYS, INDIANS, OUTLAWS AND LAWMEN. IT WAS THE DAY OF THE GUNFIGHTER.

A VAST AND EXCITING ADVENTURE... AND THEN IT WAS OVER AS QUICKLY AS IT BEGAN. THE SPIRIT OF THE OLD WEST LIVES ON TODAY IN FACT AND IN LEGEND.

JOHN E. BIANCHI

# The Powder River II

## MODEL #120

The Powder River rig is a faithful re-make of a popular, 1870's style gunbelt worn by outlaws, lawmen, and cowboys alike on the high plains. This model embodies all the rugged essential features required of the day. Our own 'Powder River' buckle, with an oval design is adapted from the heavy-duty harness buckle of the period. The holster features a 15° muzzle forward angle. All Holsters and Gunbelts are interchangeable at your option and are available as single or double outfits.

Each gunbelt and holster is a handcrafted Limited Edition
All gunbelts and holsters are interchangeable to create a customized rig.

# The Gunfighter Special

## The Gunfighter Special
### MODEL #1881

The popular Gunfighter Special is a favorite choice for members of the Single Action Shooting Society (SASS). Its rugged construction and authentic frontier period styling offer absolute historical accuracy. This is the best investment you can make in a cowboy holster. Bench made, one at a time, by the world's premier holster maker. This 1880's period holster is a fully leather lined, double loop, wet molded frontier period masterpiece. The matching straight cut, cartridge belt is fitted with a deluxe quality, solid brass, triple nickel plated, authentic period buckle and fully leather lined. Standard upgrades include fancy border stamping and custom hand rubbed, antique chestnut color. Fancy border stamping subject to change at makers choice. Available single, double or with cross draw holster.

www.frontiergunleather.com    1-877-877-4704

## The Rawhide™

### MODEL #1888

For "A Few Dollars More", we'll tell you who the tall, lanky "Man With No Name" is, and a lot more! The Rawhide Rig is an original, faithful rendition of the gunbelt worn by one of the most popular western stars in countless TV and film productions. The Rawhide outfit features a contoured, tapered gunbelt with fancy stitching design and heavy duty, solid brass buckle set. The holster has an exposed trigger guard, reinforced cylinder area and a special muzzle forward tilt for fast gun play. A real classic design. Rugged, fully leather lined, heavy duty construction top off this great outfit.

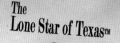

www.frontiergunleather.com    1-877-877-4704

## The Lone Star of Texas™

### MODEL #105

Popularized by the Texas Rangers during the 1880's, this excellent combination includes our straight cut 2 3/4 wide cartridge belt and Mexican Loop style holster with a Texas star medallion (standard). Belt and holster are both fully leather lined with deluxe, fancy hand stamped border.
Shown here in our hand rubbed, antique chestnut color, an optional upgrade.

## The Outlaw™

### MODEL # 1878

The Outlaw Model is typical of the Mexican double loo holster of the old west. Fancy individual, old style bor stamping, fully leather lined, and saddle stitched. Dar world chestnut oil stain finishes off this true western c Available for all makes and models of revolvers. The O was popular with cowboys, outlaws, gunfighters and law

www.frontiergunleather.com    1-877-877-4704

## El Lobo™

### MODEL #110

By popular request, we offer our classic gunfighter rig, the El Lobo. A graceful blending of the best selling Nuevo Laredo holster, with a traditional buscadero-style gunbelt. The result is a look that combines the best features of each. True to its name "The Wolf", this holster offers a sleek look with its exposed trigger guard and slim lines, along with the quickness offered in a low slung gunbelt. Truly a high-performance outfit made with the utmost custom quality as only Frontier Gunleather can deliver.
Available in single and double configurations, with a plain or border stamp finish.

## Nuevo Laredo™

### Nuevo Laredo Belt & Holster

### DEL #104N

Laredo holster is a high-ride, compact model ring an exposed trigger guard, narrow skirt slight muzzle to the rear cant. The Laredo belt is cefully curved design for enhanced comfort. Fully her lined and saddle stitched with 30 cartridge loops most sizes. Available in your choice of finish. Sterling chos on holster (optional) at additional cost. Order this ssic belt and holster combination together or separately. own in light chestnut with optional silver conchos d border stamp.

Each gunbelt and holster is a handcrafted Limited Edition
All gunbelts and holsters are interchangeable to create a customized rig.

## The Plainsman™

### Model #1884

This new model of time proven historical design is elegant in its simplicity. Our new Plainsman features a Fancy Stamped border and hand rubbed chestnut oil stain to accent the design. Available for all models of revolvers, a Cowboy favorite in the old west.

## The Bushwhacker™

### Model #1882

The all new Bushwacker model is a modified mexican loop single loop style holster designed for lightweight, minimum bulk and weight. This style was popular along the Mexican border at the turn of the century with bandits and lawmen alike. Available for all revolvers, plain or fancy stamped with a wide range of silver adornment. Single concho on holster included.
Priced as shown in Chestnut color and Fancy Stamped.

Cross Draw holsters are available for all models.

## The Wichita™

### Model #1892

The fancy style of the Wichita model became popular with cowboys and wild west show performers who wanted to dress up their flashy wardrobes and costumes. The Wichita features antique spots, fancy stamping and unique shape. Every Wichita rig is an individual work of art, choose from several different border stamps.

Each gunbelt and holster is a handcrafted Limited Edition
All gunbelts and holsters are interchangeable to create a customized rig.

### The Paladin

**Model #1957**

Relive those golden years of tv westerns with this faithful recreation of one of the most popular gunbelts of the TV west. The paladin features heavy duty construction and an authentic sterling silver chessman on the holster. Made to your exact specifications and gun model.

### The Cheyenne™

**Model #1877**

The unique shape of the Cheyenne holster possitively locks the body of the holster in the holster band. This style is attributed to an old time maker in the cattle country of Cheyenne, Wyoming in the late 19th century. Eye appealing and historically correct for the period. Priced as shown. *Silver or decorative spots extra.*

### The Laramie™

Matching Cross Draw Available For All Holsters!

**Model # 1883**

The Laramie Model Gunbelt is an extra fancy outfit to show off your favorite sixgun. The Laramie incorporates all of the desirable historical features with an upgraded billet design, extra fancy border stamping, fancy silver buckle and silver adorment are all included. Simply the best you can get.

Each gunbelt and holster is a handcrafted Limited Edition
All gunbelts and holsters are interchangeable to create a customized rig.

### Buscadero Single Gunbelt

**MODEL #103**

[...]est work of its kind in the world, this [...]arved rig is trimmed with [...] silver accents, optional, hand [...]oncho set on holster, and sterling [...]. Available in single and double [...] Shown in deluxe, western floral carved [...]also available in plain and fancy border stamped.

www.frontiergunleather.com     1-877

### The Pistolero™

**Model #106**

Nothing beats our new Pistolero for the competitive shooting edge. Fast access and muzzle forward style combines speed, comfort, and eye appealing design. The Pistolero is fully leather lined heavy duty construction with cylinder stiffener to retain holster shape. Available for most revolvers and belt styles. 4¾" to 5½" Barrel lengths. This holster works great with our tapered style Powder River Gunbelt #120B.

Each gunbelt is a custom handcrafted, serial numbered outfit made especially for you.

### The Lawman

**Model #1910**

The Lawman holster is a variation of our old favorite Laredo model and features a 'Jockstrap' style holster band that became popular with lawmen around the El Paso, Texas area after 1900. Select your choice of finish and adornment. Anything is usually possible and available for most revolvers. Priced as shown with Fancy Stamping and Chestnut color. Dress up your holster with optional silver conchos!

www.frontiergunleather.com     1-877-877-4704

### SILVER PRESENTATION MODEL #103SP-D

Many Thanks from Roy Rogers

The traditional-style of gunbelt known as the Buscadero Belt originated in the late 1920's along the Mexican border. It quickly became popular with early Hollywood western film makers. Many variations of the Buscadero Rig were produced during the last 75 years, and it remains a classic to this day. At Frontier Gunleather, we offer several rig combinations, or, build your own custom gunbelt and holster from our choices offered. We offer plain, border stamp and floral carved finishes. Color choices are saddle tan and our rich, hand rubbed, antique chestnut. Then, there's the optional sterling silver accessories.

### Double Buscadero Gunbelt

Truly the finest examples of silver and gunleather craftsmanship available. Elaborately floral carved and trimmed with traditional sterling silver, hand engraved conchos and your choice of sterling silver buckles.

Each gunbelt and holster is a handcrafted Limited Edition
All gunbelts and holsters are interchangeable to create a customized rig.

## The Hollywood™

The Hollywood Double shown as an alternative for the two gun shooter

### MODEL #115

Remember the golden age of TV westerns during the 1950's and 60's? All of your favorite cowboy stars and villains alike wore the same type of fast draw, buscadero style gunbelts. The Hollywood brings it all back from the wide, curved gun belt to the slim holster design and featuring an exposed trigger guard and unique reinforcing liner in the cylinder area. Like the originals of that very special era, the Hollywood is ruggedly constructed for long years of hard use or to hang on display with your western collectibles.

Shown in our standard offering of a deep, saddle tan. Offered with plain or fancy stamping border finish.

### MODEL #115A

This offering is the same as the #115 Hollywood, but with a muzzle forward, "walk-n-draw" style holster.

Each gunbelt and holster is a handcrafted Limited Edition
All gunbelts and holsters are interchangeable to create a customized rig.

## Navajo - Silver Concho Belt

### Model #315

Our all new collectors quality, Navajo concho belt is 2 1/2" wide with large, heavy silver overlay, hand engraved conchos and buckles. Can be worn for fashion or as a gunbelt. Custom made for men and women. No two alike, a real showstopper! The perfect gift for the person who has everything.

Features a heavy silver overlay, hand engraved buckle.

## The Johnny Ringo™

### MODEL #1876

Frontier Gunleather's all new Johnny Ringo gunbelt features heavy duty construction and old world styling to answer the needs of many SASS (Single Action Shooting Society) members who want high performance design features to meet the demanding needs of both professional and amateur western shooters. This rig captures the old world features of the 1880's, yet ever so refined to allow shooters every competitive advantage possible. Available, plain or fancy border stamped, single or double holsters and will accommodate an optional crossdraw holster. Note the special muzzle forward angle for quick access. Furnished standard, with Santa Fe Buckle.

Each gunbelt and holster is a handcrafted Limited Edition
All gunbelts and holsters are interchangeable to create a customized rig.

## Fort Apache Collection

### Model #1879

During the Indian Wars period of the frontier west, The U.S. Army Cavalry issued Nickel plated Colt Single Action revolvers with 7 1/2" barrels to Indian scouts.

Indian squaws would often make holsters, belts, and knife sheaths, appropriately adorned with decorative lacing, bead work, fringe, conchos and tribal trinkets.

We have faithfully recreated these museum quality, hand crafted relics to commemorate that colorful period of the American West. Each item is a unique work of historical significance; no two items are ever the same.

www.frontiergunleather.com    1-877-877-4704

## The James Arness™

James Arness portraying Marshal Matt Dillon on the award winning CBS TV Series, Gunsmoke

### MODEL #1953

The Arness rig is styled exactly like the gunbelt James Arness wore in the long running TV series "Gunsmoke". Where he portrayed U.S. Marshal Matt Dillon. Each rig is serial numbered and stamped with the famous James Arness Signature Block. A true collectors item, this rig is beautifully hand made, one at a time, especially for you.

Each gunbelt and holster is a handcrafted Limited Edition
All gunbelts and holsters are interchangeable to create a customized rig.

## The Wells Fargo

### Web Cartridge Belt
### Model #310

This comfortable, practical Wells Fargo style, cotton webbing cartridge belt features latigo leather strap ends and is a full 2" wide. It is ruggedly made for shot shells or large caliber rifle and pistol cartridges. And best of all, it is agreeably priced.

## The Bandito

### Bandolero Cartridge Belt
### Model 1913

No self respecting Bandito would be caught without his trusty bandoleer cartridge carry belt. This authentic system is fully adjustable for most adults and is made to accommodate all large caliber pistol and rifle cartridges. Features include a large silver concho fastening device just like the originals.

www.frontiergunleather.com          1-877-877-4704

## 7th Cav™ Troopers Outfit

### MODEL #1874

The 7th Cavalry Troopers Outfit is an accurate re-creation of the gunleather worn by Custer's U.S. 7th Cav at the ill-fated Battle of the Little Big Horn on June 25, 1876. This three piece set consists of a standard issue, heavy duty flap holster, a matching ammo pouch and 2" adjustable duty belt with a solid brass, two-piece US buckle plate. Holster design features the correct, right hand twist draw. Available individually, or as a three-piece set as shown. Offered in the old style, antique black finish.

## 1875 US Army Cavalry Holster

### MODEL #1875

The Model 1875 US Army Cavalry Holster was the transitional holster of 1875 for the US Cavalry. The holster was designed to carry both the Colt Single Action Army and the newer Schofield revolver which was used throughout the Indian Wars period of the American West. This ruggedly constructed holster is true to form of the original of the period and was issued thru the turn of the century.

*Each gunbelt and holster is a handcrafted Limited Edition*          All gunbelts and holsters are interchangeable to create a customized rig.

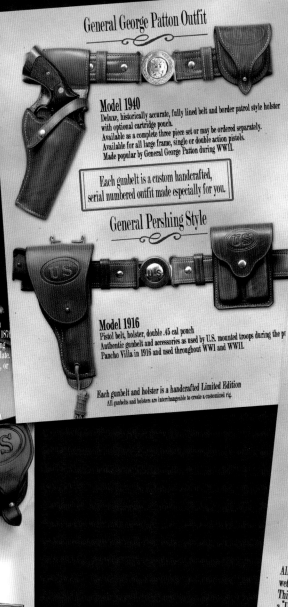

## General George Patton Outfit

### Model 1940

Deluxe, historically accurate, fully lined belt and border patrol style holster with optional cartridge pouch.
Available as a complete three piece set or may be ordered separately.
Available for all large frame, single or double action pistols.
Made popular by General George Patton during WWII.

*Each gunbelt is a custom handcrafted, serial numbered outfit made especially for you.*

## General Pershing Style

### Model 1916

Pistol belt, holster, double .45 cal pouch
Authentic gunbelt and accessories as used by U.S. mounted troops during the period of Pancho Villa in 1916 and used throughout WWI and WWII.

*Each gunbelt and holster is a handcrafted Limited Edition*

All gunbelts and holsters are interchangeable to create a customized rig.

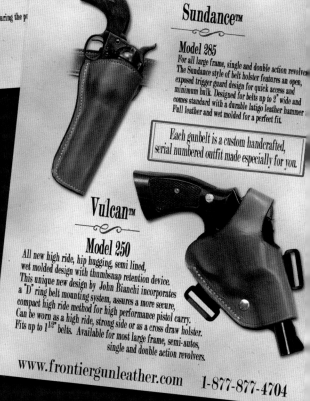

## Sundance™

### Model 285

For all large frame, single and double action revolvers. The Sundance style of belt holster features an open, exposed trigger guard design for quick access and minimum bulk. Designed for belts up to 2" wide and comes standard with a durable latigo leather hammer. Full leather and wet molded for a perfect fit.

*Each gunbelt is a custom handcrafted, serial numbered outfit made especially for you.*

## Vulcan™

### Model 250

All new high ride, hip hugging, semi lined, wet molded design with thumbsnap retention device. This unique new design by John Bianchi incorporates a "D" ring belt mounting system, assures a more secure, compact high ride method for high performance pistol carry. Can be worn as a high ride, strong side or as a cross draw holster. Fits up to 1 1/2" belts. Available for most large frame, semi-autos, single and double action revolvers.

www.frontiergunleather.com          1-877-877-4704

## Liberty "Quicksnap"

### Model #275

This Liberty "Quicksnap" model is a tried, proven, reliable design pioneered by John Bianchi almost 50 years ago, this is one of the most copied holsters ever designed. Available plain or fancy border stamped.

For most large frame single and double action revolvers and 1911 .45 cal Gov't models.

www.frontiergunleather.com    1-877-877-4704

---

### Trailmaster™

#### Model #400

The perfect shoulder for heavy duty use in the field with large caliber pistols and revolvers. Ideal for, hunters, backpackers, ATV riders, horseback riders and off road enthusiast. The trail master features a strong, comfortable "figure eight" elastic harness, fully adjustable for most sizes. Comes standard with a retention strap for added security during active use.

*Comfortable Figure 8 Harness*

### The Long Shot™

#### MODEL #305

These high grade sporting rifle slings, with padded shoulder piece and sterling silver fasteners are a perfect companion to your favorite long gun. Hand-tooled the old fashioned way with our distinctive fancy border stamping, and made to fit standard 1" sling swivels.

#### Full Custom Service

We offer a complete custom service for gunbelts, holsters and related leather products. Write, fax or phone us with your request. Please do not e-mail. We can more efficiently respond to your inquiry by phone. We offer many more holster styles and variations than are shown in our catalog. All custom work is priced according to time, materials and complexity of the project. Price quotes are valid for 30 days. All custom work is pre-paid and is non-cancelable and non-returnable. If requesting custom leather request, Call toll free...

www.frontiergunleather.com    1-877-8...

---

### Vulcan™

#### Model 250

All New high ride, hip hugging, semi lined, wet molded design with thumbsnap retention device. This unique new design by John Bianchi incorporates a "D" ring belt mounting system, assures a more secure, compact high ride method for high performance pistol carry. Can be worn as a high ride, strong side or as a cross draw holster. Fits up to 1¹⁄₂" belts. Available for most large frame, semi-autos, single and double action revolvers.

### The El Paso™

#### MODEL #1911

The new El Paso gunbelt and holster outfit is styled like the Texas Rangers and Border Patrolmen wore during the 1920's through the early 1950's. This rig features a wet molded, heavy duty, high ride, compact holster, matching, 2" tapered belt and magazine pouch. May be ordered as a complete rig as shown or individual items. Available only for the Colt type .45 Government 1911 Semi-Auto and clones. Available, plain as shown or fancy border stamped design.

### Mercury™

#### Model #1911A

A smart, compact high ride design for your 1911 .45 Gov't. Mounts securely on trouser belts up to 1³⁄₄" wide. Deluxe, full leather lined and wet molded for a perfect fit.

www.frontiergunleather.com    1-877-877-4704

---

### Gun Belts

(Top Down)
A. Model #120-B Powder River
B. Model #100-B
C. Model #1911-B El Paso (Brass Buckle)
D. Model #1911-B El Paso (Nickel Buckle)
E. Model #310-B Wells Fargo
F. Model #1881 Gunfighter Special (generic straight belt)
G. Model #120-B Powder River (tapered)
H. Model #102-B Half Breed (generic contoured belt) for use with holster models 102, 104, 105, 108, 1876

All gunbelts may be ordered separately check model numbers in catalog and refer to price list.

Please note that due to the individual nature of your Frontier Gunleather rigs, color shades will vary.

#### Tucson JB 1

In western tradition, a very elegant, tapered trouser dress belt. Border stamped and fully lined, the 1 1/2" wide belt tapers down to a very fine, highly polished 1" solid brass buckle with matching brass keeper. Strong enough to support your favorite six-gun.

#### Reata JB 2

This ideal, heavy duty pants belt is a perfect complement to your favorite gunbelt rig. A solid brass, old-style garrison buckle finishes off this rugged 1 3/4" belt. A must for every cowboy's wardrobe.

#### Round Up JB 3

A traditional style belt for all-around wear at home or on the range. This heavy duty, 1 1/2" wide belt is finished off with an old-style nickel chap buckle.

www.frontiergunleather.com    1-877-877-4704

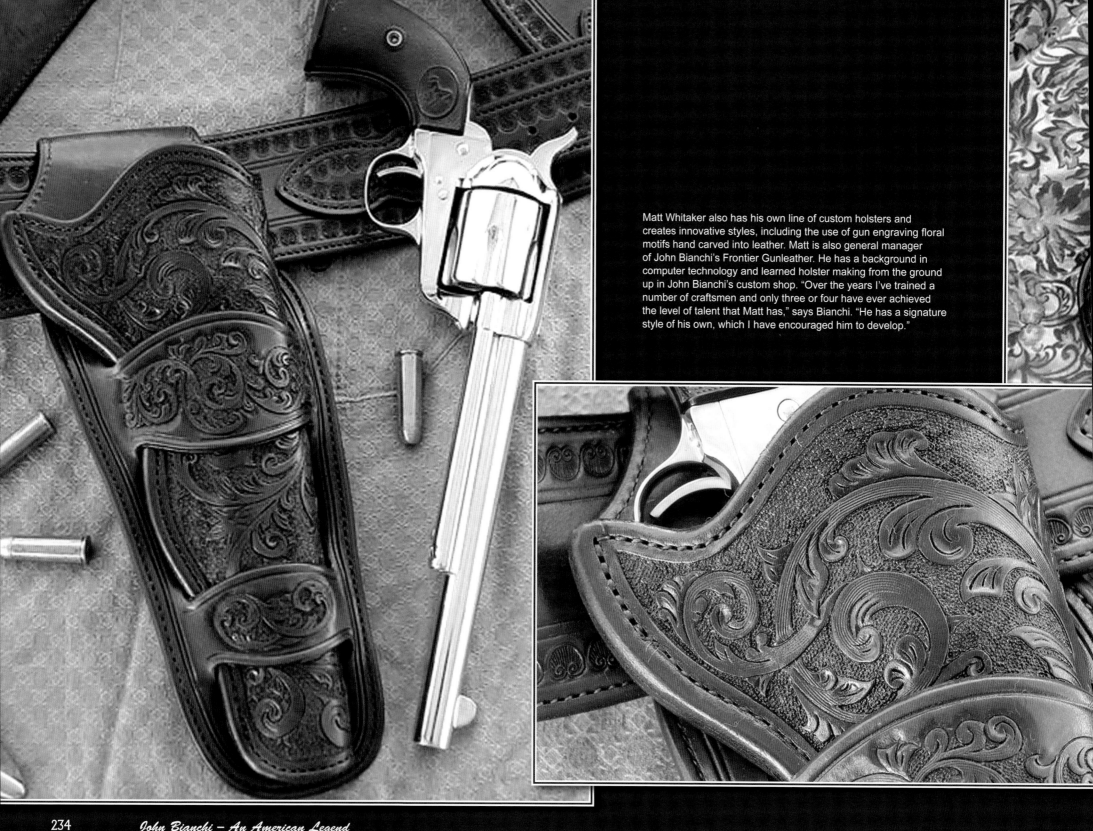

Matt Whitaker also has his own line of custom holsters and creates innovative styles, including the use of gun engraving floral motifs hand carved into leather. Matt is also general manager of John Bianchi's Frontier Gunleather. He has a background in computer technology and learned holster making from the ground up in John Bianchi's custom shop. "Over the years I've trained a number of craftsmen and only three or four have ever achieved the level of talent that Matt has," says Bianchi. "He has a signature style of his own, which I have encouraged him to develop."

MATT WHITAKER
CUSTOM MAKER

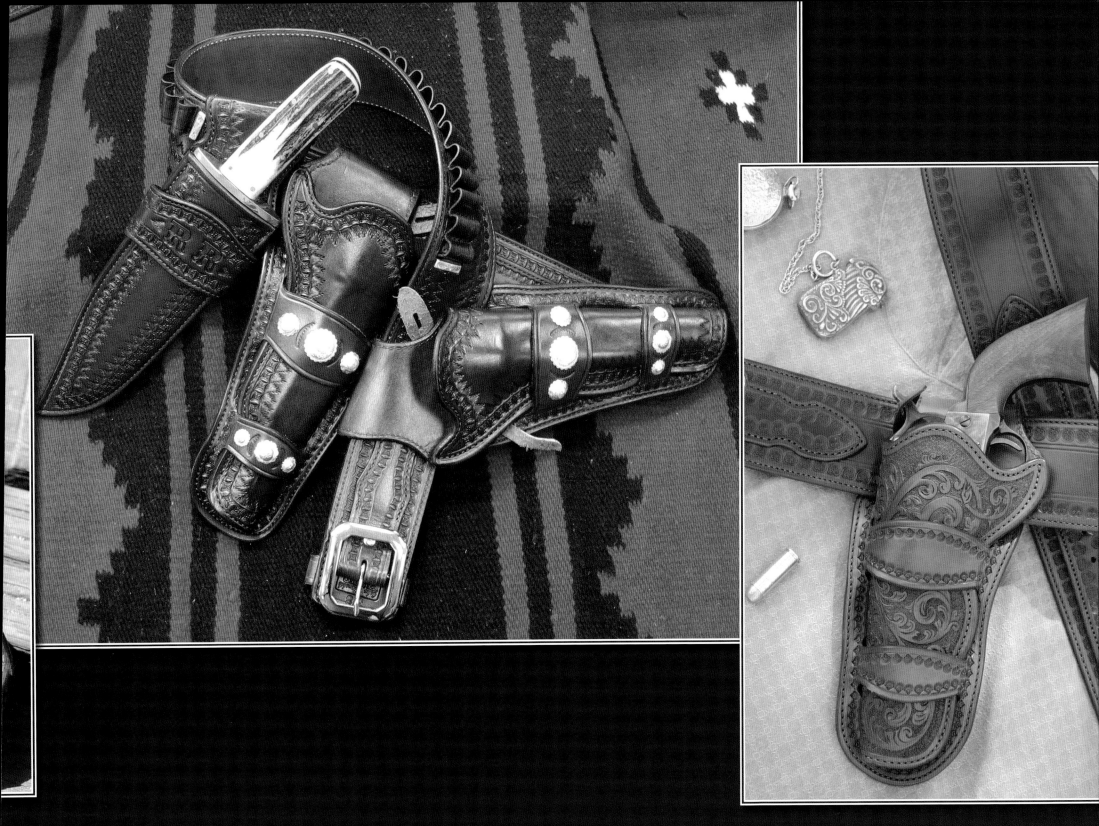

Just as in this gun store, Guns of Distinction, located in Palm Desert, California, Bianchi photos and Histographs still line the walls of thousands of gun shops and sporting goods stores around the world. More than thirty years later they are valuable, collectible pieces of art that have never been duplicated.

This is the dedication plaque from the Frontier Museum, which John kept and has mounted on the wall of his patio. "This was a philosophical summary of the mission statement of the Frontier Museum. The Autrys' declined to use it in the transition of the Museum."

THE OLD WEST LINGERS IN THE HEARTS
AND IMAGINATION OF EVERY AMERICAN.
IT WAS A BRIEF AND COLORFUL ERA IN
HISTORY BETWEEN THE END OF THE CIVIL
WAR AND THE TURN OF THE CENTURY.
IT WAS A TIME OF HIGH HOPE AND PROMISE,
GREAT RISK AND HARDSHIP.
IT BROUGHT OUT THE BEST AND THE WORST IN MEN.
IT WAS THE TIME OF COWBOYS,
INDIANS, OUTLAWS AND LAWMEN.
IT WAS THE DAY OF THE GUNFIGHTER!

A VAST AND EXCITING ADVENTURE.....
AND THEN IT WAS OVER AS QUICKLY AS IT BEGAN.
THE SPIRIT OF THE OLD WEST LIVES
ON TODAY IN FACT AND IN LEGEND.

JOHN E. BIANCHI
FRONTIER MUSEUM
DEDICATED SPRING 1982

John Bianchi still builds contemporary holsters on request for the latest revolvers and semi-autos. This example of the famous No. 2 Speed Scabbard was designed for the author's handcrafted AMT Longslide target model .45 ACP. Also shown is the original pattern, signed by Bianchi, and used to make the custom Longslide holster. The gun is fitted with an extended slide release, beavertail grip safety, tuned action, polished ramp and throat, extended 10-round magazine, muzzle break, hard chromed finish, and ivory grips custom made by Dan Chesiak.

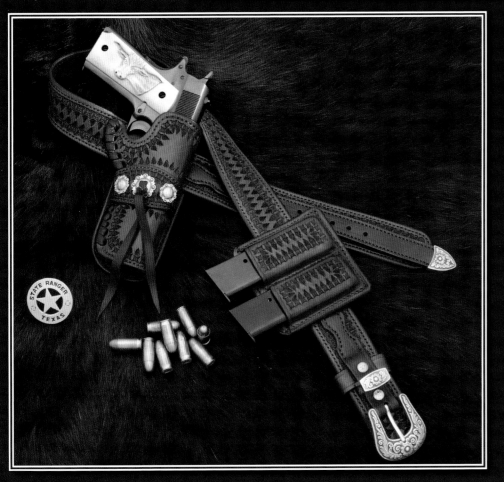

The very latest gun rig from John Bianchi is the "Wild Bunch Outfit." Reminiscent of the early 1900s gun belts for the Colt Browning Model 1911 .45 ACP Pistol, it is based on designs worn by Texas Rangers and Lawmen along the Mexican Border. The "Wild Bunch Outfit" will join Frontier Gunleather's 2011 product line. (Photo by Dennis Adler)

Recently, Major General Robert Menist (USA Ret.) escorted Iraqi Major General Sa'ad, the Provincial Police Chief for Maysan Province, on a visit to El Paso and Fort Bliss, Texas. "John learned of the visit and within 36 hours had designed, produced, and had delivered a specially made Frontier Gunleather holster and belt, perfectly designed to fit the Iraqi General (at left) and his personal sidearm," says Gen. Menist, noting that, "It was another example of John's contributions to cement great relationships between countries and their militaries."

# Appendix I

## Other Voices

Accolades From Those Who Have Worked With John Bianchi

# Ken Dodd

## Former Art and Advertising Director, Bianchi International

My career began as part of a four man crew producing a national police publication called *Police Product News*. During its first year, the magazine gained considerable attention by the law enforcement community on both coasts. Having no previous publication experience, everything we did could easily be defined as experimental. Our success grew rapidly as our editorial and product coverage was written directly to the beat cop. Anything went.

My task was to design a magazine image that projected a look of *Car and Driver* with a hint of *Playboy*. And since the design department consisted of just one person, I was free to throw in a new cartoon series called "Officer R Runner". That and a centerfold featuring a scantily dressed female wearing abbreviated uniforms such as the California Highway Patrol, SWAT Team, and the Texas Rangers – *Police Product News* was a hit.

The magazine was growing faster than the powers to be could afford, so offers to buy the magazine by various investment groups gave some temporary relief. At the same time, I had no idea that someone was about to change my life forever.

I had little to no background in law enforcement prior to working at *Police Product News*. It was for most of us a fly-by-the-seat experience. So when I learned that John Bianchi was interested in speaking to me about a position in his firm, I was quite excited; but also overwhelmed. Bianchi was a big name. Having a shot to grow my career would definitely be enhanced by working there.

It was in the fall of 1977 that I first visited John Bianchi. Upon arriving at the Bianchi Gunleather headquarters, located in Temecula, California, I immediately sensed that something very special was about to happen to me. My first impression of the company was nothing short of awe. The lobby wasn't large, glitzy, or anything near over the top. What it did have was substance. John Bianchi knew the importance of branding. And I'm not speaking of cattle branding. John made sure that his Bianchi brand, which included his promise of quality, richness, and dependability, was clearly identified from the front desk to the back door.

Upon meeting with John the first time, I knew immediately this was the place I wanted to be. John was totally indicative of the phrase, "first cabin."

My orientation to the Bianchi family and its mode of operation came to me easily as I had served just a few years earlier in the United States Navy. John's form of leadership paralleled that of my combat training and service while on the River Patrol Boats on the Mekong Delta. There was order from top to bottom. One knew what was expected.

My first tour of the Bianchi operations was extremely educational. To begin with, I couldn't help but notice that strong leather smell. John stated, "I would eventually not even smell it." Over the years, that good smell unfortunately became unnoticeable just as John foretold.

As we ventured from John's office we entered the shipping department. It was apparent that these folks bought into the Bianchi mystique lock, stock and barrel. Every station was smartly designed for ultimate proficiency and all employees were totally involved in their task.

Venturing further into the plant, we came upon the leather workers. Here, they were sizing, cutting, gluing, sewing, trimming, sanding, polishing, and loading thousands of holsters of all styles and shapes onto holding racks.

As we approached each section of operation, a lead person (supervisor) would immediately receive us. And as we left and entered a new section, the same action repeated itself. I know this could easily be interrupted as ego, but soon I learned this action was the sign of individual pride and precision. Here was the heart of the Bianchi brand. These folks truly appreciated what they were a part of.

When John took me up to my new digs, I was really excited. The space provided was just that, space. It was going to be my job to completely outfit this new department. That meant digging out catalogs and sitting for hours with the purchasing department. And as with everything else, John wanted me to have the best. He taught me the value of purchasing good tools that combined with my talents would produce excellent results. I felt like a kid in a candy store.

It was time to get down to business. John had a habit of calling me down to his office periodically as an idea hit him. I loved these one on one exchanges. We would gather around his coffee table and review past ads, posters, and promotions seeking to improve whatever we did. The most important business was to bring the Bianchi brand alive in the minds of the consumer. What better than to instill a demand for quality leather handcrafted by experts. Craftsmen who had mastered the art of producing highly sought after holsters, belts, scabbards, and leather accessories.

The Bianchi brand had already achieved considerable equity prior to me coming on board. It was a name known throughout the shooting sports, law enforcement, and military industries. But like they say, "Being on the top and staying on top are two very different tasks." We knew we had to stay out in front with an image John had begun in the 1970s but now needed to be reinforced. Thus began a series of ads, posters, and catalogs that truly established the Bianchi legend.

John Bianchi without a doubt loved being the "brand." So with my marching orders, I sat down and began a series of concepts that would be seen in our ads, sales sheets, and promotions. The biggest advantages I had going for me were John's continued support, a wealth of old Western props, and perfect geography all around us.

John provided me unbelievable encouragement to come up with the wildest of ideas. I could expect having a visit from John most anytime of the day. He loved to see what

I was up to and how he might get involved. We were bringing in several outside sales teams at the time. John had a great idea of introducing these guys with a one sheet promotion whereby John and the new representative would appear properly outfitted in the best of the Old West. Sometimes we could bring in a small buckboard wagon or saloon table. A fitting title would be: "Jack Storm rides for Bianchi." The reps loved this. Any time a new guy came onboard, they'd ask me, "When do we do the promotion sheet? What will I be dressed like?" John's first cabin treatment would follow. He would have me set aside a promo sheet and have it laminated onto a nice wood plaque and set it off with a metal plate stating the name of the ad.

My first and foremost responsibility was to our annual sales catalog. This was serious business and required significant planning and prep time. I was terrified with the production of the 1979 catalog. Producing a magazine was one thing; producing a catalog was absolutely another world of surprising issues. I didn't care what I had to do to get that book finished on time. That included bringing the book home and working on it into the early hours. It got done and it looked great. Having put that first book behind me, I could then establish an experienced plan.

Experienced plan or not, of all the books I produced, none went together without its hitches. Those hitches included John, John, and John. The Bianchi brand was on every holster stitch, dye lot, product photo, catalog text, headline, and more. We often approached deadlines with John stopping the presses to make one last adjustment to that perfect holster. Was this a bad thing? Absolutely not, it all came down to having it right.

I was extremely fortunate to be where I was. I had total access to a world of old Western clothing, gun belts, hats, saloon tables, and the list went on. I considered it my own personal paint pallet for painting some of the most interesting and effective ads, posters, and promotional materials of our time.

Of significance is the fact that computers were far off into the future. Graphic software programs, electronic effects, digital scanning — none of these were on the market. We produced our marketing images the same way holsters were made, with handcrafted care and perseverance, and unrelenting trial and error.

"Everybody is reaching for Bianchi" was one particular ad that gave me great pleasure to design and produce. First of all, every idea was brought to John for his input. John enjoyed this as he loved having an opportunity to work with me in developing the scene. I sketched out a display that included a rusty old jail cell complete with wall clock, crank phone, bunk, and sheriff's desk. This set was built three dimensional providing me the opportunity to really bring a sense of reality to the project. I needed to ensure the cell itself would be as close to reality as possible, but using actual brick and mortar was out of the question. Especially since we needed to move this project out of the machine shop once we were finished. Thank goodness they had brick wall paper. With a little smudge work here and there my jail cell looked ready for the worst of outlaws. As in all of the ads, John was the center focus. In this set he was standing next to his desk speaking on the phone. At the same time, I placed my jailed cowboy with one knee on the floor and

his left arm reaching through the bars for John's gun and holster.

Set building was very enjoyable, especially with so much to work with. In yet another ad, we took advantage of this beautiful authentic Tombstone saloon bar. Simply exquisite, this elegant piece of furniture was complete with beveled glass mirrors, deep cherry wood, and all of the accessories needed in making this a wonderful saloon scene. John had spent a fortune on obtaining the exact clothing designed for film star John Wayne. Continuity was maintained in every production we worked on with John wearing his leather vest, red shirt, tan pants, and light suede hat with black band and silver studs. That was topped off with his red scarf and patented cigar. We pulled off two ads using the saloon bar as our backdrop.

"Everybody is fighting over Bianchi" took considerable effort as we brought in four members of the company, dressed them in the part and directed them how to stage a rip roaring fight, complete with black eyes, bent noses, broken beer bottles and flying teeth. John had the more cozy part, as he was properly seated front and center playing a single hand of solitaire. This project required considerable study in the complex process of breaking a glass bottle and gluing the parts together in a pattern that would fit over the skull of a man. The entire set was built inside of the machine shop requiring me to cover everything with large canvas covers. Once again, I was extremely lucky to have my world of props to pull from. John had these large Buffalo Bill Cody's Wild West Show canvas paintings. These worked perfect as the reflection of these paintings fell onto the bar's glass casings giving it a wonderful warm effect. My strong guys were positioned just behind John holding their arms in the air with fists smashing into each other's chin. They really got into it and enjoyed groaning and shouting as though they were in a live action movie.

"Bianchi Doesn't Gamble on Quality" was the second ad we produced using the saloon. Frank Boyer, the curator of John's Western collections, was my favorite go-to-guy and was always a tremendous help. In this ad, Frank was called in to be our bartender. With his beard and long white hair, Frank was absolutely perfect for the part. I placed him behind the bar drying a glass and John once again sitting at his favorite table in front of the bar. On the table were placed several poker chips with John holding his cards. No level of attention to detail was enough as each ad became a collector's item upon publication.

Shooting "Bianchi Takes the Bull by the Horns" was probably the most fun day I had while with Bianchi. I remember coming into John's office to present my latest ad concept that included John wrapping his right arms over the neck of a very large bull while hanging on to its horns. At the time, Temecula was served by a veterinarian who just happened to have an extremely robust bull in his corral. Nebs was the vet's pet, having had it since it was born. Nebs was a fitting name for the bull as it was born already having small nebs for horns. Those nebs were now extending out about thirty-six inches in all directions. At least that is how John envisioned it. John's eyes were quite wide when I showed him the layout and described the scene. I enjoyed this moment as it pushed the envelope for this cowpoke probably a little more than I dared. To my delight, John said absolutely. Great idea.

We arranged a day and time with the veterinarian who fortunately was very helpful in our arrangements. We brought Nebs into a tight corral and the vet did me one big favor. He slipped a shot of calm-me-down into old Nebs. Knowing that helped John gain the requisite confidence to place himself between a thousand pound bull and safety. Nebs was perfect. He just stood there thinking when the heck is this going to be over and we got our shot. John was glad to get out of there, but more glad that we had pulled off yet another masterpiece. His openness to pushing the envelope was just what I needed to bring these ads to life.

The Bianchi Histograph was probably the most challenging and time consuming project I worked on outside of the annual catalog. The Histograph was a four color poster printed on high-end quality collector paper, measuring approximately 24 x 36 inches. These works of art presented historical milestones in America's Old West. Prior to me coming on board, John had produced three Histographs, so I had the advantage of seeking out his and others' advice and support when preparing for these projects.

"The Pony Soldiers Wore Bianchi" was produced in Monument Valley, Utah. Phil Spangenberger, Western historian and close friend of John's, provided significant assistance to me in preparing for this project. His uncompromising knowledge of the "time" and "event" of the Pony Soldier was invaluable to me. His working actively in the industry and participation in a Western history re-enactment group made it even better. These folks owned authentic Union soldier apparel and more importantly knew the history behind it. Our challenges were in all sizes. The concept included a company of Union soldiers, accompanied by artist and sculptor Dave Manuel, who played the part of Frederic Remington. Remington made his name as an illustrator, mostly of Western and military subjects, for most of the widely circulated magazines of the late 1880s and 1890s.

John had come upon a photographer by the name of Jerry Jacka. A resident of Phoenix, Arizona, Jerry was a renowned photographer known for his work in *Arizona Highways* magazine. Of significant importance was Jerry's personal respect and trust by the Navajo Indians located in Monument Valley. Having that rapport with the natives was invaluable. We were dealing with sacred ground and not just everyone could come in and pitch camp.

I journeyed to Hollywood, California, to seek out and procure an 1886 Gatling gun. It was the same as the model 1883 with improvements in the ejector and cartridge guides. This gun was a ten-barrel .45 cal. fully encased in a bronze jacket. A side mounting hand crank produced a rate of fire of up to 800 rounds per minute but could be rear mounted to increase the rate up to 1,500. Internal components were strengthened to withstand the punishment from the higher rate of fire. I was thrilled to find this Gatling in a back lot of the Burbank film studios. After signing my first born away, I hauled it in the back of the Bianchi company pickup back to Temecula and readied it for our trip to Utah.

I first set out for Phoenix to meet up with Jerry at his home. Jerry and his wife were extremely warm people bringing me into their home as though I was family. Their home was an amazing collection of Navajo artifacts going back hundreds of years. You could tell this man was a welcomed and trusted friend of the Navajo people.

Jerry and I collected supplies which included about ten 4 x 6 foot light reflector panels, an 8 x 10 view camera, and loads of film. Our trip took us up into Southern Utah where we entered God's country. Monument Valley welcomed us with the most majestic landscapes I had ever seen. We checked in to a small motel at the foot of a steep mountain and entrance to the Valley and spent four days searching every spot we could find for the perfect location. During this time we also came across a Navajo family that owned a pony. I needed to rent that horse for the photograph and agreed upon a price and time for the horse to be on the set. Like any business deal, the horse price nearly doubled upon arrival – or else. You have to love capitalism.

Finally our large entourage of Union soldiers, Phil Spangenberger, Dave Manuel and John and Donna Bianchi arrived at the motel that I had reserved for our stay. At the time, this place was the only one available. John was eager to get out into the Valley to see the locations I was recommending. We narrowed it down after a few hours to two spots, each spectacular.

Jacka and I had ensured our horse and his owner would arrive a few hours before the shoot and we began clearing the ground. Pulling the Gatling gun into position wasn't the easiest of tasks. Especially after discovering a rattlesnake in the exact spot John was going to be standing! Jacka educated me on the facts dealing with snakes and other wildlife stating the Navajo were highly opposed to hurting any one of them – nature was considered God in Monument Valley.

Developing a concept is one thing, pulling off the shot is quite another. With every move of man, machine, and/or camera the image would change, often taking on a completely different concept of its own. Clicking the camera was relatively easy compared to deciding the best view. Monument Valley was a dynamic living being and you simply had to just let it lead you. We worked the two sets throughout the two days of shooting. Having come so far, we really didn't want to miss anything. The final product is one of my more favorable projects, and I feel extremely fortunate to have been a part in producing "The Pony Soldiers Wore Bianchi Leather."

My tour with Bianchi International left me with a lifetime of memories. Especially, as it relates to my personal involvement with the Bianchi Frontier Museum. I can't tell you how many times I crawled in and out of tight spaces within inches of the most valuable Western artifacts money could buy. Look to the left and it would be John Wesley Hardin's revolver, to my right, Wyatt Earp's, next up, the leather jacket of Buffalo Bill Cody. Naturally as the museum took shape, my closet of toys was quickly becoming unavailable to me when needing something for an ad photo shoot. I spent a ton of time handmaking artifact description signs, plaques, direction signs, and more. It truly was like building the set for a major Hollywood movie. John was a fanatic over detail. If anyone thought John was an overly obsessive perfectionist with holsters, they soon learned the museum did not hold second place. And why not, this was his life and dream. Nothing would go into that museum unless it was truly perfection at its best.

During pre-grand opening week, it was like the Queen of England was on her way. Every single issue became the Titanic. This ship was NOT going to hit any snags or a hidden iceberg. VIP opening day was like the opening of Disneyland. We were tired beyond belief and every one of us were busting at the seams with pride. The John Wayne family were John's most proclaimed guests. In the main lobby was a larger than life size bronze statue of the Duke himself. Upon unveiling the statue, John and family declared the museum officially opened. This was the first time that I had truly experienced firsthand a man and his family enjoying an accomplishment others could only dream of pulling off.

As stated above, my tour with Bianchi International has a personal meaning to me. John was the epitome of a military leader. It was in his walk and his pride of ownership. Having served immediately alongside naval officers, I recognized this swagger and was extremely comfortable with it. John was a living brand. John knew he had much to accomplish and would never accept less than perfection in whatever he did.

Donna Bianchi was just as professional and worked relentlessly to shape those in management into a proficient machine each working on the same page. At one stage of my career with Bianchi, I reported directly to Donna, assisting her to establish and implement a marketing department that served the short and long term direction of the firm. I bought into everything she spoke of, as I had made a personal decision to pursue and finish my degree in marketing. We had called a marketing meeting that would include several other departments of the company; marketing being a diverse subject which combines experienced application with theory. This "science" was now going to lock horns with those involved in leather design, sales, inventory, and budgeting – in one meeting. John came in after it had begun and took his lead chair. I will refer to the following as the "Lieutenant General George S. Patton" moment. John was without a doubt reflecting on other issues a lot more important than round robin table talk on marketing. Upon reaching his limit on patience, he slammed his fist hard on the table and yelled, "Damn it people, there's a war out there!" While this scared the hell out of everybody in the room including Donna and myself, we were used to John speaking his mind and when he did, stand back . Important or not, that particular time and place was a lot like throwing rocks in a glass house as everything in that room was expensive and fragile. Unfortunately, I didn't truly understand or appreciate his meaning, but his explanation never left me.

I retained and treasured that momentary outburst into my own business career when forming and operating my own marketing firm founded in 1987. I had plenty of days when I thought back to John's eloquent expression and wanted to scream the same to my own staff. Business survival is a war and John had it right. He never minced words due to possibly hurting someone's feelings, and it made us a better team and company for it.

John and Donna Bianchi gave me something no others have. They provided me the opportunity and financial support to finish my college degree. Their personal concern for their employees went well beyond what is normally expected. I remain forever in their debt. Personally, we share a most tragic loss of a son. Within a year of the loss of their son, John Jr., my wife and I tragically lost our own son, Brian. The Bianchis' spared nothing in coming to our aid in helping us endure this most horrific time in our lives. We truly appreciate them and feel it an honor to have been part of the Bianchi family. ✍

# Massad Ayoob
## Author, Firearms Instructor, Magazine Editor, and Columnist

Not for nothing has John Bianchi been called "The Master of Gun Concealment." He studied the history of his craft both ancient and modern, and essentially made it into an art form. Sometimes he resurrected and distinctly improved older designs, such as the Berns-Martin Lightning – and when he did, he gave attribution to the original designer – and sometimes, he came up with his own unique ideas.

One of the most useful gun concealment tools is the elastic belly band, designed to be worn "over the underwear and under the overwear," concealing the handgun beneath a tucked-in dress shirt. I first saw John holding his prototype in the 1960s in the pages of *Gun World* magazine, and like a gazillion other people thought, "Why didn't I think of that?" John didn't manufacture that rig right away, and another company, in New York, came out with it first. I got one while still in college, and literally wore it out. When John Bianchi did finally bring out a belly band, in his fabric Ranger line, I bought a couple and found them by far the best of their breed. My last well worn Bianchi Ranger Belly Band, which also serves as a money belt, is still a constant companion when I travel far from home, especially overseas.

John Bianchi was, to my knowledge, the first to line an ankle holster with wooly sheepskin to not only soak up perspiration, but cushion the ankle bone from chafing. This made ankle carry tolerable for some who wouldn't have had that protection otherwise, and I know two men personally whose lives were saved by John's design. His ankle holsters have proven to be the ideal choice when the good guys have to draw while supine and fire quickly to survive. I can also point to several lawmen I know personally who survived what would have been fatal gun snatch attempts, because they were wearing John Bianchi-designed security holsters that did not yield the weapon to unauthorized hands. Today, in a time when open carry is becoming popular among those who once carried concealed, the namesake holsters of John Bianchi include several models that work for concealment *or* open carry, and offer added security against being disarmed.

There are too many fine designs that came out of the head of John Bianchi to list here in their entirety. Suffice to say that classics, by definition, endure.

I had the privilege of having some design input into the inside-the-waistband Bianchi No.3 Pistol Pocket back around 1977. I only had one suggestion to make, but was pleased to see it implemented. That design remains available today, and it is probably the finest thumb-break inside the waistband holster (particularly for a service-size handgun) ever made. Some of mine are thirty years old and show it, but none is anywhere close to wearing out or failing. They're still timely, they're still comfortable, they still conceal big handguns superbly…and they're still fast. A couple of years ago, I had the pleasure of shooting a Master score on the tough IDPA Classifier 90-shot course with a K-frame S&W revolver out of a thumb-break Bianchi Pistol Pocket.

I've owned many shoulder holsters, but there's none I've worn more often than John Bianchi's iconic X-15. It pulls a gun in tight to even a slender body as if the holster and .45 Auto had been painted onto the shirt, yet there's no faster draw than starting with your arms folded, and your opponent not yet realizing that your hand is already grasping your 1911 in its Bianchi X-15.

It is good to know that Dennis Adler is writing this long-overdue tribute to Bianchi, both the man and his designs. Both have stood the test of time. Whether you're talking about the man or his products, the name Bianchi stands for enduring quality and trustworthiness.

*[For over thirty years, Massad Ayoob has been Handgun Editor of* Guns *magazine, and Law Enforcement Editor of* American Handgunner. *He is the author of numerous books and training films on handgun use, and has written thousands of articles over the past thirty-six years. A former police officer, he served nineteen years as chair of the firearms committee for the American Society of Law Enforcement Trainers, and twenty-eight years as director of the Lethal Force Institute. He designed the Ayoob Rear Guard holster for Mitch Rosen and LFI Concealment Rig for Ted Blocker, and has the distinction of having fired the first shot at the first Bianchi Cup in 1979!]* ✍

# Bob Arganbright
### Firearms Historian and Author

I first learned of John Bianchi in the late 1950s through his small advertisement in *Gun World* magazine for his Protector Brand holsters. I read and re-read an article that he wrote on holsters in an early issue of the magazine. When I became interested in so-called Combat Shooting, I mail ordered a state of the art Cooper Combat holster directly from John.

Eventually, those small ads were replaced by full page ads. I recall one with John posing as a James Bond type with appropriate Bianchi holster and a beautiful young lady. I remember Bob Downs, former president of Brauer Brothers Holsters, telling me how everyone in the holster industry, where sales were to wholesalers rather than direct, thought that John was "crazy" to be spending all that money on advertising. But they changed their minds when they found that his ads were generating enough mail order retail sales to pay for them.

I was also honored to be one of those receiving an invitation to the first Bianchi Cup competition. Looking to promote the hand gunning sports, John envisioned a professional shooting match for a large purse that would be handgun neutral by favoring neither revolver nor auto-pistol. John chose Ray Chapman, the first World Combat Pistol Champion, to design the course of fire and be the match director. I shot in that initial Bianchi Cup, which was dominated by IPSC shooters with their custom .45 auto 1911 style pistols. John's vision was proven to be true when the NRA took over the Bianchi Cup as the NRA National Action Pistol Championship.

At one of the early Bianchi Cups, John related his involvement in the early days of the fast draw sport. Approximately twenty years ago, I obtained a copy of a theatrical sports "short feature" titled *Golden Gunfighters,* which covered the Colt-Sahara Hotel National Fast Draw Championship held in Las Vegas, Nevada, in 1962. I was surprised to see a young, handsome John Bianchi as one of the re-enactment gunfighters in the opening gunfight. In a later scene of the actual competition, John was seen as a level judge.

John acquired a large collection of Western guns, gunleather, and Western artifacts and established the Bianchi Frontier Museum, which I had the pleasure of touring. Many of the Colt SA revolvers were authenticated to lawmen and outlaws of the Old West. The museum collection was eventually sold to the late Gene Autry and used as part of his museum. After retiring as president of Bianchi International, John could not stay away from leather work (the smell of fresh cut cowhide is addictive), and soon founded John Bianchi Frontier Gunleather and produces the finest in Western rigs. By the way, it was John that originated the term "gunleather."

It has been a fast-track fifty years, with John officially celebrating half a century in the industry in 2010. John Bianchi has proven to be "one to ride the river with." I am proud to call him friend.

*[Bob Arganbright has been a respected gun writer for over thirty-five years as well as a competitive shooter and author of the 1978 book,* The Fastest Guns Alive: The Story of Western Fast Draw.*]* ✍

# Debra Benton
### President, Benton Management Resources, Inc.

Working with CEOs all of my career, I have a real standard of comparison by which I look at them. John Bianchi is a special breed – and I hope for the sake of our country not the last of the breed.

Just one example: When he was just starting to create a company, he'd frequently drive by one specific corporate facility and noticed how neat, organized, and clean the grounds were — the parking lot, the buildings, and the rest. Out of curiosity one day, he stopped to find out what it was. Turns out it was the famous German manufacturing company Braun, which had headquarters in Alhambra, California.

That cleanliness, organization, disciplined approached he saw there became a guide for his own operations. He took that same approach inside, even to the employee desks. There was a "rule"that at night each desk was allowed to have a phone, a half-inch thick pad of paper, two pens, two pencils, six paper clips, etc.

He carried out that organization, discipline, perfectionism, and general standard of excellence into his facilities, onto the assembly line, into the company cafeteria, through his ethics and integrity, and into the people he surrounded himself with – from his mentors to his executives to his friends to his employees. Everybody's "game'" was raised around John because that is how he lived and worked and that is the example he set. That's why his product, company, and personal name are legendary.

Today's young, creative, high-flying, risk-taking CEOs could greatly benefit by adding a component of "Bianchism" to their structure, their way of doing business. It's solid. He's solid....both of which is needed as much or more than ever.

*[Award-winning author and motivational speaker Debra Benton has known John Bianchi for over thirty years and often refers to his business acumen and management style in her lectures. She has helped professionals worldwide design subtle changes in their presentation, attitude, and leadership styles to increase their personal and professional effectiveness – and subsequently their financial status.]*

# Patrick Curtis

## Actor / Director / Producer

Let me tell you a bit about our friend, John Bianchi, and his lovely wife, Nikki. During the last several decades, John has been my go-to guy when I really needed a friend. When my wife Annabel's ailments became catastrophic, John and Nikki were the first to tell us to move to the desert, and let the warmth of the sun help heal her. We did, and it helped!

For three or four months of the year, John and I are the same age, but for the rest of the year, he is, and always will be, the big brother I never had. He's continually there with the perfect words of encouragement. John is a true friend, in every sense of the word.

Frontier Gunleather became my personal "home away from home" on an almost daily basis. John let me pitch in and help him with his magnificent leather works, and after a while, I became slightly proficient in the small tasks that he assigned me. Then one day, as I was elbow deep in black leather dye, I had an epiphany. Wait, wait, John's doing the ol,'"let's have fun painting the fence gag on me." He hated working with black dye, once

you got it on your skin, it lasted forever. And there I was, soaked in dye, even with gloves on. To this day, as the dye slowly fades away, I must admit I had a hell of a time.

A few years ago, John and I were both honored with stars on the Palm Springs Walk of Stars. We made sure our respective stars were opposite each other, about a gunfight distance away. I just know if the sun's in his eyes, I could take him!

*[Patrick Curtis was literally born into acting in 1939 as "Baby Beau Wilkes," in* Gone With The Wind. *During the next twenty years, he appeared in almost sixty motion pictures and countless television programs. Many of his early roles were at Republic Pictures, where he was usually the fourth kid on the right. He was fortunate to work with Roy, Dale, Gabby, Wild Bill, Rocky Lane, and many of the other Cowboy Heroes of Our Youth. His production career started in 1965, with the filming of* A Swingin' Summer, *starring his then-wife, Raquel Welch. This led to Europe where he produced many of Raquel's most successful films, including the memorable Western,* Hannie Caulder, *directed by Burt Kennedy. Patrick has produced over thirty-five major motion picture and TV programs.]*

# Rick Baratta

## Former Police Officer, Monrovia Police Department

## Firearms Instructor

I was driving to the station to start the swing shift at Monrovia P.D., and entering the busy traffic downtown, when I saw Officer Ron Buck running across the main street chasing after a young man that was dodging traffic. The traffic had come to a stop and Ron and the suspect disappeared into the crowded sidewalk. When traffic cleared I continued to the station and reported in.

The duty sergeant turned to me and said, "Help Ron book the suspect in." He laughed and informed me that two Boy Scouts has seen two juveniles steal a handgun from a display case at the local sports store. The Scouts had informed the owner, who, without making a fuss, called the police. Ron and his partner had arrived just as the suspects were leaving the store. They spooked and ran into traffic with Ron racing after them. Ron caught one, but the other had escaped.

I placed my gun into a gun locker and pocketed the key, then walked into the booking room where Ron was busy searching the youth, who appeared to be about sixteen years old. Just as he was finger printing the suspect I heard a commotion at the front desk, where two young boys in Scout uniforms were pointing out of the station and yelling that they had found the other suspect hiding in a car parked in front of the local school, a block or so from the station.

I grabbed the suspect and pushed him into a holding cell, and yelling to the duty sergeant to roll a backup I jumped the front counter and followed the Scouts out of the building. "He's in that car parked in front of the school," one of them shouted. I could see the school from the station two blocks away, and started running, followed by Ron and the two Scouts.

Reaching the suspect vehicle, I looked into the back seat area and saw a young man trying to make himself invisible on the floor. A patrol car rolled up and parked behind the vehicle, and Officer John Bianchi got out with his hand on his holstered gun. "No need," I said, and opened the door, telling the suspect to get out. As he climbed out and stood up, Ron pushed his face close and said, "You want to try running now?" The kid put both hands on Ron's chest and pushed hard. Ron hit the ground and the suspect was off and running between the school buildings. I raced after him with Ron and John Bianchi close behind me. As we ran between the buildings I could see the suspect racing across the playing field. Two young men shooting baskets stopped to see what was happening and I yelled at them to stop the kid. One jumped into the suspect's path but the kid dodged around him and kept running.

I jumped when a gun went off behind me, and the kid seemed to increase his speed. The gun fired again and again, but I was too busy running to look behind. The kid headed towards an eight foot chain link fence surrounding the school. I was nearly up to him when he leaped at the fence and pulling himself up threw one leg over the top. I jumped and caught the other leg and pulled. The kid screamed and cursed as his crotch was pulled into the steel points of the fence. Ron arrived and also grabbed the leg. This brought on another scream from the kid, who couldn't go forward and would not drop back. Ron and I were all but out of breath when John ran up. He had his gun in his hand and was ejecting shells. As he punched new rounds into his gun he stared at the kid and whispered, "Hold him steady, I want a clear shot." The kid screamed again and panicked, jerking his leg free, and dropping down the other side to the concrete. As luck would have it, a brawny man in work clothes appeared and promptly grabbed the kid and sat on him. "I saw the chase and thought I'd help," he said. None of us were in shape to climb the fence, so I passed my handcuffs through and asked the man if he would please cuff the suspect to the fence while we picked up the patrol car and drove around the school. While walking back to the car Ron and I both asked John what he was thinking of, shooting at an escaping juvenile. John just grinned. [During the pursuit John had slipped in a mud puddle in the middle of the football field and landed face down, his second uniform of the day, and when he got up he began firing warning shots. He actually only fired three, but with the echo it sounded like more].

We picked the suspect up and sat him in the rear of the car between Ron and myself. The kid had got over his fear and started telling us how he was going to sue us and the department for trying to kill him. "Kid," John says, looking over his shoulder at the boy, "You are absolutely right, and I'll be a witness that they tried to shoot you. Count on me." "John," I said, "neither Ron nor I have guns, we locked them at the station when we were booking the other suspect." John smiled, not a bit fazed. "Probably used a throw-away. I'll still testify for you kid." The suspect shrank back in the seat with a fearful expression on his face. I think he was wondering if we were really cops. I occasionally wondered myself after riding with John.

Ron and I decided to keep quiet about the gun accidentally going off…three times.

*Officer Rick Baratta was one of John Bianchi's partners while he served on the Monrovia Police Department. Rick later went on to become a respected firearms instructor and presently teaches firearms tactics in South Africa.* ✍

# Robert Menist

## Major General (USA Ret.)

In 1982, I had the good fortune to meet then Lt. Col. John Bianchi in a rather unusual way. As part of the committee tasked to review his doctoral dissertation in business management, I was impressed with John's intellect, grasp of history and was later to learn, his ability to see into the future. I looked forward to the completion of the oral phase of his dissertation, so that we might continue the conversation.

We discovered that we knew many of the same folks in the military, had similar business backgrounds, common goals for our military careers and for the future of the Army. As the years passed, we connected on many occasions to include some joint training missions between the California State Military reserve, when John was a Brigade Commander and I was Commander of the 91st Training Division's Command at Camp Parks, California.

On an annual basis, we spent time at the Association of the United States Army's (AUSA) conferences held in Washington, DC. It was at one of the early AUSA conferences that John presented me with one of his prototype UM84 holsters, what was to ultimately become the M9, the standard military sidearm holster for the United States. He asked me to field test this holster and I took it on a camping trip with my son, then a teenager, now an Infantry Battalion Commander on his third tour in Iraq. It had rained for that entire woodland adventure and I soon discovered that the prototype could hold water. A later conversation on the subject with General Robert C. Kingston, commander of United States Central Command, also a tester of John's holster, found us both talking of a need for a drainage hole in the new holster.

John was relentless on his journey to create the perfect all-service military holster. Visiting the Bianchi plant in Temecula, California, was like seeing a high test space age research center. The attention to detail and the energized artisans working there attested to John's aggressive pursuit of excellence. Even in the face of cancelled funding for the government's holster development project, John continued to work on the design at his own expense. Later, when funding was reinstated, he stepped up with the winning holster design after the Beretta M9 was selected for the U.S. Military's new standard issue sidearm.

In later years, John and I were both serving on the National Advisory Board of the United States Marshals Association, a time when Henry E. Hudson was Director of the U.S. Marshals Service. Again, it was an opportunity to work closely with John, and also to watch his rising to the rank of Major General as the Commander of the California State Military Reserve. During his tenure as Commanding General, he spent an inordinate amount of time and resources, and was able to hone the unit into a highly professional organization that proved to be a force multiplier for the California Army National Guard for years to come.

Most recently, I was to escort Iraqi Major General Sa'ad, the Provincial Police Chief for Maysan Province, on his visit to El Paso and Fort Bliss, Texas. John learned of the visit and within thirty-six hours had designed, produced, and had delivered a specially made Frontier Gunleather holster and belt, perfectly designed to fit the Iraqi General and his personal sidearm. It was another example of John's contributions to cement great relationships between countries and their militaries.

John Bianchi's reputation and his numerous accomplishments made his name well known throughout many countries around the world. So, while traveling in foreign countries, dealing with their militaries, the mere mention of the name, John Bianchi, opened doors, and created mutual friendships. With a relationship of almost thirty years, one could not find a better or more devoted friend. ✍

# Dennis M. Kenneally

## Major General (USA Ret.)

I knew of John Bianchi long before I met him. His reputation, signature leather work, and his design of a new and unique military holster were legendary. Then I met the legend. I was struck that this man, who was synonymous with corporate excellence, was the consummate gentleman who had humble beginnings. He was the embodiment of the American dream; a man with native intelligence, a passion for excellence, and the determination to be the best in his field. He started his business in his garage and thus began the steady but determined rise to worldwide recognition and success.

Even as I got to know John I learned he was one of the most compassionate, intelligent, and dedicated persons I had met. He had that uncanny and enviable ability to remember everyone's name and never forgot to follow up on the smallest of requests. At one point, I was convinced he had sticky notes as part of his brain matter.

John had an unquenchable thirst for history, especially weapons, the Old West, and the military. His attention to detail was always higher than museum standards, it was to the Bianchi standard. He started a series of historical prints and created his own museum of Western artifacts long before it became fashionable to do so.

John was more than an aficionado. He was a practitioner of military service. He unselfishly dedicated himself to service in the volunteer California State Military Reserve of the California National Guard. He quickly rose through the ranks and became a general officer and the commander of the California State Military Reserve. After a distinguished record he retired and settled into his life in Rancho Mirage, California, where he continued to make custom, handcrafted Western holsters. Then 9/11 hit and the world changed. I was asked to assume command of the California Army National Guard and begin the process for mobilization and deployment. The first call I made was to John Bianchi. I asked him to come out of retirement and take command of the California State Military Reserve. I remember thinking I couldn't blame him if he said no. He had already given more than most and was comfortable with his life in Rancho Mirage. However, not to my surprise, he never questioned my request, he simply responded. The next day he was in my headquarters in uniform and looking as if he had walked off a Hollywood studio set or off a recruiting poster. His presence alone was like a flashing marquee. In short, he had charisma and the intangible quality of a remarkable leader.

Although lost in history, General Bianchi contributed immeasurably to the success of our mobilization and deployment of troops to Afghanistan and Iraq. After two years, John completed his assignment and as he told me, his "duty was done." And not unlike the classic Roman citizen soldier Cincinnatus, his duty complete, he returned home.

It was my honor to soldier with General Bianchi. I will always remember him for what he truly is – a legend in his own time – an American legend. ✍

# Thomas A. Swidler

## Brigadier General (Ca.) Ret., Former Deputy Cmdr., California State Military Reserve

In his first tour as Commander, Major General John Bianchi assumed command of a State Military Reserve force with a large number of substandard personnel who had failed to meet acceptable levels of performance. In an unprecedented move, Maj. Gen. Bianchi initiated an entire reorganization by eliminating non-performing personnel and then established rigorous professional military standards for reenlistment and appointment to the new organization. The selected small cadre formed the basis of the rebuilding of today's 800 soldier strong force. For these accomplishments, Maj. Gen. Bianchi received the Order of California, the State's highest honor upon his retirement.

In his second tour as Commander, Maj. Gen. Bianchi was called out of retirement to meet the challenges facing all military forces in the United States after 9/11. During this tour, I was honored to serve as his Chief of Staff and then Deputy Commander. The National Guard was being restructured from a strategic reserve to an operational force and deploying to Iraq. Under Maj. Gen. Bianchi's leadership, the State Military Reserve was transformed into a fully trained and capable force upon which the California Army National Guard relied. During his tenure, more than 15,000 National Guard servicemen were mobilized and this would not have been possible without Maj. Gen. Bianchi's strong leadership in commanding the State Military Reserve in support of the Guard's deployment.

As Maj. Gen. Bianchi stated to his Command at his retirement, "Together we have risen to meet the critical challenges assigned us by the California Army National Guard. We have succeeded in being an effective, professional, and reliable 'force multiplier' during this time of national crisis. We made a difference." ✒

# Major General Paul D. Monroe, Jr. (Ret)

## Former, The Adjutant General

## California National Guard

I have known John Bianchi for twenty years. I was aware of his reputation long before that. When we met, he made me feel that we had known each other for years. John has this reserved presence that puts people at ease. At the same time, he displays a calm, pleasant demeanor. He is relaxed, confident, and enjoyable to be around.

During his military career, John commanded the California State Military Reserve on two separate occasions. I was the Adjutant General for the California National Guard during his second tour. John organized the State Military Reserve to assist the Army National Guard during its mobilization process. The Army Guard could not have accomplished its mission without the assistance of General Bianchi and his State Military Reserve.

John worked with his staff and that of the Army Guard to provide physicians, attorneys, and mental health specialists. The California State Military Reserve became the national model for the mobilization of National Guard and Army Reserve units.

At the same time, John worked with me and the commander of the California Army National Guard, to modernize the State Military Reserve, to make its purpose more relevant to that of the Army Guard's mission. The State Military Reserve now provides support to Army Guard units.

Finally, John's value to the California National Guard extended to the halls of congress. Whenever a project, beneficial to the California National Guard, was stuck in some congressional committee or office, John was our go to person to get the project moving again.

It has been my sincere honor to have known John, and also have the privilege of working with him. ✒

# Phil Spangenberger

## Author / Western Historian / Movie Consultant

As the sun slowly rose over the broad open valley, rich shades of red and gold gradually revealed themselves through the dark shadows of early morning. As they played over the ancient panorama that lay before me, thoughts of ghostly riders galloped across my mind – a scene I had thrilled to so many times on the big and small screens in countless Westerns. This was John Wayne and John Ford country. A harsh, but beautiful expanse of red buttes and sandy plains, where dusty columns of blue-clad cavalrymen and bronzed and painted Indian warriors had ridden to do battle in the winning of the West of imagination – only this time, I was one of those troopers!

It was just a few months earlier, during the winter of 1980 as I recall, while on a visit to Bianchi Leather on behalf of *Guns & Ammo* magazine, where I was serving as a staff editor and feature writer, as well as their Black Powder columnist, when John had asked me to help him put together a poster with a frontier U.S. Cavalry theme. At the time, as president of Bianchi Gunleather, John, who's long had a deep passion for the Old West, had already published three colorful posters of the frontier experience. Called Histographs, these full-color photographs depicted colorfully costumed characters from a segment of the panorama of the Wild West of the late 19th and early 20th centuries. I had previously lent a hand in the production of the Histograph of the Mexican Revolucionarios, and would later supply some ideas and costuming for his fifth and last poster of "The Cowboys."

However, for this fourth poster in his series, John told me that he had envisioned one on the Indian fighting cavalry as not only a colorful addition to his growing collection of Histographs, he also wanted "The Troopers," as this one was to be named, to be a tribute – not only to the spirit and memory of the cavalrymen of the Far West of the 19th century, but also to pay homage to the classic films of John Wayne and John Ford – a salute as it were, to their trilogy of U.S. Cavalry films, *Fort Apache*, *She Wore a Yellow Ribbon*, and *Rio Grande*. "The Troopers" poster depicts a small patrol of the 6th U.S. Cavalry in the 1886 American Southwest. Being an Indian Wars cavalry enthusiast, a member of a recreated 1886 Apache Wars cavalry unit, and knowing the dedication that John Bianchi brought to a project, I was eager to help in any way possible.

In order to capture the spirit of the wide open spaces so often patrolled by the horse cavalry of the frontier, historic Monument Valley in southern Utah was selected as the site for this image. This ruggedly beautiful area not only provides a classic background for "The Troopers," it is also rich in the flavor of the Old West as seen through the many motion pictures filmed here. Above all, this was John Wayne country! To a man, we were deeply touched and inspired to have been portrayed as cavalrymen on the same ground trod by such memorable Wayne characters as Captain York of *Fort Apache*, Captain Nathan Brittles in *She Wore a Yellow Ribbon*, and several other of the Duke's unforgettable heroes. To those of us both in the Histograph and behind the scenes, this was a unique project, being created in a special place.

My particular role in this project, besides being one of Bianchi's troopers, was to see that all of the uniforming, firearms, accessories, and equipment were authentic. The casting of the actual troopers themselves was also left up to me. Each man was handpicked not only for his physical appearance, but for that intangible quality that only comes with years of experience in the saddle. All of the troopers that were used were friends of mine that had been actively involved with the cavalry re-enacting hobby and, in Bianchi's Histograph, are wearing their own uniforms. In fact, at one time or another, each of these "campaigners" had actually served in "C" Troop, 6th U.S. Cavalry Memorial Regiment. Along with "Captain" Bianchi and yours truly as the sergeant in this Histograph, the cavalrymen are (in alphabetical order) Troopers John Costanza, Bill Evans, David Goen, Scott McMillan, and guidon bearer Jay Van Orden. With a total combined record of over sixty-five years of mounted drills, weekend campaigns, troop maneuvers, public displays, and various military, shooting, and riding skills acquired through this rough and tumble pastime, we felt that these men represented the old horse soldiers as closely as possible.

There were several talented and knowledgeable people involved "behind the scenes." Ken Dodd, Bianchi's art director at the time, worked enthusiastically, not only on layout and design, but also coordinated all of the location arrangements and logistics of this "epic" cavalry picture as well. Jerry Jacka, one of the nation's foremost scenic photographers, whose works were often featured in *Arizona Highways* magazine, put his creative talents to work on "The Troopers," and my long-time pal, Jay Van Orden, who was then the head curator of the Arizona Historical Society in Tucson, Arizona, contributed many invaluable ideas used in this poster. Further, during the actual location shooting, much valuable assistance was given by the wives and sweethearts accompanying "Captain" John Bianchi's troop. It was truly a group effort and both guys and gals threw themselves into its production with an eagerness that was hard to beat!

While on location in the late spring, the cast and crew of "The Troopers" stayed at Goulding's Lodge in Monument Valley. This is where the major players of many of the later John Ford productions were quartered during filming. Since Goulding's is around thirty-plus miles from any amenities, meals are served at given times in the dining hall – you either ate at the specified time or you missed a meal. Ironically, the dining hall was the same building that had served as the sutler's store in *She Wore a Yellow Ribbon*. This structure was still standing and was located next to a small stone building that was used as a potato cellar and had doubled as Capt. Nathan Brittles' quarters in that movie as well.

The filming was more like a motion picture production than that of a still photo session. Photographer Jacka brought in a slew of lights and reflectors, along with other equipment that would give him the best possible images for Bianchi to select from for the final product. We created two different setups during the day's filming, with one of the first setups becoming the final choice for the published Histograph.

Besides the troopers, the image features a couple of other colorful characters to round out the scene. One was a local Navajo, who we only knew as Tom (we never got his last name)

and was brought on board to pose as an Apache scout. Tom was a pleasant young man who spoke virtually no English and had to take instruction through an interpreter. A second addition to the cavalry soldiers was renowned Western artist, Dave Manuel, who earlier had been commissioned by Bianchi to create a sellout limited-edition bronze of John Wayne (which was also officially sanctioned and authorized by the Wayne family and bears the Wayne Enterprises logo on the bronze). When Dave heard about the poster, he wanted to be a part of it, so John asked me if I could come up with some way to incorporate Manuel into the image. Since he did not have the appearance of a saddle-hardened cavalryman, I felt it would add flavor to the Histograph to have Dave dressed in civilian attire – complete with high-topped leggings, an 1880s-style, tweed Norfolk jacket, a broad-brimmed hat, and a sketch pad – to give the impression of a Frederic Remington-type character accompanying the small patrol, much as the famous Western artist himself did in the late 19th century.

Having owned and operated Red River Frontier Outfitters, a pioneer company in the reproduction of frontier clothing and gunleather, I presented John with a special cavalry officer's bib-front shirt that I designed especially for him to wear in this photo. This blue wool bib-front blouse (as they were called then) was based on the type privately purchased, and often worn on campaign, by army officers of the era. It boasted a double yellow-embroidered and braid-bordered bib, braid-trimmed collar and cuffs, authentic vintage, cream-colored vegetable ivory buttons. For a final touch of flavor, yellow crossed sabers were embroidered on each collar, adding a unique and authentic look to Bianchi's officer portrayal.

Although the troop appears dismounted in the Histograph, we decided that there should be at least one horse in the photo, since we were representing the cavalry. It was too costly to transport one of our own mounts from California or southern Arizona, where the troopers all hailed from, so it was decided that a local animal could be "recruited" into the cavalry for the day of filming, and a McClellan saddle, bridle, tack, and equipment was brought along for our token mount. Here's where the fun began.

As the rest of the "troop" dressed and prepared for the day's shoot, I was sent out "on patrol," along with Art Director Ken Dodd, to find a suitable horse for the photo. We drove through the Monument Valley dunes and rough country for some time in the early morning looking for an animal that would look like a cavalry mount. I was already in my sergeant's uniform, since we would start our setup as soon as I returned, and after searching in vain for some time, we finally came across a ranch with two likely horses. They were stabled in a ramshackle corral, made up of chicken wire, barbed wire, crooked mesquite poles, and old tires, all loosely strung together to create some semblance of an enclosure. One of the horses was a chestnut sorrel that, at least as far as his reddish brown color and average size went, met the cavalry specs. Although he definitely was not what you would describe as "prime horseflesh," I determined that once saddled, his less-than-ideal confirmation could be concealed.

As we approached the little ranch, I saw three Navajo children playing in an arroyo next to the house. In full campaign uniform, I got out of our vehicle and began walking toward the kids, who by now were making their way up and out of the ravine toward me. One little fellow who looked to be about ten or eleven years of age, was armed with a bow and arrow and was pulling the bowstring back, and aiming his arrow directly at me! I have to say, for a little guy, he looked enough like a warrior to get my full attention. As he slowly approached, he said sternly, "What you want, Yellow Legs?"

I answered that I was looking for a horse. With a burst of laughter, the kids started jumping up and down and dancing around playfully, as the boy with the bow and arrow chuckled, "Yellow Legs lost his horse!" "No," I replied smiling as I walked toward him. "I didn't lose a horse, but I do need one. Now put that bow down. I come in peace. I'm looking for a horse for a picture. I'd like to take a look at your horses." Lowering his bow, the youngster motioned for me to proceed to the ramshackle corral. Feeling as though I were the straight man in a Western comedy, I walked over to the corral and checked out the red horse. I concluded that by covering his ribby, pot bellied torso with our cavalry saddle and saddle blanket – coupled with the fact that he was the only horse we'd seen that morning that even came close to what a cavalry mount would look like (the others were all paints, palominos, and other colors that would not be appropriate for the cavalry). Properly outfitted, he could pass for a horse that had been on campaign. I said we'd like to rent him for the day, and the interpreter stepped out of the truck to strike a deal with the youth's parents. Shortly thereafter, I was told that I could put a halter on the horse and we could use him.

Of course, Murphy's law was in full force that day and the closest thing to a halter was about four feet of a beat-to-crap nylon lariat, hanging stiffly, like a steel cable, from the fence. "How are you going to catch him?" Ken asked me. "I'm sure I can slip this old lariat over his head. It should be good enough to hold him 'til we put a military halter on him," I replied as I picked up the raunchy piece of rope. As I pushed the gate open and stepped inside, a big – and I mean big –billy goat, obviously protecting his little domain, quickly put his head down, started pawing the ground, and with his horns aimed at my rear end, started to charge me. Having been around domestic animals, I quickly figured this was not the first time he'd tried this aggressive stunt. Turning to face him I threw my hand forward like a traffic cop and shouted forcefully, "Don't you dare!"

As the goat got about two feet from me he suddenly stopped dead in his tracks. He tried to bluff me, but I had bluffed him…this time. "Wow," cried Ken, "Buffalo Bill! You stopped him!" Still facing the disoriented billy goat, I said to Ken, "Some animals you can bluff, others you can't." Then I proceeded to slip the stiff rope over the horse and with one eye on the threatening goat, led him out of the corral. I then turned him over to a Navajo who had accompanied us and had agreed to lead the horse to our nearby location. Once saddled for the photo, he did offer an acceptable appearance of a cavalry mount that had been on campaign, subsisting on a small ration of grain and lots of local forage.

Another humorous occurrence during the actual setup and placement of everyone in the picture happened. Once the positioning and actual posing of each person was determined, we held our poses for what seemed like hours, while the lighting and other technical details were attended to. Finally, almost ready to shoot the photograph, we were told we could take a break. We could move around a bit, but we had to stay in our general position. As Dave

Manuel rose from the flat stone he'd been sitting on, he stretched and commented, "Oww…I sat on this rock so long that I thought my butt was going to sleep." Always quick witted, teasingly Scott McMillan wryly quipped, "I believe you. I thought I heard it snoring!"

Although the photo shoot went off pretty well for the most part, we did have one minor crisis. This was when Tom, our "Apache" scout, who as I mentioned earlier, spoke almost no English – other than the international language of money — went home when we finished the first setup and had returned to Goulding's Lodge for lunch. I had told Ken not to pay him until the end of the day, when the work was done. However, Tom told Ken that he had to leave to tend his family's herd of sheep, which was grazing about five miles away. Ken, not being used to Indian ways, paid him as we broke for lunch, then realized that we just lost our Indian scout.

When he frantically told me what had happened, he and I, along with a Navajo interpreter, jumped in the truck to see if we could hire another Navajo for the second setup. I told Ken that he had been "bamboozled" and that five miles was nothing to these locals, since this land was their back yard. After about forty-five minutes of scouring the countryside and trying to persuade the locals that this was not a major motion picture, rather a single still photograph, we returned to our group empty handed. However, on our return, we found that the man who had originally gotten us Tom in the morning was able to entice him to return for the second setup – for another full day's pay! So thanks to the lure of more money, Tom was able to leave his sheep to graze without him, and that second day's pay for the one-day's work would aid him in finding his way back home in the dark wilds of Monument Valley!

All in all, the shoot went well and was a huge success, with "The Troopers" poster being perhaps the most popular of Bianchi's Histographs. I've seen it in restaurants, bars, gun shops, and other establishments – as well as in people's homes all over the country. I was extremely proud to have seen it on display in the Roy Rogers Museum, then in Victorville, California. When I later mentioned to Roy that I was proud to have my photo in his museum, he replied "Yes, but you're not stuffed." 'Nuff said. The only problem I ever heard about this cavalry poster was when a girlfriend who had showed it to her mother said that when she read the title which read, "The Troopers wear Bianchi Leather," she, not being familiar with the world of firearms, commented that she thought it was an advertisement for a men's cologne!

Now, more than three decades later, I look back on working with John Bianchi on this and several other projects, and have nothing but fond memories of each and every one. However, "The Troopers" was an adventure that struck a special cord, not only in this trooper's heart, but all of us who participated in the making of this Histograph. We'll always feel that we were involved in something special, and that each of us was able to play a part in this colorful tribute to the cavalry of the real West and to those of the "reel" West. Garry Owen! ✒

# Index

(Photos/captions in *italics*)

— C —